The Clinton Chronicles
BOOK

Third Edition

Patrick Matrisciana
Editor-In-Chief

Jeremiah Books
P.O. Box 1800
Hemet, CA 92546

Printed in the United States of America.
10 9 8 7 6 5 4 3

The Clinton Chronicles Book
Patrick Matrisciana, Editor-in-Chief

ISBN 1-878993-63-1

Published by:
Jeremiah Books
P.O. Box 1800
Hemet, CA 92546

TABLE OF CONTENTS

CITIZENS FOR HONEST GOVERNMENT STATEMENT OF PURPOSE

Citizens for Honest Government, founded in January of 1994, is a non-partisan, non-profit, grass roots organization whose purpose is to promote honesty in government.

Founder and president, Patrick Matrisciana, recognized the need to offer an alternate news medium to the American public, and as an independent documentary film producer he has been able to help fill this need through the medium of video journalism.

Mr. Matrisciana states, "I believe that regardless of our diverse political views, we, as Americans, must join together and demand that the men and women who represent us at the government level be of the highest possible caliber of honor and integrity. This is not a partisan issue; it is a moral issue upon which the strength and the very future of this great nation must stand."

ACKNOWLEDGMENTS

I would like to dedicate this book to the people who have put their reputations and their lives on the line to speak the truth. To those of you who have been hurt by Bill Clinton's abuse of power, yet have bravely stepped forward to tell your story; to you journalists who have dared to write the truth when your associates shrank back; and to those of you in the political arena who have spoken up in front of your colleagues, daring to challenge the reigning power structure—America owes thanks.

Specifically, thanks go to the numerous talk show hosts who, although skeptical of our story at first, cared enough to check out the information and then chose to provide us a forum in which to present our message to the American people. Your names would go into the hundreds were they all to be listed. The impact of your programs is clearly demonstrated by the ground-swell of Americans who are now asking for full and open hearings into the allegations against Bill Clinton and his "circle of power." I thank you all.

Accolades also go to those who contributed in the writing and assisted in the compilation of this book.

I deeply appreciate the dedication of my associates at Citizens For Honest Government (especially our selfless publicist), who all helped bring the video and now the book into being.

Lastly, but most importantly, I am grateful to Almighty God, without Whose guidance and protection this book would never have been written.

Pat Matrisciana

INTRODUCTION

As citizens of a republic, we consider it a solemn privilege and obligation to select qualified, responsible and honest people to represent us in government. In the event we elect a leader who fails in these crucial areas, we know that the same Constitution which allows us to vote allows us to impeach.

The President of the United States must be a man who will uphold the Constitution and the Bill of Rights, a Commander in Chief who can lead our armed forces with honor, and one who is trustworthy. We do not believe Bill Clinton is this man.

Since leaving the governor's mansion in Arkansas and its politics of secrecy, Clinton has been scrutinized under the bright lights of the White House. The heat of this light is melting his media-generated image, allowing the American people to see their real President for the first time. "Don't ask, don't tell" is an even more appropriate motto for President Clinton's life than for his policy of including homosexuals in the military.

Surprise, shock, then outrage describes the reaction most Americans have after viewing the video, *The Clinton Chronicles.* Its alarming testimony alerted the public to the serious charges against Bill Clinton. Concerned citizens have responded, calling for open and complete investigations into these allegations.

Detailed chapters in *The Clinton Chronicles Book* describe first-hand accounts of Clinton's criminal activities and expose the controlling bias of the liberal American media and their failure to report the truth about Clinton.

The comprehensive, endnoted chapter outlining Clinton's woeful treatment of the military as well as documenting his ominous slant toward a socialist, globalist design for the U.S.A. produces outrage in even the most hesitant of patriots.

We've included an extensive listing of sources, fully documenting the allegations made against Bill Clinton and his "circle of power" in *The Clinton Chronicles* video.

Finally, actual documents from the files of the FBI, DEA, police and other investigative agencies, which incriminate Clinton and his associates, are presented for your examination.

This book is a chronicle of the life and lies of Bill Clinton. As you will see, Clinton's claim of "there is no proof" will soon become his most blatant lie of all.

PREFACE, CHAPTER 1

Bill Clinton, not even two years into his first term, has become one of the least popular sitting Presidents in history.

Who should be blamed for the President's inability to win the confidence of the American people? Not Bill Clinton, the White House spin doctors want us to believe. The blame has fallen instead on "obstructionists" like Rush Limbaugh, Jerry Falwell, and "that video."

As founder of Citizens for Honest Government, Pat Matrisciana's extensive background in film making helped him spearhead the production of *The Clinton Chronicles* video and the companion book.

Twenty years of producing cutting edge documentaries seasoned Matrisciana for this project. His daring films exposing such cult leaders as Bhagwan Shree Rajneesh (who subjugated people in a remote guarded compound in Oregon) demonstrate Pat's willingness to step "close to the edge" with his camera to find the truth.

Matrisciana's beliefs as a loyal American compelled him to provide the American public with the truth about Bill Clinton.

CHAPTER 1

AMERICA NEEDS THE TRUTH

by Pat Matrisciana

Thirty thousand feet above the earth, President William Jefferson Clinton sat in his flying Oval Office, Air Force One. It was June 24, 1994, and Bill Clinton was being interviewed on St. Louis' KMOX radio call-in program.

Declaring that "there is too much cynicism and too much intolerance," Clinton lashed out at the "violent personal attacks" made against him by the likes of talk radio hosts, notably Rush Limbaugh, as well as allegations made in a video distributed by, among others, Dr. Jerry Falwell.

The public was getting a glimpse of the real Bill Clinton, the one intimate friends know, the one described by Bob Woodward in *The Agenda* as a man who could turn in a moment from a light-hearted mood to a fit of absolute rage.

The President was screaming into the phone about "that video." Two days previous to this outburst, a copy of *The Clinton Chronicles* video had been hand-delivered to him by one of his trusted friends.

This best-selling documentary brought to the surface allegations of criminal wrongdoing by Bill Clinton and his political machine that began while he was governor of Arkansas. Clinton, no doubt, had become concerned enough by the video's accusations that he felt the need to deflect them.

However, the video has not been easy to dismiss as it includes testimonies of credible individuals, from police officers to a former Arkansas Supreme Court Justice.

13

Hundreds of thousands of the videos have been sold and millions have watched it.

Thanks in no small part to the video, Bill Clinton, not even two years into his first term, had become one of the least popular sitting Presidents in history. Despite Democratic majorities in both houses of Congress, most of Clinton's legislative agenda—including his health care proposals—had floundered.

Who should be blamed for the President's inability to win the confidence of the American people? Not Bill Clinton, the White House spin doctors want us to believe. The blame has fallen instead on "obstructionists" like Rush Limbaugh, Jerry Falwell, and "that video."

Usually a person in Bill Clinton's position doesn't answer the critic's charges—unless he is in a corner, caught. Clinton made one mistake when he attempted to repudiate his chief critics—he hollered into the phone. He allowed the public to get a glimpse of the real Bill Clinton. The White House press office would later say that Clinton was simply elevating his voice because of the noise of the jet engines.

I have talked to others on the phone many times while flying in jet planes and I have never once had to raise my voice. Maybe Air Force One is different. Maybe the universe is different for Bill Clinton.

He would like it that way. He wants to judge others by accepted rules, but not to have these same rules used as a standard against his own behavior. Take, for example, his response to the accusations made in *The Clinton Chronicles:* "Look at who [the video] is talking to . . . does [the video] make full disclosure to the American people of the backgrounds of the people that he has interviewed that have made these scurrilous and false charges against me?"

Then, closing his sermon, Clinton asked, "Is that in a good Christian spirit?" Bill Clinton doesn't want to argue with the facts and truth of the video—he wants to discredit the witnesses through "full disclosure." Then he wants us to judge him with "a good Christian spirit," a standard which has eluded his own behavior.

Clinton's remarks about the video came just at the time the major media began viewing *The Clinton Chronicles*. Instead of investigating the allegations of the video, the press took part in a well-organized campaign to discredit the film. Again, not by proving any of the allegations to be false, but instead, like Clinton, attacking the Christian spirit of the video. When the press gets religion, we know something must be up.

On August 1, 1994, *Time* magazine published an editorial, which was disguised to look like a news article, attacking the video. This article, entitled, "The Clinton Hater's Video Library," concluded by suggesting that Bill Clinton might remind those who distribute the film, like the Rev. Falwell, "of the Eighth Commandment:[sic] Thou shalt not bear false witness against thy neighbor." But what about bearing false witness to the American public? Did *Time* bother to speak to our witnesses or check our sources? No, they did not.

Similarly, *U.S. News and World Report* did a hatchet job on the video. Not surprisingly, the reporter, Greg Ferguson, refused to come to Arkansas to meet with our sources.

"Don't confuse me with the facts, folks, I have a story to write," is the attitude of the American press.

As for "full disclosure," we need to look at how some media giants have been doing Bill Clinton's bidding, supporting his allegations while destroying the credibility of his critics.

Time magazine has been a stalwart supporter of Clinton since the 1992 campaign. A *Time* editor, Strobe Talbott, is a former Oxford classmate of Clinton's, who was rewarded with the position of Ambassador-at-Large to the former Soviet Union.

U.S. News & World Report is owned by a strong Clinton supporter, media mogul Mort Zuckerman. *U.S. News'* editor was none other than David Gergen, who was tapped to be Clinton's chief advisor.

No wonder Clinton and his press supporters have gotten religion (In flailing against the truth in the *Clinton Chronicles* tape, they have even begun to quote the Bible.) They're obviously worried. They know millions of religious Americans of every background have watched *The Clinton Chronicles* video. Many of these people are leaders in business and civic life across America, and many more serve in our armed forces.

The critics also know that these people use the principles of the Bible to structure their lives, prompting them to stand against corruption in public officials. The liberal establishment finds these dedicated religious people a threat because their value system is based on absolutes.

The millions of patriotic Americans who have watched *The Chronicles* video realize they must make a decision. Either all the individuals testifying in the video (and the many more that are ready to testify under oath) have fabricated this intricate web of criminality, or Bill Clinton is lying.

I personally believe that public officials of both parties should be held accountable for their actions, and be held to a high standard of ethical behavior.

As an independent film producer, I have seen the impact that documentary videos have in the commercial arena and have come to realize the importance of using this medium to inform the public of the misdeeds of their elected officials. That's why Citizens for Honest Government was formed, and why the video, *The Clinton Chronicles*, was made.

Some time in 1993, I began communicating with a man by the name of John Hillyer, an investigative reporter and a former cameraman for NBC. John told me that he had met many people in Arkansas, credible people who had much to tell of the criminal activities which took place when Bill Clinton was governor.

With great skepticism I went to Arkansas to meet with John and some of his sources in February 1994. What I learned shocked me. This book contains some of that same alarming information about our President, Bill Clinton (and his circle of power) that I observed and which the mainstream media has chosen to ignore. You'll read "first-hand" testimonies about drug running, money laundering, illegal payoffs, abuse of power, the improper use of law enforcement authorities and yes, even murder.

These allegations are backed up by copies of actual documents from the Arkansas State Police intelligence files. These documents, some from the Drug Enforcement Agency and FBI, corroborate the illegal drug trade in Bill Clinton's Arkansas. These documents also show that Clinton's *two biggest campaign supporters* were the kingpin figures in the drug trafficking and money laundering activities.

The video first demonstrated how Bill Clinton, in his private and public life, abused the power of his office. Contrary to what those in charge of damage control would have us believe, the President's character and morals are important to us. Just as the immorality of an adulterous father injures his children, so the immorality of a President victimizes us all.

Even the liberal Joe Klein wrote a scathing piece on the President's morality in *Newsweek* (May 9, 1994) entitled, "The Politics of Promiscuity." Klein admitted the serious problems with the President's morality: " . . . it seems increasingly apparent that the character flaw Bill Clinton's enemies have fixed upon—promiscuity—is a defiling characteristic of his public life as well. It may well be that this is one case where private behavior does give an indication of how a politician will perform in the arena."

Klein elaborated, saying that not only is the President promiscuous in his own affairs, but in public affairs as well. Klein depicted Clinton's foreign policy as a shambles, from Bosnia to Somalia to Haiti—because Bill Clinton's word is not trusted.

In an equally devastating piece about the President's morals, Michael Kelly wrote in *The New York Times Magazine*: "The President's essential character flaw isn't dishonesty so much as a-honesty." Truth is not something real for Bill Clinton; he creates his own.

The Clinton Chronicles probes much deeper than just the President's character. It raises an important question: Has his distorted character permitted him and his friends to break the law?

Bill Clinton and the media have mentioned "the Christian spirit" of our video. Yet, no one seems to challenge the spirit of Bill Clinton and his political fixers in Arkansas. Here again, I never believed the ruthlessness of the Arkansas establishment until I witnessed it firsthand.

The first time I met Larry Nichols was at a restaurant in Arkansas. Nichols, a former Clinton aide, now a Clinton critic, warned me that we might be under surveillance.

"They follow me everywhere," Nichols said. At first I thought his comment leaned toward paranoia. Yet, twenty minutes later two state troopers came in the restaurant and proceeded to watch us from a nearby table. I soon realized that Larry's fear was justified; he is followed almost unceasingly.

This type of harassment is petty compared to the circle's other forms of terrorism. Larry has been beaten twice recently. The second time his already-broken ribs were painfully re-injured by two Little Rock policeman.

A few weeks later he was arrested on fallacious charges. After a public outcry, the charges were dismissed. The purpose of the arrest became clear when an informant told us that a bounty had been placed on Larry; $1,000 was offered to the prisoner who could beat or kill Larry while he was incarcerated. Fortunately, before that could happen, Larry was quickly bailed out and his life was spared.

These occurrences of physical assault are not isolated incidents. Another vile act was the savage beating of Gary Johnson, a next-door neighbor of Gennifer Flowers at the Quapaw Towers in Little Rock.

Gary, a respected attorney, had a security video camera monitoring his door, which inadvertently filmed Flowers' door as well. When someone discovered that Johnson's camera had, on many occasions, actually taped

Bill Clinton entering Flowers' apartment, thugs were sent to do some "damage control." Two men entered Gary's apartment and demanded the video tapes, which he quickly gave them. Then they brutally beat him—leaving him for dead. Yet the press showed no interest in investigating the attack nor the reason it occurred.

Johnson wasn't the only one to be beaten. L.J. Davis, a writer for *The New Republic*, was in Little Rock completing his exposé on the Rose Law Firm ("the firm" in Arkansas whose partners included Hillary Clinton, Vincent Foster and Webster Hubbell).

As Davis entered his hotel room, someone hit him over the head, rendering him unconscious for several hours. Davis' doctor later confirmed that Davis had been struck on the back of the head.

After Davis' story started gaining publicity, the hotel claimed he had consumed several drinks before returning to his room that night. This was used to discredit his story (although the drinks can't explain how he received the debilitating blow to the back of his head while standing in a carpeted hallway).

At first, when John Hillyer told me of the strange goings-on in Arkansas, I found the stories hard to believe. But it was not my imagination when I found six listening devices ("bugs") in an apartment Citizens for Honest Government had rented in Little Rock.

It was also not simply the imagination of the Parks family that their father, former head of security for the Clinton campaign headquarters, was brutally murdered; that their home was broken into three times; or that recently, a man broke down the door to Gary Parks' apartment in the middle of the night.

The Wall Street Journal shed some light on these incidents in its review of *The Clinton Chronicles* video, concluding with: "Pondering the string of violent coincidences, we feel some duty to share with readers one factor that colors our own thinking about the Arkansas connections. In particular, with drugs does come violence and also money laundering."

Considering the pattern of violence, it shouldn't surprise us that many people are afraid to tell their story. To some, the allegations contained in this book appear extraordinary because the press, by and large, has refused to acknowledge them.

Many people think, *If I haven't seen it on CBS News, it probably isn't true. If it were true, it would certainly have been published somewhere.* As logical as that thinking seems to be, it doesn't fit reality.

Recently, a caller to a late-night talk radio program asked a very simple question of a host we'll call "Albert." The caller questioned, "How could the events outlined by Larry Nichols and presented in *The Clinton Chronicles* video completely escape mass public inquiry?" The answer the syndicated host gave was astonishing: "There is nothing to the allegations in that video. We know this because if there were, the mainstream media would have flushed it out."

The fallacy in this host's conclusion is easily demonstrated by his own actions. Let me explain. We at Citizens had received phone calls from Albert's radio audience asking why Larry Nichols refused to go on Albert's show. They informed us that the host was bragging on the air: "Larry won't come on my show. I've asked him repeatedly, but he's afraid to face me."

We believe the phone callers' questions and reports of Albert's bragging are extremely revealing. We'd been *trying for three months to schedule Larry Nichols on Albert's show*, but he wouldn't speak to Larry's publicist, return our phone calls or acknowledge any of our letters.

What does this reveal? Simply put, sometimes people in the media lie. They have a list of standards that doesn't include honesty, especially when the truth interferes with their agenda. But why is there such an extreme protectionist attitude in the media toward Bill Clinton? A couple of factors may explain this.

First, the Clintons have very cleverly manipulated and compromised the press in Arkansas, a small state with only

one major newspaper, the *Arkansas Democrat-Gazette.*
(While its editorial policy may have been critical of Clinton,
it surely has not been known as an unbiased investigative
newspaper.)

Despite revelations of scandal after scandal regarding
the Clintons, the Arkansas press has been in a state of
denial, portraying most of the revelations as attacks on the
people of Arkansas themselves. Let's face it, they are
certainly not going to admit to their readers that they have
been negligent.

Second, we have the national media. The liberal bias
of the establishment media is no secret. It was clearly
apparent during the '92 presidential campaign that the
media had, after twelve years, endured enough of the
Reagan and Bush Administrations and wanted someone in
office who would promote their agenda.

That is why, I believe, the major media have looked
the other way from the Arkansas story. Clinton is a master
at manipulating the media, but they have succumbed
without a whimper because he represents their best hope.
He has pushed for homosexuals in the military, a nation-
alized health care plan, an invasion of Haiti, abortion, and
other litmus-test items of the left.

Some media, very much in Bill Clinton's corner, have
been quite aggressive in publishing articles that would
discredit and destroy those who might bring down "their
man."

Nearly everyone willing to speak the truth has been
defamed. Paula Jones was depicted by the media as a
gold-digger and a pawn of the "religious right." Yet, Anita
Hill, whose allegations were completely unsubstantiated,
was declared a modern-day Joan of Arc for feminism.

Consider also the testimony of five state troopers (all
of whom had served on Clinton's security details) who have
given eyewitness testimony of how Clinton not only engaged
in numerous sexual affairs, but how he abused his office by
using Arkansas state officers, vehicles and finances for his
trysts.

Soon after coming forward with their testimony, two troopers were falsely charged with insurance fraud (charges were later dismissed); a third was asked by Clinton to change his story.

Another law-enforcement officer who was beginning to uncover official corruption in Arkansas was first demoted to patrol duty and then forced to resign. Nevertheless, courageous people have spoken out and continue to do so.

Many who have been victims of Clinton's "hit and run" intimidation tactics related their devastating experiences in *The Clinton Chronicles* video. Now in this book, they, and others who have been "run over" by Clinton and friends of Bill (FOBs), add more information. We want people to investigate these stories and check out the facts.

These testimonies are more than just compelling reading; how we respond to this information could determine the future of our nation. If we ignore the tribulations of Americans in Arkansas and the corruption they're trying to expose, we will be permitting this cancer to grow throughout our federal government.

The Clinton Chronicles, both the book and the video, tell a true story about one man's abuse of power. The founding fathers so feared the abuse of power by any one person or group of persons that they created a unique system of checks and balances within our government, designed to prevent tyranny.

Let us suppose that Bill Clinton and his circle desire to abuse the vast power they now hold: to use federal agencies and the immense resources of the presidency to accomplish their goals, as they did in Arkansas. Where will this lead? Can our system of government, as we know it, survive their assault?

These are serious questions. Our desire is that America's once-objective, judicial and legislative system will honestly investigate, fairly adjudicate, and justly resolve these allegations. Fellow Citizens: we must not rest until this is done.

PREFACE, CHAPTER 2

Clinton is a user. He uses people. He used Arkansas, and he'll use the United States. He is capable of anything . . .

The Honorable Jim Johnson served his home state of Arkansas with distinction for many years, both as a senator and a Supreme Court judge. Throughout his tenure of public service and political crusading, Johnson has consistently backed causes and leaders he's believed would be best for his state. He's chosen to promote candidates not by their party affiliation but by their quality and integrity.

Judge Johnson's insightful, personal observations provide a glimpse into the workings of Arkansas politics and a foundation from which we can understand and evaluate the President from Arkansas, Bill Clinton.

CHAPTER 2

JUSTICE—ARKANSAS STYLE

by the Honorable Jim Johnson

Bill Clinton is one of the most charming men I have ever met. He's not just intelligent, but brilliant. Yet, when he left the governor's mansion in Arkansas to go to Washington in 1992, he had created the most corrupt and powerful political machine in the history of Arkansas, and maybe in the whole country.

When Bill Clinton ran for President, his campaign advisors were the best in the country. This was no small feat. Bill and Hillary Clinton used Arkansas and its people to achieve their goals. They were merely using this small state; they were only passing through.

Many people knew about the corrupt machine Bill Clinton had going while he was governor, but he was a master of control and manipulation. Even so, when he ran for President, he only carried the state by fifty-three percent; that's only three percentage points above midpoint, and that was with the Republicans conceding the election. Had the Republicans run a real campaign, Bill Clinton would not have gotten a majority.

I have spent most of my seventy years being involved in Arkansas politics, and for most of the last fifteen years I've been trying to get the word out about the Clintons.

I was raised in a little town in south Arkansas called Crossett, just nine miles from the Louisiana border. My parents were country merchants. A country store is always a center for politics, and I guess politics came almost naturally to me.

My area of Arkansas was strongly influenced by the

legend of Huey P. Long, the long-time political boss of Louisiana (as both a governor and senator). My mother was a Long; she had a brother named Huey and another one named George. But I never checked to find out whether our family was related to the Longs of Louisiana.

One of my great disappointments in life was a trip I took with my father into Louisiana to hear Long speak. The speech was cancelled because Long had gotten drunk in Monroe, Louisiana, and couldn't make it.

Arkansas political life in the New Deal era and after was greatly influenced by the populism of Huey P. Long. He was an electrifying speaker. Clinton in many ways followed in the footsteps of Long. He certainly nestled up to the people in a way no politician since Long had.

Shortly after World War II, after serving in the Marine Corps, I got my law degree and became quite active in politics; Arkansas was a one-party, Democratic state. In 1948, I was the South Arkansas coordinator for the presidential campaign of Strom Thurmond, who ran on the States Rights ticket. Two years later, in 1950, the people of that area made me the youngest person ever elected to serve in the Arkansas State Senate.

In 1956, I ran unsuccessfully against Governor Orval Faubus in the Democratic primary, but I, with the help of great States Righters, like Notre Dame's Dean Clarence Manion and Texas' J. Evetts Haley, ran Faubus one heck of a race, getting the most votes against him of any challenger in a Democratic primary while he was governor. It was not a total loss because two years later in a state-wide election, the people of Arkansas made me the youngest man ever to serve on the Arkansas Supreme Court.

While a member of the court, I became the only state-wide elected Democratic official in the nation to endorse the Republican candidacy of Senator Barry Goldwater for President of the United States. I appeared on a South-wide telecast with the senator, and individually on a number of other television programs on his behalf.

In 1966, I was the Democratic nominee for governor.

My major Democratic primary opponent was part of the Faubus machine, and after I had defeated him, the Faubus people turned their support over to Winthrop Rockefeller, one of the richest men in the world, who ran on the Republican ticket. He spent untold millions to successfully become governor, becoming the first Republican to become governor of Arkansas since the war between the states.

The Rockefeller people wrote the book on dirty tricks and probably opened up a new era for Arkansas politics. They knew all the tricks. Phone tapping and car bugging went on all the time, but you couldn't live if you worried about it.

Many years after the campaign, Lyn Blaylock, a former Republican chairman, was being roasted. He got up and made some comments about me. He said that the most terrifying time in his life was when he was assigned the duty of going to my house to copy down the license plates of the people attending a party there. Well, Lyn met my St. Bernard, who scared him to death.

The thought of them assigning a man of his caliber, of any caliber, to stake out another person's house to check on license plates, is unbelievable. The Rockefeller people didn't leave a stone unturned.

These people also went out and bought off Democratic chairmen and defeated primary candidates in the various counties, especially the ones with deficits.

After losing the race to Rockefeller, two years later I ran against Senator J. William Fulbright, and again almost forced him into a runoff. Several years later I ran as the Republican nominee for the position of Chief Justice of the Arkansas Supreme Court. It was a squeaker. All of my campaigns have been squeakers.

There has always been a power structure in this state which has controlled the political activity in Arkansas. I spent my life fighting that power structure—a structure largely built around the Stephens empire.

I have known the Stephens family over the course of my lifetime. I knew the grandfather, Jack Stephens, and his sons, Witt and Jack.

Stephens had the financial connections to control the politicians. He brought the banks and other financial people together, creating the power structure. Stephens, Inc. is one of the biggest financial firms in the country, having been responsible for Wal Mart, Tyson Foods, Dillards, Hunt, T.C.B.Y. and other Arkansas-based national business powers going public.

Bill Clinton eventually became part of that power structure. He boasts that his first paid employment was as a campaign worker against me in my 1966 campaign for governor.

Meredith Oakley in her biography of Clinton, "On The Make," states that Clinton first met me during that campaign, and after he heard me speak, he so violently disagreed with my conservative premise that he came up and told me that I made him ashamed to be an Arkansan. I never remembered either the remark or Clinton at that time, but it was interesting to note the constructive influence my response had on Clinton's political future as related by Oakley.

Bill Clinton tells people he is a product of Hope, Arkansas, that small town off Highway 40. This isn't true. Clinton is a product of Hot Springs. He moved there from Hope at a very young age with his mother, and that's where the young boy was raised and his "character" was formed.

Hot Springs is a place apart. It's like the corner of every barnyard where all the manure is piled. You know where it is, and if you get in it, it's by choice. It was a town where many people operated beyond the law. There was open gambling, open prostitution, horse racing, and quite a few saloons and clip joints. The Hot Springs credo was, "If it feels good, do it." The town's celebrity was the gangster, Oney Madden, of the Harlem Cotton Club fame.

Clinton came up in that atmosphere of smoke and mirrors, where the fix was in. The rules that applied to other people didn't apply; he never played by the rules. The city was a "con."

When I was in the State Senate, a colleague of mine was from Hot Springs. He was a charming man just like Clinton. But this fellow would find out how I was going to vote on a piece of legislation, and then he would go out and sell my vote to the people who had an interest in the outcome of that legislation, appearing as if he had gotten me to vote a certain way. If I found out what he did and confronted him, he'd be sorry he did it. But it wouldn't stop him from doing it. The main thing that bothered him was that I found out about it. He was amoral, just like Bill Clinton.

Of course, Clinton's mother was part of that fast and loose Hot Springs life, too, as so daringly disclosed in her autobiography.

I remember meeting Clinton during the 1972 presidential campaign, the year George McGovern ran as the Democratic nominee. The convention was in Miami. I and most other Arkansans were supporting the powerful Ways and Means Chairman, Congressman Wilbur Mills, for President. Wilbur was my wife's cousin, and my son worked in his office.

On the plane to Miami, I recall meeting this young man, Bill Clinton—an affable fellow. He told me he was supporting McGovern. He also told me—and this shocked me—that he had asked Mills for permission to work for McGovern. I thought to myself, *the audacity of this young man, to ask someone for permission to work for their opponent.* I imagine Wilbur probably looked at him like he was a bug. But it was vintage Clinton—looking to cover every side.

Even though McGovern lost the election, working on the McGovern campaign was probably one of Clinton's most important political experiences. In high school, Clinton, I'm told, kept a list of everyone he met and kept in contact with them. His contacts with the McGovern people would be the foundation for his runs for office in Arkansas. These McGovern hippies were like termites; political junkies who would sleep on the floor to get their candidate into office.

But they also were sophisticated and knew how to raise money.

Clinton, with his McGovern friends, lost his first race for office in 1974 against Congressman John Paul Hammerschmidt, a long-time Republican from north Arkansas. However, it was a very clean race. Clinton impressed many people by the way he handled himself, developing an impressive network of people to run for state-wide office.

In 1976, Clinton ran for attorney general virtually unopposed. He ran on image (something that wasn't really there and was never earned).

As attorney general, Clinton had overspent his budget and had been involved in some other items of scandal. This might have stopped him, but by 1978 he was already a nominee for governor. Nothing came of the scandal, and the brakes were put on the ensuing investigation.

Clinton was very lucky because there was no incumbent running for the governorship in 1978, and no one else of quality was running. He became Arkansas' youngest governor. Soon enough, he shocked the people of the state by surrounding himself with a bunch of hippies.

In two years, the voters literally threw him out of office. I helped in that effort. A Republican by the name of Frank White challenged Clinton for reelection in 1980. I was working full-time on the telephone for the election of Ronald Reagan for President. During the course of my conversations with the Democratic leaders across the state I made it a point to say that this boy, White, had a good chance to be governor. This planted the seed that White could be elected and gave him a credibility he didn't have up to that time.

This endorsement was important because business people around the state were afraid to oppose a sitting governor, even if they hated him. It was one thing to privately be opposed to a person in office; it's quite another thing to actively support his opponent. A businessman has a lot to lose if he votes wrong because the governor has control over almost every business. Boards and commissions for highways, utilities, banks, securities, game and fish, trucking—all have members appointed by the governor of this state. If a businessman supports a candidate who loses, he has to live with an enemy in the governor's office until the next election and pray that he can survive in the meantime.

The "circle of power" in Arkansas is awesome because of the power the governor holds and the appearance of power he wields.

In 1980, Clinton was at his weakest because he had not appointed many members of the boards and commissions—compared to 1992 when Clinton had obtained nearly absolute power. By then he had appointed every member of every board and commission in Arkansas.

Clinton returned in 1982 by default because, by that time, the people of Arkansas had literally "chunked" White out of office. By then Clinton had learned his lesson and had created the most sophisticated political operation this nation had ever seen. He cultivated all the people he didn't use the first time, enabling him to take almost total control in the state.

I had opposed Clinton during his entire time in office. There were many of us who realized he was just concerned about his "inner circle" in preparation for his run for President.

Also during this time, the Arkansas media were an embarrassment. Clinton knew there were probably only five key journalists he needed to pacify, and he played them like a fiddle. He stroked them; he counseled them; he lulled them. They became so carried away, they didn't know what was happening. Apparently, by the articles they printed, they didn't want to know either. Clinton spoon-fed these journalists the information he wanted them to print. He made them fat and lazy.

There is no independent press in Arkansas. Nowadays, thanks to the national press, we are finally learning of the corruption which had been going on the whole time right under the local media's noses. The locals can't admit it even to this day because it's almost an admission of their own corruption. I don't believe they really sat down and planned to cover up corruption, but it happened. This is why the *Arkansas Democrat-Gazette* and others have to ridicule and destroy people like Larry Nichols who have bravely come forward and exposed these journalists for not having done their job.

If you read Oakley's biography of Clinton you'll see how Clinton manipulated the state's media, and how the media in turn did Clinton's bidding.

In 1988, when Larry Nichols first made his charges that then-Governor Clinton abused his office, carrying on numerous sexual affairs at state expense, the Clinton spin doctors set out to destroy Nichols. They did a marvelous job; his credibility was indeed destroyed.

Nichols' charges were so outrageous, even I found them unbelievable. They fell on deaf ears. Then in 1992, Gennifer Flowers came out and said Nichols was telling the truth. Sally Perdue of Pine Bluff also said it was true. Then the state troopers came forward.

I thought to myself: *Dear God, Larry Nichols was right. There's more credible evidence supporting his allegations than exists against ninety percent of the people on death row today.*

I made a public statement that someone ought to help Larry Nichols to get his good name back. Right after that, the producers of *The Clinton Chronicles* asked me if I would put that statement on film; I said *I would put it anywhere because it's true.*

Many people think Clinton was cleared during the presidential campaign of all those charges Nichols and others brought up against him. But that's not true; the media just wanted people to believe Clinton was cleared. When some negative information like his womanizing and the Flowers affair was released, the media would say that a particular state primary, in this case New Hampshire's, would be the jury for whether this should be held against him. Clinton would come close or win the primary, the media would declare him not guilty, and the charges would quickly fade from public scrutiny.

I believe Clinton was elected President because of the lack of a Democratic candidate who had the ability to inspire the people. He sailed through the primaries with the media helping him get through the scandals.

One scandal that got lost was the letter Clinton wrote to Colonel Eugene Holmes, the head of the University of Arkansas ROTC program. Clinton not only dodged the draft, but he (in the tradition of Jane Fonda), with his anti-war activities, gave aid and comfort to the enemy while America's finest young men were fighting and dying in the stinking jungles of Vietnam. Even though the letter to Holmes was written, as Clinton admits, to "maintain his political viability," he couldn't honestly resist saying he "loathed the military."

After the primaries I asked Jim Lindsey—a friend of mine from Fayetteville, one of the most prominent business-men in our state and a former All-Pro football player for the Minnesota Vikings—to go out and see Colonel Holmes. He urged Colonel Holmes to write out an affidavit on Clinton's draft-dodging.

During the presidential campaign, it was arranged for Holmes' affidavit and Clinton's letter to be placed in the hands of President Bush. I'm told that Bush cried when he read Clinton's letter and the affidavit, and at a speech shortly thereafter, brought up the letter. But he evidently handled it in such a clumsy way that he blew the whole thing and was soon apologizing for attacking Clinton's patriotism (even though Clinton had demonstrated that he had none).

Many people were afraid to speak up during the campaign about Clinton's wrongdoings. They no doubt saw the heavy price people like Larry Nichols had to pay for telling the truth.

Another person who has had to pay a big price is Judge David Hale. Hale is currently working with Independent Counsel Kenneth Starr on his dealings with Clinton and the Whitewater scandal.

I have known David most of his life. He honored our state by being national chairman of the Junior Chamber of Commerce (Jay-Cees). The Hale family comes from Yell County (a rural county), where they have been very active in politics.

Clinton found the Hales' rapport with rural voters useful, and subsequently used David and his family to help in his campaigns. Clinton later appointed Hale to a municipal judgeship in Little Rock.

In 1978, David started a business called Capital Management Services. It lent money to small businesses which were owned by minorities or disadvantaged persons who could not get credit from any other source. The federal Small Business Administration guaranteed the loans.

It turned out that the Small Business Administration got wind of some fraud at David's office. David's company had been lending money to people who were not disadvantaged. (David had become part of Clinton's machine, and Clinton had asked him to lend money to political cronies.) One of David's loans went to Susan McDougal, wife of Jim McDougal. The McDougals were 50-50 partners in the Whitewater land deal with the Clintons.

Clinton personally asked Hale to give Susan $300,000 (with much of the proceeds to go to the Whitewater partnership). At the time she and her husband were reputed to be worth $3.5 million, yet David qualified her. She didn't repay the loan, and that's when the federal investigators began looking through Hale's records.

They brought this information before a grand jury, which returned an indictment against David for conspiring to defraud the government, a felony. Hale went to prosecutors and offered to tell about Clinton (his co-conspirator) and the others involved in defrauding the government. But the prosecutor, Fletcher Jackson, according to the *Arkansas Democrat-Gazette*, said he was "not interested in prosecuting anyone else"; that he just "had a relatively short time until retirement" and that he was not going to "rock the boat."

I dropped Hale a note and told him it looked like they were going to nail his hide to the wall; that they meant for him to take the fall for all the wrongdoers. He came to see me the afternoon he got my note and told me he had enough documented evidence to put both Clinton and Governor Jim Guy Tucker in the penitentiary. I told him his only chance was to go public.

I encouraged David to get in contact with the national media, and his story began to be picked up by the *Los Angeles Times*, *The New York Times*, *The Washington Times* and *The Wall Street Journal*. The media coverage helped Hale, and Robert Fiske made a plea bargain deal with him. I have always believed that Fiske made the deal with Hale because Fiske wanted to cover up for Clinton. He did not want David's information to come out before the public.

Fiske had gotten Clark Clifford off without even a trial for his role in BCCI, one of the biggest scandals of the century. I believe Fiske was owned by Clinton. His White House Counsel, Bernard Nussbaum, was a friend of Fiske's. We also know that Fiske recommended to Nussbaum that Louis Freeh head up the FBI. William Sessions, you may recall, was fired as head of the FBI the day before Vince Foster was found dead.

No doubt David did what was best for him, and with the advice of his lawyer, agreed to help Fiske. I have not spoken with David since he was relocated by Fiske's staff in March of 1994. I never approved of David's activities at Capital Management Service, but at least he wanted to come clean—something Bill Clinton refuses to do.

Something that really needs a closer is this. On the same day that the subpoena was issued for all the documents in David Hale's office, Vince Foster died. The subpoena that went out that morning would uncover documents that contained tremendously incriminating evidence. In the same afternoon, Foster, who was the personal counsel for the Clinton's and knew about all Clinton's dealings, was found dead. Everyone had gotten in bed together and they were just about to put the covers on.

❖❖❖

Bill Clinton is a user. He uses people. He used Arkansas and he'll use the United States. He is capable of anything as demonstrated by this next story which screams to be told.

When my friend Jim Lindsey went up to see Colonel Holmes during the 1992 presidential campaign (to get the affidavit verifying Clinton's method of sneaking out of the draft through a ROTC deferment), Holmes had told Lindsey this story.

As Jim was about to leave, Holmes, a decorated war veteran who was in ill health, said, "I want to tell you about something that happened about the time Bill Clinton manipulated me." Holmes proceeded to tell me about a young man named Kim Johnson who was a member of the ROTC who had graduated, married and had two children.

The Vietnam War had heated up and Kim was called up. Holmes told Johnson that since he had family responsibilities, he could get him a position out of harm's way.

Holmes remembered Johnson's loyal retort: "No, sir. Airborne, sir; all the way, sir."

Three months later, Holmes attended Johnson's funeral. Holmes told Lindsey, "Thank God that for every Bill Clinton in the history of this country, there has always been a Kim Johnson to take his place."

PREFACE, CHAPTER 3

Imagine a man obsessed, willing to do anything for power. A little boy who would be king, who rages and throws tantrums when his whims are not met.

Now imagine such a man controlling the FBI, the DEA, the IRS, the CIA, the Justice Department, Customs, the ATF, and even the armed forces.

In other words, the corruption and the subjugation of the will of the people which took place in Arkansas **can now take place in America, only on a far more bold and frightening scale.**

Long-time acquaintance of Bill Clinton, Larry Nichols, received the perk of working at the Arkansas Development Finance Authority. Clinton mistook Larry to be "one of the boys" who would cooperate in crime in exchange for favors. During Larry's job at ADFA, he discovered Clinton's criminal activities. At great personal risk, he copied documents which exposed Clinton scams.

Vicious personal attacks against Larry (aimed at discrediting his testimony about Clinton) have been proven in court to be unfounded, yet the liberal press still prints this slander as truth. Larry Nichols went to court to prove his innocence, and he challenges Bill Clinton to do the same before Congress. Against the tide of liberal press control, threats and physical attacks, Nichols has doggedly sought to warn the American people about the true nature of their President, Bill Clinton.

CHAPTER 3

CLINTON'S CIRCLE OF POWER—THE EPICENTER
by Larry Nichols

Little Rock is the center of the universe to the rest of Arkansas, and it was there that two Arkansans, drawn to the big metropolis from different small towns and from somewhat different backgrounds, met in the late 1970s. One of these small-towners was Bill Clinton; the other was me.

Having a commercial production company in the late '70s caused me to cross paths with many up-and-coming politicians, such as Clinton. Most politicians sooner or later found their way to this establishment since it was one of the only commercial production companies in Little Rock, where they could get everything from radio commercials to bumper stickers.

Because of this business, many of the young political climbers and young business people would meet after hours for dinner and drinks. While running the bars and night-clubs together, none of us ever dreamed that one of the group was destined to become President of the United States.

In hindsight, maybe we should have at least con-sidered that possibility. Bill knew how to use people. For, although most of us thought at the time that he was little more than a spoiled brat, Bill Clinton was the greatest "networker" we'd ever seen. In fact, he was the first person we'd ever heard use that word, and now everybody realizes what an immensely powerful tool networking is.

Each one of us was one little connecting piece of mesh

39

in Clinton's huge network. Other small but essential links in Clinton's vast net were Sheffield Nelson, Jim Guy Tucker and a host of others who made up Little Rock's "who's who" of politics.

Exactly what Clinton might have done to all those others, who knows, but he eventually betrayed everyone in one way or another. Sheffield Nelson, for example, was promised by Clinton that he wouldn't run again for governor in 1990, leaving the way open for Nelson. Well, he broke his word and ran against Nelson anyway, who, incidentally, came close to beating Clinton.

If you knew Clinton long enough, you came to realize that lying wasn't second nature to him; it was first. You didn't have to be a psychiatrist to see that his lying almost seemed compulsive—like his internal gyroscope was off.

A woman author once said of a rival: "Every word that comes out of her mouth is a lie, including *and* and *the*." Bill Clinton was the same type of liar. Claiming that he came from humble Hope, Arkansas, was one of his countless lies; he really grew up in Hot Springs.

Bill and I first met when he was Arkansas' attorney general, an elective office he won in 1976. He became, at twenty-eight, the youngest attorney general in state history.

Here was a classic example of how his networking method paid off. Clinton apparently realized early on that even if one isn't wealthy himself, he can achieve the same political results as a rich man just by organizing well-heeled people, the press and politicians.

Later you could see that Clinton had been creating his own "circle of power," which would become more corrupt as he used state law enforcement agencies for witch hunts against his opponents.

One of Clinton's first political connections was Jim MacDougal, who was later to reward the Clintons with a full partnership in the infamous Whitewater Development scheme, although the Clintons put up almost no capital. Clinton first met MacDougal when they both worked on the Washington staff of U.S. Senator William J. Fulbright of

Arkansas.

Influential people like Fulbright were like a narcotic to Clinton. He'd become transfixed around powerful men, like someone who plays the slots at Vegas and just can't stop.

Everyone thought Bill was a strange character. If you could ever get someone who was close to him to level with you, they would always say the same thing: The man is strange; he's "different" from the rest of us.

Take his womanizing. It's not just his alley cat morals; it's the way he came apart when his sexual demands weren't met on the first encounter. When he didn't get what he wanted when he wanted it, he'd go berserk. Angry; mean; rude.

Whenever he insulted some woman who refused to satisfy his sexual appetite, we'd remark that he just lost another ten votes: the woman he abused, her parents and her friends.

Bob Woodward wrote a book called *The Agenda,* and it went over big because it divulged that Clinton sometimes went into rages and fits. This is news? Woodward must be slowing down or getting lazy, because any number of women who refused Clinton's demands over the last twenty or thirty years could have told you that.

This isn't said to be mean. Bill is the leader of the most powerful nation on earth and people have a right—no, an obligation—to know who he really is. You see, the humble guy with the "Oh shucks" look, unpretentiously biting down on his lip, is not the real Bill Clinton.

❖❖❖

Many people say that Bill is really a nice guy and that Hillary is the real villain. Such observers are wrong. Bill and Hillary are of the same cloth; the difference is that Hillary can't hide her evil designs (at least from anyone who is not totally naive), whereas Bill is a master actor.

They have survived and thrived together because they both believe in the same radical politics they loved and embraced when they worked on George McGovern's 1972 presidential campaign. The only difference is that Bill, because of his extraordinary talent for deception, can assume the mantle of a moderate, or even a conservative, while clinging tenaciously to his radical roots. Hillary, on the other hand, appears false when she tries to hide her radical beliefs.

Hillary's radical feminism was probably a big factor in Bill's losing his second race for governor in 1980. When first meeting her, you found you couldn't even call her Hillary Clinton. She insisted on being called Hillary Rodham (better known as the Dragon Lady).

Some analysts have mistakenly attributed her unpopularity with many Arkansans to her being a sort of Yankee outsider, someone Bill met at Yale Law School. That was not the case. She was disliked because she was arrogant (her in-your-face feminism was only part of it). Her contempt for the folks of Arkansas was beyond her ability to conceal.

Hillary entered our picture when she was beginning her career as a member of the Rose Law Firm in Little Rock. She was not a "fun" person, at least not with us native Arkansans. She saw us as hicks and her contempt often broke through in the form of rudeness. She especially despised Arkansas police officers—they can tell you stories galore about her arrogance. To her they were all rednecks.

When Clinton was elected governor in 1978, things changed. He made new friends and developed new habits that offended many of us. He, as the youngest governor in the country, doubtless had much bigger goals in mind, goals that didn't lend themselves to such things as genuine friendships and loyalty.

Don Tyson, the poultry magnate, is one long-time friend of Bill who has kept his closeness with Clinton. In Bill Clinton's moral universe, that can mean but two things: either Bill hasn't yet found anyone to take Tyson's place whose friendship is more exploitable than that of Tyson's, or Tyson knows too much about Clinton to be thrown overboard.

Clinton's acquaintance with Tyson goes back to the days before the attorney generalship. They met when Tyson's business was unheard of outside of Springdale, which is not far from Fayetteville, a sleepy little college town in the Ozark Mountains near the Missouri border. They developed a mutually beneficial relationship: Tyson would fund Clinton's campaigns and assist his quest for power; Clinton, in turn, would throw state help and money to Tyson while looking the other way when Tyson and his people were in conflict with the law. It became clear over the years that Tyson was more than just a money man for Clinton; he was one of his political godfathers.

While it may have shocked most Americans when Hillary made nearly $100,000 on a $1,000 investment in cattle futures (relying on "investment advice" from James Blair, the attorney for Tyson), it came as no surprise to anyone who knew of the coziness between the Clintons and Tyson. Any sane person would call that "investment profit" an out-and-out bribe. It's only fitting that Don Tyson's office at his Arkansas headquarters is an exact replica of the Oval Office—for Don Tyson might just as well be sitting in the real Oval Office.

The arrangement worked like this: in exchange for the money Tyson gave Clinton for his political ambitions, Clinton gave Tyson the rivers and streams of Arkansas.

You heard it right: Tyson Foods' one billion farm animals produce waste equivalent to that of forty million people (approximately the population of America's two biggest states). That amounts to a lot of waste to *properly* dispose of. So Tyson Foods just did the next best thing, which was to simply dump the chicken droppings and the like in Arkansas' rivers and streams, while the state government more or less looked the other way.

By 1990, Arkansas' Department of Pollution and Ecology tested the rivers and found that ninety-four percent of them were unusable for swimming and fishing. The waterways had become breeding grounds for bacteria and disease.

Bill Clinton liked the sort of relationship he had with Tyson, so he built some other friendships along similar lines in his calculated march to the White House. Prominent among these relationships was the one he had with Dan Lasater, a Kentuckian, who came to Arkansas after becoming a millionaire several times over. He achieved this in his mid-twenties through starting the Ponderosa steakhouse chain. In Little Rock he became a "bond daddy," running one of those bond-brokerage firms hawking bonds through high-pressure tactics in boiler room operations.

According to local wisdom, he first met Bill's mother, Virginia Kelley, and Clinton's half-brother, Roger Clinton, at the Hot Springs racetrack. Roger would later become an employee of Lasater's in the capacity of well-known local "go-fer."

Lasater had a love for horses and breeding stock. He was also, in gambling parlance, a high-roller. He was known as a druggie as well—a weed smoker (a user of marijuana and hash). Later he developed a taste for cocaine (as did Roger Clinton, whose cocaine debts Lasater helped pay).

Lasater always had drugs and lots of women, young women. There was one party Roger Clinton and Lasater threw where you could only come in an outfit made from one yard of cloth; one yard doesn't go very far.

Clinton's circle of power was growing. Lasater, like Tyson, would be a major contributor to Clinton's comeback campaign for governor in 1982.

Clinton was a genius in melding money with politics; he realized more than anyone that money could buy the right political friends, quash embarrassing investigations, and even cultivate a friendly press—in large part by having the big advertisers wield their leverage at the newspapers. Newspapers that didn't comply saw ads run by Clinton's business friends disappear.

But everyone has a weakness, and even Clinton's most powerful friends couldn't hide the fact that he came across as a smart aleck, a stuck-up spoiled brat. So in 1980, the voters of Arkansas, fed up with the arrogance of the first-term Governor Clinton and his wife, elected Frank White, a Republican, as governor.

As much as Clinton kow-towed to powerful business interests who would play ball with him, he alienated others who perhaps weren't willing to go along. One such alienated powerhouse was Jackson Stephens, Inc., the largest financial firm in Arkansas and one of the largest in the country. Stephens was not at all pleased with the Clinton's liberalism.

After Clinton's loss to Frank White, a big change came over him. It was then that we learned of his cocaine problem. Back in those days, taking a sip of whiskey was a big thing; cocaine was out of this world, at least in Arkansas. He really had changed—like a kid thrown off his high-horse and desperate to get back on—willing to sell his very soul to get on again.

Sometime in 1981, in a restaurant down in a community in south Arkansas, a group of us were working on a marketing plan for a local bank. Witt Stephens, brother of Jackson Stephens, told Bill Clinton (in front of the mayor of that community) that they would back him for governor in the race for '82, but they insisted he would have to dry out from cocaine first. Subsequent to that meeting, Clinton went somewhere in Minnesota and supposedly dried out.

From that meeting in the restaurant, Clinton developed a real hatred for the Stephens family and would stab them in the back many times after that.

In his second term, Clinton was smart enough not to repeat some of the blunders of his first term. He replaced his wise-acre kids with a mature group of aides, one of whom was Betsey Wright from Texas. Betsey had worked with the Clintons on the McGovern campaign and had the discipline Bill lacked. She became his chief of staff and really ran everything—especially in light of Bill's recurring cocaine problem.

We'll get back to that point in a minute; first, it has to

be pointed out that Clinton had complained for a long time that he could never run for President on the basis of his record in a flea-bitten state that didn't accomplish anything. So he and Hillary began telling his backers that Bill needed to make a mark in education if he was ever to ascend to the Oval Office.

During his first term, the forward-looking Clinton established the Governor's School for Gifted and Talented Students, which was later to come under fire for showing explicit sex-ed films. One Christian group described the school as Clinton's propaganda outlet dedicated to "humanism, pessimism and feminism."

But shrewd Clinton wasn't overly troubled by that; his thinking was that here you have a dirt-poor state like Arkansas and you pull all the brightest kids into one school where you can mold them the way you want—thereby eventually controlling the future elite of the state. Clinton's circle of power concept extended all the way down to the kids.

In 1983, the Clintons asked that a marketing plan be designed for the Arkansas schools. The marketing plan developed was "The Pepsi Challenge for Education," whereby children would exchange bottle caps for Apple computers and other items at their schools.

Next, the Clintons decided they would push for a new education standards program throughout the state, something he'd unsuccessfully tried to do in his first term. That plan had involved consolidating a lot of small school districts—which was resented in small towns because people wanted their own community schools, no matter how small. This scheme offended small-town folks so much that it contributed to his 1980 election defeat to Frank White.

This time around Clinton wasn't going to make the mistake of being perceived as unresponsive to the people. Betsey Wright put together a marketing program for the supposedly independent Education Standards Committee. In reality it was made up of Clinton public relations people, whose alleged purpose was to seek the views of Arkansas' people.

We would get the Democratic officials in each county to organize a public meeting for the Standards Committee, and then we'd turn out the local people when Clinton showed up. He visited every one of the seventy-five Arkansas counties to hold "open" meetings—*and every last meeting was rigged.* The education plan passed.

Hillary learned from this experience. She had "public" meetings for the Health Reform Task Force that she was later to chair from the White House—every meeting was similarly staged.

❖❖❖

Whenever something went awry, Clinton called us in to fix it. Betsey was used to control "emergencies" involving Bill's behavior in what were later to be known as "bimbo eruptions." We managed to cover everything up—always emphasizing to Bill how imperative it was to never allow himself to be photographed with any of his girlfriends.

One strategy developed for these bimbo eruptions, as well as for official problems, was called "rope-a-dope." Whatever the problem, Clinton was urged to lie low. "Let them hit you," he was instructed. "Just get out of town. In three or four days it will pass. Something else will intervene and it will be forgotten." We knew if he stood there arguing about it with the media, the thing might never blow over.

In addition, we would have "scripts." Friendly politicians would say anything we wanted to the public. For example, if some girl claimed Clinton had harassed her in Jonesboro, Arkansas, on a Saturday night, we'd have some state senator lie to the press saying "that was impossible" because Clinton was in Fayetteville that night.

Here's a perfect example of how these prepared "scripts" worked. During the '92 presidential campaign, a young lady named Connie Hamszy told *Penthouse* magazine about her having had sex with Clinton. Hamszy was a rock groupie who used to sneak into the North Little Rock Hilton to use the hotel's pool. One day—August 31, 1984, to be exact—she was sunbathing when Clinton caught a glimpse of her. He sent an aide to ask her to come meet the governor—with her wearing nothing more than the bikini she had on.

The young lady agreed, and Clinton began a frantic search to find an empty conference room to use for a quick encounter. He finally located one; it was over in a matter of minutes. Then, as if nothing untoward had happened, Clinton returned to the Capitol—the total statesman—and all was forgotten.

Well, not quite all. Years later Clinton was faced with the young lady's allegation. What did he do? Well, Bill was a lawyer and he knew that to win a case you need to discredit the witness. So his people swung into action. Clinton's press aide issued a statement declaring that three witnesses would testify that "Hamszy accosted Clinton" in the lobby of the Hilton, and that being the dignified statesman and loyal family member that he was, "He rebuffed the advance."

Here's one of the "scripts" from none less than an Arkansas state legislator, Jimmie Don McKissack: "I was dumbfounded. He [Clinton] turned red. She reached for his groin and backed off."

As scripts go, that wasn't the best of creations. What sort of fool would believe that a bikini-clad girl would walk into an uppity hotel's lobby and grab the governor's groin? But, somehow, it worked.

A big problem for people trying to protect Clinton was that he would never level with anyone as to what had actually taken place. He would not only lie to the public but also to those trying to help him. For example, he'd say that he'd never been in the town where he was accused of having harassed some woman, when in actuality he had been.

These are the two recurring sicknesses of Bill's: his obsession with women and his inability to stop lying—to anyone, no matter how trusted or how close.

❖❖❖

In a remote area of western Arkansas, you'll find the small town of Mena. It's about an hour's drive south of Fort Smith. In the 1980s, Mena, Arkansas, was principally known for its airstrip, which had a "garage" (a hangar where planes were retrofitted and repaired). The garage was owned by Rich Mountain Air, but appeared to be a CIA front or "cut-out."

Many of the pilots who were part of the Contra supply operation would regularly fly into Mena for repairs at Rich. You couldn't have picked a more "out of the way" spot, which of course, is exactly what the CIA would be seeking for such an operation.

For related reasons, convicted drug dealer Barry Seal (one of the CIA-contracted pilots) saw Mena as an ideal spot for drug smuggling. He had noticed that planes returning from Central America didn't have to go through customs upon landing at Mena for retrofitting—a perfect cover for smuggling. Of course, Arkansas also had a sleazy governor who would cover for him. Soon Seal had half of the pilots in the operation bringing drugs back on their conveniently empty return flights.

Seal was murdered in February 1986 while preparing to testify against the Medellin cartel. The three-man hit squad that located him in a halfway house in Louisiana was said to have been sent by a Colombian drug lord.

In reality, Seal knew far more about drug trafficking in Arkansas and "where the bodies were buried" than he knew about Colombia. His testimony sure could have put many American officials in jail.

As it turns out, the Mena airport in Arkansas was a main thoroughfare for much, if not most, of the drugs flowing in from Central America. Russ Welch, the Arkansas State Police investigator looking into Mena, stated publicly, on the record, that Mena was just one link in a whole network of drug drops throughout the state.

Now we know there were hundreds of millions of dollars worth of cocaine coming into the small state of Arkansas. This was creating a great problem. How do you distribute so much contraband without getting noticed? How do you launder the immense profits from such an enterprise?

This is where Clinton's friend Dan Lasater came into the picture. Lasater had his bond business, Lasater & Co., which became one of the main points to launder the drug money. (Lasater used ADFA, the Arkansas Development Finance Authority to help in this laundering.)

Don Tyson, another close friend of Clinton's, also has links with the cocaine industry in this state. Files from the Arkansas State Police, the FBI and the Drug Enforcement Agency document Tyson's role in drug trafficking. Here's an excerpt from one DEA document: "On July 5, 1984, [Confidential Informant] telephoned concerning narcotic trafficking by Donald J. Tyson in and around the area of Fayetteville, Arkansas. The informant had information concerning heroin, cocaine, and marijuana trafficking in the states of Arkansas, Texas, and Missouri by the Tyson organization."

The DEA report goes on to describe key lieutenants in the Tyson drug organization as well as a place near Fayetteville called "the Barn," which was used by Tyson as a stash for "large quantities of marijuana and cocaine." Another memo from the state police files tells of one informant's testimony that Tyson's plane was used to ferry drugs between Florida and Arkansas. Still another DEA report details how Tyson smuggled drugs from Central America by putting the contraband inside horses that were being shipped to Hot Springs, Arkansas.

In 1984, Tyson registered a relatively modest eighteen million dollars in profit. In 1994, his company, with almost a quarter of the total United States chicken market, was expected to reap over $600 million. It's highly questionable for a company to expand that fast in the highly competitive poultry industry—even with a governor turning a blind eye to that business' mass pollution.

✧✧✧

Jack Stephens of the Stephens Investment Company was (and still is) powerfully connected with many Republicans in Washington.

Stephens Investment Company owns twenty-six percent of Worthen Banking, which owns Worthen Bank. Worthen Bank had direct links to the state development agency (ADFA) that was used to launder the drug money. At a critical point during the presidential campaign, Worthen would provide Clinton with a line of credit for three million dollars. This type of loan is considered choice by any bank since it is backed up by matching funds from the federal government.

Lasater, too, became tremendously wealthy from laundering cocaine money. In his seemingly limitless affluence, he became arrogant, throwing drug parties and inviting everyone in town. At these gatherings, lines of cocaine would be laid out on coffee tables and would be distributed in bowls and ashtrays.

So blatant did he become, together with his sidekick, Roger Clinton, that the state police (caught in a federal-state task force) had no choice but to act. Dan Lasater was arrested and convicted of cocaine distribution. He was sentenced to two and a half years in prison, but not too surprisingly, considering who his friend was, he served only six months.

What really nailed Lasater was the testimony of a sixteen-year-old girl from North Little Rock. She was a virgin until she met Lasater, who then plied her with cocaine. She became his mistress; he sent her to his doctor, who put her on birth-control pills. The last anyone heard of her she was a prostitute in Lake Tahoe, Nevada. Her life had been destroyed.

Bill Clinton, a man who of late has tried to acquire a reputation as being tough on crime—and properly contemptuous of child abusers—*gave Lasater a full pardon.*

❖❖❖

Of course, Clinton knew about Lasater and his brother, Roger. Roger had a four-gram-a-day habit. Everyone knew.

Clinton reaped tremendous second-hand benefits from the entire cocaine operation. Among other things, Bill and Hillary took frequent trips on Lasater's jet. It was during this period that Clinton himself went through another bout as a cocaine abuser. If you snort enough cocaine, it burns the membranes in your nose. Those tissues are delicate and Clinton lost all of them—he blew out his soft tissues. This is why he has so many allergies and he rarely visits Camp David. This is also why he takes regular shots of cortisone, which give him the red, puffy look.

✧✧✧

When state police investigator Russ Welch and IRS investigator Bill Duncan found evidence of drug smuggling and money laundering at Mena, one would have expected the governor of that state to pitch right in with substantial law enforcement support. Clinton didn't.

By 1988, Charles Black, Deputy Prosecutor for Polk County (which covers Mena), had collected *over 20,000 pages of evidence in his criminal file on Mena.* He then asked Clinton for help—not knowing Bill's friends were the brain trust behind the whole thing! Clinton ignored Black and the gigantic drug operation he'd uncovered, although Clinton later claimed he allocated $25,000 in special funds. The record shows that he never came through even with that relatively paltry amount.

It should be known that Clinton himself probably was not part of the brain trust behind the Mena drug operation. As long as he was able to get his own dope and have his lady friends, what did he care about his associates' activities at Mena? Clinton stopped being a "passive" player at Mena when it became a potential albatross with Welch and Duncan breathing down his neck. No doubt he wanted to cover it up for his powerful friends.

Welch would eventually be forced out of the investigation. At one point in the investigation he was poisoned with anthrax by an unknown party. Fortunately, he managed to survive this attempt on his life.

Duncan would be taken off the Mena case by 1986—and eventually forced out of the IRS entirely.

It was then, in early 1988, that a job at the Arkansas Development Finance Authority opened up—a job that would change my life. The position of marketing director at ADFA (a position created especially for me) put me in a technician's slot for $21,000. Then they went to the legislature to boost my salary to $46,000 a year.

The job began in earnest by February 1988. I worked under the president of ADFA, Wooten Epes, who was a very scholarly-looking fellow with horn-rimmed glasses and a bow tie . He looked around twenty-seven, but in actuality was about forty-five. He was one of the yuppie crowd around Clinton.

ADFA's office was in an ultra-modern building in downtown Little Rock, my office being next to Epes'. He knew of my abilities and relationship with Clinton. (When ADFA was first formed in 1985, its offices were in Jim MacDougal's Madison Guaranty Building.)

In the first two weeks at ADFA, my job description should have been to create awareness for this little-known agency that could create jobs for Arkansans. Clinton always wanted to let people know what he was doing for them.

You see, the stated purpose of ADFA was to give loans at below-market rates to start up businesses, churches, schools, and other institutions that couldn't get loans from banks. ADFA would put the full credit of the state of Arkansas behind its offerings because ADFA, in turn, would create new jobs for Arkansas. It all sounded good, but that's not the way it worked.

For one thing, no one could get access to anything. The agency was basically involved in a civil war between the two parts from which it was formed, the former Housing Authority, and the Industrial Development Agency. They wouldn't even talk to one another.

Clinton and Epes decided they could privatize the Housing Authority to gain control of the $8.5 million it received each year from mortgage payments. At the same time they took the Housing Authority out of the hands of the legislature, merging it with the agency's industrial development program.

In 1985 the legislature, through Act 1062, created ADFA. It was a slick trick, because it became Clinton's private piggy bank—while still having the credit and name of the state of Arkansas behind all its bond offerings. It was the only agency of its kind in the country. As a private agency, it worked perfectly because its dealings were with private companies, many of which were run by Clinton's friends and supporters,who, in turn, could get loan applications without being concerned with anyone looking through their paperwork to ascertain whether they merited such loans.

Each month the board of ADFA would meet—once in the morning and once in the afternoon. At the morning meeting, applications would be "reviewed" and approved. This was done in private. It was the bureaucratic equivalent of the judicial kangaroo court. Clinton appointed everyone.

In most bonding agencies, appointees are divided between the legislature and other state officials, or members are given staggered terms, allowing for no one person to dominate the proceedings; but not here.

As for the afternoon meeting, all that took place was the announcing of who were awarded the loans. The loan application was a joke. It was just a simple set of documents to which Clinton supporters attached a profit and loss statement. ADFA never even bothered checking out these applications.

As if that weren't easy enough, you could make *sure* the loan was approved if you paid $50,000 to the Rose Law Firm in Little Rock. Hillary was a partner there, as was Webb Hubbell, who would later join the Clintons in Washington as associate attorney general, and as did another Rose partner, Vince Foster, whose mysterious, supposed suicide and its blatant cover-up is an ever-growing stain on the Clinton Administration.

From 1985 to 1988 there were only five issues for industrial development bonds. That was over a three-year span! It looked funny. They were all friends of Bill—people like Webb Hubbell and his family. The Stephens were in on the act too.

Apparently Clinton saw no impropriety here; after all, it was all in the family. *Clinton personally signed off on every loan.*

Who wrote the legislation creating ADFA? Webb Hubbell—which explains it all. Who got one of the first ADFA loans (for $2.75 million)? None other than the Park-O-Meter Company, owned by Hubbell's brother-in-law,

Seth Ward. Hubbell was also an officer with the company. Who wrote up Park-O-Meter's application? Again we see the same names—Webb Hubbell and the Rose Law Firm.

In any other state, this would have been a severe breach of the law. But guess who wrote Arkansas' so-called ethics-in-government law in 1988. Mr. Webb Hubbell!

❖❖❖

Even though Clinton had a closet full of skeletons, my understanding of ADFA's role was still naive. After pushing Epes, saying that we should hustle more loans, he said to me: "You don't understand. Your job is not to get loans. It's damage control."

It was the dawn breaking through—realizing this job and ADFA itself was part of the Clinton politics-as-usual game. ADFA was just another prop for Clinton's campaign literature, to tell Arkansans how much he'd done for them—when in fact it was used almost entirely to enrich him and his friends. ADFA was in the epicenter of the circle of power, where the network of kickbacks, paybacks and corruption emanated.

If you should go to ADFA today, the personnel would take out big volumes of only twenty-five companies they say they've made loans to. L J. Davis of *The New Republic* went there and saw an application for a twenty-sixth company, but they immediately removed that one from his sight, probably because it proved more wrongdoing.

Davis believes they made anywhere from sixty-five to seventy-five loans in seven years. Not all that many for an agency dedicated to the single purpose of making loans. Where are the records for the forty or so missing loans? Probably shredded. Here's why:

After two months of putting together the annual report, it became apparent that *no one was paying interest on these loans.* The question arose, where are the payments from these companies on their loans? After checking with everybody concerned, it became apparent that there weren't any.

It should have been obvious: the job of marketing director was to cover for the good ol' boys system, to put out fires. This was the fire.

ADFA was profitable for everyone (except, of course, the taxpayers). Rose would get its $50,000 per application. Then the deal had to be "structured." Clinton's old law firm of Wright, Lindsey, Jennings would get another $50,000 for that. In addition, the Clinton campaign would get another $50,000 as a kickback for the loan.

One afternoon during a luncheon with the ADFA board in the Quapaw Towers, James Branyon, ADFA's chairman at the time, yelled down the table to one of the members, asking if the applicant had put his $50,000 into the campaign. The board member shouted back, "No!"

Branyon responded in an equally loud voice, "Then hold up the loan." It amazed me that he had yelled that kind of thing out in a public restaurant.

❖❖❖

From 1985 to 1992, ADFA would loan out 719 million dollars, allegedly to help the disadvantaged of Arkansas.

Instead, the money went to profitable companies who made the required donation to Clinton's campaigns.

The *Los Angeles Times* looked into the payoff system and discovered that Clinton's 1990 campaign for governor received over $400,000 just from companies that benefited from ADFA (That was just the 1990 campaign and the money that could be directly traced).

Another thing that really piqued my interest—and led to troubles galore: "Who bought these bonds?" It made sense that whoever it was, they were going to be looking for blood when they didn't receive their payments. Problem was, you couldn't locate even one owner of ADFA bonds. Laws were definitely being broken.

In late August 1988, my concern over what seemed to be a major problem prompted me to say to Bill one day in his office: "Bill, there's something real wrong here. This agency is breaking the law." He made a comment that seemed to express genuine concern, and said that he would clean it up and make it right. He then said he had to go to Japan on a trade mission for two weeks and that when he got back he'd tend to it. (Before confronting Bill, I'd spent lots of time copying documents in ADFA. Not knowing how all this was coming down, it just seemed like the smart thing to do.)

A week later the media broke a story about me, alleging I had been using state funds and property to make telephone calls to raise money for the Contras—that I was guilty of "theft by deception." Every day brought a supposed new revelation about my "wrongdoings"—TV, newspaper headlines, the radio, you name it.

When Clinton got back from his trip, my words to him were: "Call this off. My daddy has a blood pressure problem; this will kill him. Just tell the truth."

He told me to go home; that he'd arrange it. The next morning, the message coming from Clinton to me through a conference call from Wooten, Clinton and Betsey Wright was, "The only way this will stop is if you resign." They promised my resignation would close my personnel file and the attack would end.

My question to them was, "Why resign when it wasn't me that did something wrong?" There was, of course, no answer given to that, and it became plain that the only choice was to cut losses and get out of there. Only a few minutes after my signed letter of resignation was placed in their hands did the voice of Bill Clinton enter my car, via the radio, saying at a press conference that he didn't know me; that Larry Nichols was just some guy who'd been taking taxpayer dollars to help the Contras, and that a full investigation into this wrongdoing was underway. I pulled over to the side of the road in a fit of rage. The only thing I remember saying was, "This ain't over."

Clinton kept up the attack, and for six months every imaginable allegation was made about me in the press. At the end of three months, Wooten Epes was canned from ADFA for supposedly mishandling me. He then took a job in the Stephens building.

Clinton then put in his longtime aide, Bob Nash, to run ADFA. Nash later became undersecretary in the Department of Agriculture under Mike Espy—who was brought under investigation for accepting gifts from none other than Don Tyson. Nash has probably been Tyson's guy in the U.S. Department of Agriculture all along. What's funny is that Espy got sacked, and if Nash ever gets the job, he'll clean things up, all right, Clinton style.

Meanwhile, all these guys were in cahoots with the ADFA scam, and they knew some of their dirty little secrets had been discovered. They planned to roast me. It was clear that they were worried about ADFA, judging by the unprecedented, unrelenting attack the Clinton people were inciting the media to make on my credibility, .

At that point, the magnitude of the ADFA scam still hadn't dawned on me. It wasn't until a year or two after leaving ADFA that Bill Duncan, the former IRS investigator of Mena, came to my home. It was Duncan who explained how some of the money trails out of Mena led to Dan Lasater, and from there to central Arkansas. He wondered if I could help him and if ADFA could be connected. From what Duncan told me, I started reviewing documents I had made copies of. What I found was that Lasater was indeed using that agency to launder his drug money, and Clinton had signed off on every bit of it.

Millions of dollars in bonds were purchased by Lasater, then sold and rebought through trading accounts in Lasater's firm. The upshot was that untold millions were being laundered without using banks directly or acknowledging it to the IRS.

The problem was that just having this information was not enough. The media had to help in getting the information out—which they showed zero interest in doing. With all their resources for establishing such things, they wanted me to search it out and just hand it to them all finished—which probably was just stonewalling on their part.

In 1994 a credible witness, Dennis Patrick, stepped forward and told his story to the *Economist* magazine and to Ambrose Evans-Pritchard of the *London Telegraph.* Back in 1985, a friend of Patrick's who worked at Lasater & Co. talked him into opening a brokerage account at the firm. At the time, Patrick had no more than $60,000—but he was startled to find that Lasater's company had laundered over $50 million through that account! He was understandably besieged by the IRS, and since Lasater was then in jail on cocaine charges, Patrick complained to the individual running the firm, a young woman named Patsy Thomasson. He was assured everything would be corrected, but he soon learned there was a contract out to kill him. Eventually federal agents told Patrick of three attempts on his life. Patrick went into hiding, and he's still there.

Why? Because Lasater is the President's friend and that young woman, Patsy Thomasson, is now a special assistant to the President. Wouldn't you be worried, especially after watching the mass cover-up which has attended the death of someone far, far bigger—namely White House Deputy Counsel Vincent Foster?

Patsy keeps popping up in all sorts of strange settings.

She's one of Clinton's main fixers. She was one of the people who went into Foster's office the night he died, even before his body had cooled. Those entering even admitted they took out documents.

Patsy, whose name has appeared in various law enforcement files for being involved in drug trafficking is, believe it or not, *in charge of security clearances and passes at the White House.* She dropped random drug testing for White House employees—which is understandable for someone like her, who had trouble getting a security clearance because of her involvement with Lasater.

✧✧✧

In 1990 it was time to bear down on Clinton. One thing that hadn't been exposed yet was how Clinton kept a slush fund using ADFA money to pay for his sexual high jinks. I filed a lawsuit against Clinton and ADFA in September 1990,which hit smack in the middle of his reelection campaign for governor against Sheffield Nelson. In my press release issued with the suit, the womanizing was highlighted like this: "For as long as Clinton has been in power, he has engaged in a scheme to divert state funds for personal gain and specifically to entertain girlfriends."

My belief was that the media would be more interested in the womanizing than in the boring financial story about ADFA being used to help Clinton run for President.

The idea that Clinton might be aiming for the presidency became an issue during the 1990 campaign for governor when a reporter picked up on my statement. He asked Clinton at a debate if he was planning on running for President. "Will you guarantee all of us," the reporter asked, "that if reelected, there is absolutely, positively no way that you'll run for any other political office, and that you'll serve out your full term?"

Here's Clinton's response: "You bet. I told you when I announced for governor that I intended to run, and that's what I'm gonna do. I'm gonna serve four years; I made that decision when I decided to run. I'm being considered as a candidate for governor. That's the job I want. That's the job for the next four years."

Obviously Clinton will do or say anything it takes to get elected. Remember, Clinton has a different idea of honesty than most folks.

❖❖❖

The lawsuit exposing Clinton's wrongdoings was transferred to a Clinton-appointed judge. The judge quashed and sealed my case.

On October 19, 1990, my first and only press conference was held on the steps of the state Capitol building. The conference exposed the truth about Clinton's women and how he abused his power by using state facilities and ADFA funds to conduct these relationships. Five women were named who Clinton had used state funds to romance: Gennifer Flowers, Debra Mathis, Elizabeth Ward, Lencola Sullivan and Susie Whittaker. Not one word of this got printed in the press! Bill Simmons, the Associated Press bureau chief in Little Rock went around telling people that not a word of it was true and not to print it.

In April 1991, Robert "Say" Macintosh, a black activist, sued Clinton. In his suit he said that Clinton didn't fulfill his promise to pay him $25,000 for denouncing me to the media regarding my information that Clinton slept with black women.

At about the same time, a reporter for the *Arkansas Democrat-Gazette* decided to check on the status of my case—just for kicks. He called and informed me that my case had been opened on November 17 and then resealed. Since one must appeal within thirty days of a decision, and this was already April, it was apparent these guys had slam-dunked me. The only choice was to move my suit to federal court in order to keep the case alive and to make an issue of it during the presidential campaign in 1992.

The media came to me asking for proof. Again, they wanted me to do the work for them, and again they were unwilling to do the digging themselves. They wanted me to get a woman to talk, but they'd all been paid for their silence. Susie Whittaker had landed a cushy job working as a liaison between Arkansas and Washington. Also, Elizabeth Ward had bee hired by the Clintons' close friends, Hollywood producers Harry Thomason and Linda Bloodworth Thomason.

Star magazine sent a reporter to ask me if I could get any of the women to go public. My recommendation was that they talk to Gennifer Flowers. In working with *Star* magazine, my idea was to have them interview and print my story first, before they broke the Flowers story. They agreed to this.

When my story appeared in *Star*, Bill Simmons ran an AP story saying that I couldn't prove my allegations. Simmons said that he had personally interviewed all of the women and that he knew that it was not true. Then the *Star* piece came out about Flowers, making a fool of Simmons while proving the veracity of my charges. It also showed that Simmons was a part of the Clinton propaganda machine rather then an unbiased bureau chief for the Associated Press. To this day, when Clinton needs a lie put out nationally, Clinton's people go to their friend Bill Simmons in the AP.

❖❖❖

Later we would learn just how concerned the Clintons were about Gennifer Flowers. According to *The American Spectator*, Betsey Wright hired a private detective to dig up dirt on Flowers. Interestingly, the detective asked one of Gennifer's friends, "Do you think Gennifer is the type to commit suicide?" Fortunately for her, Gennifer had no history of depression and by not fitting the suicide "type" was spared Vince Foster's fate.

With the breaking of the Flowers story, the media were inundating me and my family. The pressure was so great I decided to drop the suit, since the media had it all anyway.

On a call to Buddy Young, Clinton's main henchman

and head of the State Police detail around Clinton, I ended our dispute. Clinton agreed to meet me and to apologize to my family, and he did. However the harassment against me and my family went on.

Consequently, I made a promise to Bill Clinton that one day he and I would meet at high noon and one of us would get out of town. I also promised to report a scandal a week until everyone in the world knew who and what he was.

Since that time it has been almost exactly as I promised, with one scandal after another being released, each one revealing a little more about Clinton and his corruption. No one could have believed everything about him if it had come out all at once. Now more and more people are starting to understand this man and his wife.

No President has been disliked or mistrusted more than this one. The American people are just getting proof of what most of them have already known in their hearts about Clinton.

I'll take the hits. There's nothing anyone can do to stop that. But, there is still time to stop him. You see, Clinton hasn't closed the circle of power yet, but each day he gets closer. I'm not talking here about opinion polls. The Clintons know they are meaningless. The circle of power is about control: controlling the media and the law enforcement agencies.

That's why Clinton put Webb Hubbell in as associate attorney general; he needs to control justice. That's why Janet Reno, as her first act in office, fired every U.S. attorney—without having a single replacement ready. That's why William Sessions had to be fired as director of the FBI, and why the heads of the Secret Service, and the Bureau of Alcohol, Tobacco and Firearms had to be replaced.

You get a glimpse of the circle of power through Whitewater: Clinton's best friend, Roger Altman managed that mess and the attendant Madison Bank problems, taking temporary control of the Resolution Trust Corporation, which was investigating Madison. He subsequently got caught in lies and had to step down from his job as Assistant Secretary of Finance.

Clinton sought to put a close friend in as head of the FDIC. A friend of Bill (FOB) is Comptroller of the Currency, overseeing all the banks.

Imagine a man obsessed, willing to do anything for power—a little boy who would be king, who rages and throws tantrums when his whims are not met. Now imagine such a man controlling the FBI, the DEA, the IRS, the CIA, the Justice Department, Customs, the ATF, even the armed forces.

In other words, the corruption, and the subjugation of the will of the people that took place in Arkansas *can now take place in America, only on a far more bold and frightening scale.*

Telling the truth about this man who will stop at nothing isn't easy. The jailings, the threats, the harassment, and the slander my family has suffered—has it been worth it? The price is sky-high: we've paid it, and are paying it now, and may pay it for the rest of our lives.

If I could say anything to Bill Clinton, it would be that it's bound to be a great burden to walk around lying from one thing to another.

Bill, tell the truth. You may not be able to remain President, but the truth will set you free. It sets all of us free, and it will save this nation from "the boy that would be king."

PREFACE, CHAPTER 4

The police told me recently that this will be just another one of "Arkansas' unsolved mysteries." My mother and I can't accept that; we won't. That's why we are speaking out.

Gary Parks presents startling information revealing the calculated cover-up of his father's murder. Due to some unique circumstances (including being in charge of Bill Clinton's security during the *Clinton for Presidency* campaign), Gary's dad, Jerry Parks, compiled a damaging file on Bill Clinton. When Jerry's silence could not be bought, someone stole the files from Jerry's home. Later, in broad daylight, a professional hit man riddled Jerry's car, finishing the execution at close range. Gary outlines Clinton's involvement in this and the abuses of power documented by his murdered father.

CHAPTER 4

HIT AND RUN EXECUTION

by Gary Parks

On September 26, 1993, my father, Jerry Parks, the former head of security for Bill Clinton's presidential campaign headquarters, was brutally murdered.

That day will live in my heart until I die.

It was a Sunday in Little Rock. Dad was driving home after grabbing a bite to eat at El Chico Mexican Restaurant, one of his favorite places. I wasn't living at home at the time, and Mom, who suffers from advanced multiple sclerosis, couldn't cook. El Chico was a good place for us to meet, so we went there often. Unfortunately, on this Sunday I was busy, so Dad ate alone.

Police say that Dad left El Chico at about 6:30 p.m., while it was still daylight. About six miles from our house in rural Pulaski County, he made a left turn from Chenal Parkway onto Highway 10, just on the outskirts of west Little Rock.

This was the most direct route home, but unfortunately it was also the most predictable, so as a precaution Dad had avoided going this way for months. He had reason to believe that people were out to kill him. He knew that if assassins were out to set him up, he had to keep his activities, such as the route he took home, irregular. I remember how he would take the back roads home, which many times took him thirty miles out of the way.

I can only speculate that on this fateful day he must have felt more relaxed than usual, since he and Mom had just gotten back the day before from a week-long vacation in the Bahamas. He may have figured that since it was

Sunday evening, the only people on the road were going home from church. He was wrong.

Although almost all the eyewitnesses present at the scene the night of my father's murder have changed their stories, one eyewitness, a thirty-year police veteran, has not. Through him we have been able to determine basically what happened.

As my dad made the left turn to Chenal Parkway, a Chevrolet Caprice traveling two cars behind his vehicle suddenly shot ahead, crossed the intersection and cut Dad off.

There were two people in the Caprice. The passenger began firing at my father with a 9mm semi-automatic pistol. By the time Dad's car had stopped, the killer had already shot him three times.

My father apparently tried in vain to get hold of his .38 Colt "Detective Special," which he kept between the car seats. Then, as he exited his car, one of the assailants leapt from the Caprice and fired another four shots into his body. Dad dropped to the intersection, blood pouring from his wounds.

The gunman—who eyewitnesses say was a white male in his forties, six feet tall, with salt and pepper colored hair and beard—jumped back into the Caprice and took off west on Highway 10.

Of the seven shots that hit Dad, at least four were lethal: two shots to the chest, one to the lower left side of his abdomen, and another bullet which hit a major artery in his leg. But I am sure he did not die easily.

My dad was six foot three inches tall, weighing nearly 300 pounds (photo in Appendix A). He wasn't fat, just powerful—a second degree black belt in karate. I tell people he could bench press a small European automobile. He used to work out regularly with a "Mr. Arkansas" and could typically bench press one hundred pounds more than his professional workout partner.

Mom says:

"Jerry was a wonderful man. He was so funny and laughed a lot, like a big old teddy bear. He also loved God. He would go to church, and you'd see this big old guy with his arms lifted up. It was like seeing a mountain up there."

The cowards who killed my father wanted to make sure they brought him down. We later learned that the Caprice had been seen driving around the area of that intersection for three hours before the attack. My father had been stalked.

When police arrived at the scene, they flew Dad's body to Doctors Hospital in Little Rock. Although, the paramedic told me that Dad was already dead when they got to the scene, the hospital medical team tried desperately to revive him. But after two hours, they officially declared him dead. I was told later they were hoping to get him conscious just long enough to say who might have done this terrible thing to him.

There's a lot of graft in Arkansas, especially around Little Rock. There's lots of people paying off other people. That's why people feared Dad, because he was a good, honest man. You see, there are many people who are benefiting from Clinton being President.

Some very influential Arkansans have told me that my father was probably the only person in the state who could have brought Clinton down. I have no doubt that Clinton himself, or people behind Clinton, had my father murdered.

"I can't tell you that President Clinton ordered my husband to be murdered. But I can tell you that what Jerry had in his files could have unseated this President of the United States."

Dad was a police officer by profession, but had left police work in 1976 to work as a private investigator. He later became an executive with one of the country's largest private security firms, Guards Mark. In 1986, Dad, with a business partner, John McIntire, opened up his own security and janitorial business, American Contract Services. However, his investigation of Clinton had begun before this in 1984 and lasted until at least 1990.

At that time in 1984, my family was living in the Vantage Point Apartments near downtown Little Rock. Mom was the manager of the apartment complex.

That was also the year Governor Clinton's half-brother, Roger Clinton, was arrested for cocaine use. In the summer of 1984, Bill Clinton's friends decided to hide Roger away from the public scrutiny of the press.

Bill was friendly with the owner of Vantage Point, Thomas Winterger. Winterger apparently offered Roger use of a one-bedroom corporate apartment free of charge.

My mom's office was created from two bedrooms that had once been part of the apartment Roger was living in. She was practically "living with him" for a few months that summer of 1984, separated only by the paper-thin walls of the corporate apartment and a bedroom door secured with a deadbolt lock.

My mother had no choice but to hear what was going on. Roger and his friends were very loud and were always partying.

> *"You could hear through the walls and through the vents, and almost from the moment Roger moved in, the party started."*

I visited Roger's apartment several times. On one occasion he offered me marijuana. I was only thirteen; Roger was about twenty-eight.

Roger's apartment became the hangout for the young girls who lived at Vantage, girls between the ages of thirteen and eighteen, many of whom were my friends.

> *"What really started concerning me, about a week and a half into his residency there, were the*

young girls who came to the door. Roger would visit with them. These girls were young—fourteen, fifteen and sixteen years old."

Roger constantly enticed the teenagers up to his place for parties with marijuana and cocaine. The cocaine was plentiful and was visible each time I was there, spread out on a mirror which rested on a coffee table. Usually three or four girls would be in the apartment.

"There was such an odor coming from Roger's apartment . . . that I went over there to see what was going on. There was cocaine on the furniture, the coffee tables. It really scared me."

Many tenants of the complex complained about Roger's activities, particularly about the loud music which sometimes went on until after midnight.

Residents also complained when Roger and his party-goers ran out into the pool—on more than one occasion—buck naked. People would watch, thinking it was really funny, because the buildings of the complex all faced the pool. One time, Roger was so drugged out by the pool that Mom had to take him physically by the arm back into his apartment.

"When [Roger and I] opened the door to the apartment, Bill [Clinton] was there. He was stoned. He wouldn't have known what was going on. He was basically sitting there on the couch with his arms down, just staring into the air. There wasn't anything but cocaine in the apartment. It was on the living room coffee table when I opened the door."

I never saw anyone have sex with any of the girls, but one girl who lived in the complex claimed to have had sex with Roger and Bill at the same time. She was only fifteen.

*"One day Bill Clinton came to the apartment.
He had an argument with Roger. Two women then
came in two different state trooper cars. The girls
were probably in their late teens. They couldn't
have been twenty. It wasn't fifteen minutes before
the noise started in the bedroom, and it was vulgar.
It was Bill's voice and they were having some sort
of sex party in that bedroom. The noise that came
out of there I had never heard before. The 'F—'
word was used real often. 'I'm going to sc--w your
head off' was used too, but that was just minor.
God's name was taken in vain over and over."*

Bill would come over frequently, two or three times a
week at any time of the day or night, usually in a state
police car. Roger would usher all the teenagers out, and
frequently a whole wave of adult party-goers would then
show up.

Dan Lasater, later convicted for distributing cocaine,
showed up many times as well. Roger had been working for
Lasater, who was also a big contributor to Clinton's campaigns.

I remember one time when Bill came and Roger went
through his routine of clearing his apartment. A few
minutes later, a state trooper pulled up and dropped off a
young lady, who went into Roger's place.

About ten minutes later another state police car
showed up, and another young lady popped out to go in.
Both were good looking.

*"On one of the occasions when there were
some young girls there, Bill Clinton's driver dropped
him off. You could hear the loud talk through the
walls. Bill made the comment, 'This is really good
sh-t.' He was referring to the cocaine which had
been dropped off earlier. A young man had come by
the office looking for Roger Clinton. I just happened
to be going around the corner when Roger opened
the door and said, 'You've got my sh— with you?'*

*The guy said, 'Yeah, I've got it.' He held what
appeared to be a bag of cocaine."*

My mother asked my father if he would begin taking
notes of the comings and goings at the apartment. She was
afraid that if Roger was busted dealing drugs out of his
apartment, she could be held responsible, especially since
he wasn't paying rent.

Dad's observations were real casual, just enough to
keep Mom out of trouble. He made notes of times, people,
and car tags.

By the fall of 1984, Roger Clinton had moved out and
had begun serving time in federal prison. Soon after that,
Dad said he'd been hired by someone to begin a full investigation on Bill Clinton.

My father always wanted me to follow in his footsteps.
Whenever he went out on a stakeout, he took me with him.

Over the next few years, I'd go out with him to a
number of spots frequented by Bill Clinton. Usually this
included the governor's mansion, Quapaw Tower Apartments, or Governor's Park Apartments. We'd sit and wait for
hours sometimes. Dad also took pictures.

Dad knew Bill Clinton's schedule like the back of his
hand. Clinton, for example, would usually show up at
Quapaw Towers around 11:30 at night, entering through
either the back or front door. Sometimes he would show up
driven by a state policeman, and at other times he'd drive
alone in an unmarked car.

Dad said Clinton was visiting either Gennifer Flowers
or Dan Lasater, both residents of the Quapaw Towers. Dad
often spoke with the security guard who worked the door at
the Towers to get more information.

We would wait three or four hours for Clinton to come
out, passing the time listening to the radio. We'd just sit
and drink Pepsi and eat peanuts. Dad loved doing that.

The last time I went out with Dad on a stakeout was
during the summer of 1988. We were sitting across the
street from the entrance to the governor's mansion. Clinton

pulled out at 12:30 at night in an unmarked state police car.

We followed Clinton down to Roosevelt Road, a low-income area of Little Rock. Clinton circled the block a couple of times and yelled over to a prostitute, a black woman. She got into Clinton's car. Dad just shook his head when that happened. Clinton drove off, and we went back home.

It also happened at that time that Dad was a special deputy for Pulaski County. He carried a badge he got in 1983 when Tommy Robinson was the sheriff of Pulaski County. Tommy ran for Congress as a Republican and served one term.

Dad met with Robinson many times during this time period. I have always believed that Tommy Robinson hired my father to investigate Clinton, but I believe that he was only the intermediary for someone much wealthier. He couldn't have been the one paying Dad the hefty fee he was getting.

Robinson was a favorite of the Jackson Stephens Investment Company, Arkansas' most powerful company. However, in 1990, Tommy Robinson lost in the Republican primary to Sheffield Nelson (whom the Stephens greatly disliked). Because of this, the Stephens switched their support to Clinton.

Stephens Incorporated is made up of some pretty tough people. They like to own and control the politicians that they back.

In 1987 Dad was appointed by Governor Clinton to the State Board of Private Investigators and Security Firms, a division of the Arkansas State Police.

People always ask me how Dad got appointed by Clinton to a state position during the time he was investigating Clinton. It was easy because Clinton didn't know he was being investigated.

The funny part is that the people who were paying Dad to photograph and document Clinton's illicit activities were supposed "friends of Bill." The deal worked like this.

They gave Clinton money in return for favors, and then made sure Bill came through with the favors by reminding him of what they had on him. It really amazed Dad how Clinton was able to manipulate the people of Arkansas; but Clinton himself was also being manipulated.

Clinton's friends now say that Clinton never knew Dad, but not only was Dad appointed to the State Board by Clinton, he also eventually became chairman of the board and often met Clinton at civic dinners and roasts.

As far as I know, Dad ended his active investigation of Clinton around 1990 (I was serving in the Navy as a submarine navigator at that time). As luck would have it, however, Dad would again be put in Clinton's path during the 1992 presidential campaign.

Dad had already had some run-ins with Clinton's buddies. His business partner, John McIntire, was a drinking buddy of one of Clinton's top aides, state police officer Buddy Young, who headed up Clinton's trooper security detail. Young and McIntire always wanted my dad to get involved in shady business deals, but he never would do it. They really wanted him to be a front man for a strip bar they planned to open in Hot Springs, but Dad refused. That was in 1990.

Dad never bid to get the contract for security services for the Clinton presidential campaign because he already had the contract for the building. The Clinton/Gore campaign rented space from the *Arkansas Democrat-Gazette*, which owned the old Gazette building. When the Clinton campaign signed the lease, they got Dad, too.

Dad ran building security and was given a contractor and staff badge by the campaign, giving him total access. The campaign hired Pinkerton Security to control doors and access to the building.

I helped Dad by working the press room, checking visitors with metal detectors, and seeing that no media equipment was being used to bring in weapons.

Soon the Pinkerton security guards became a problem for the campaign. Women campaign staffers complained that the guards were making dirty remarks to them. Just before election day, Pinkerton's contract was terminated, and Dad took over the whole account for the rest of the transition period from the time Clinton was elected until his inauguration.

During this time my father had about twenty employees from his company, American Contract Services, manning the Clinton campaign headquarters—quite a hefty payroll to meet each month. That's when his problems began with the Clinton people. Dad began complaining that he was not getting paid, that he had a huge payroll to meet, maybe more than $30,000 a month. He was given the runaround from the campaign staff.

Dad went to see Dee Dee Myers, who showed him the cancelled checks proving he had been paid. But the checks were cashed by a third party who was absconding with the money.

> " 'Well, Mr. Parks. I have the company's signature on the back of the checks,' Jerry told me Dee Dee Myers said to him.
>
> "Jerry said, 'We don't sign checks. We stamp them with our account number.' Dee Dee Myers then told him there was some embezzling going on, and she didn't know who was doing it. She showed Jerry the checks he was supposed to have gotten. Evidently someone at the campaign had cashed them. She went on to say that this had happened to several other companies as well. She asked him to keep this confidential. He didn't. He came home and immediately told me. He also documented it.
>
> "After two months of running security at the headquarters, Jerry became scared. In fact, he went to a Republican attorney he knew, not knowing that the attorney would later sell him out. The attorney later said that the only thing Jerry talked to him about was that many unauthorized people were coming and going and that there was heavy use of alcohol. His guards had to walk drunk

*people to their cars. That's all the attorney alluded
to. But I'm sure Jerry told him about the
embezzling."*

Dad was told that they discovered that his money had
been embezzled. He was asked to keep quiet about it
because it would be embarrassing. They promised to pay
him fully.

But after the inauguration in January, Dad was
fuming because the campaign had offered him some deal to
pay him thirty cents for every dollar owed. He wouldn't go
for it because he needed the money to pay off outstanding
signature loans he had taken out to meet payroll.

I checked through Dad's ledgers and found that the
Clinton-Gore campaign never completely paid American
Contract Services until the last week of July 1993.

I later read in the *Arkansas Times* that during the
campaign and transition period both Betsey Wright and
Buddy Young were trying to get Dad's contract terminated.
They looked for things they could use to disqualify him.
Apparently they didn't like Dad's complete access to the
headquarters. But I think they also didn't like Dad as a
person, but not because he was bad. It was because he was
honest, and they knew they couldn't trust him to lie for
them.

Dad was a deeply religious man, a member of the
Assembly of God church. He attended on Sundays and any
other day the church doors were open. He was a good man,
a changed man.

Before 1977 he had been known for his meanness; the
White House people seemed to rouse that old anger in him.
Dad knew he was dealing with a rough crowd.

The day after Vincent Foster's death on July 20, 1993,
Dad and I were eating at El Chico. We were watching a
television news program about Foster's death. I remember
Dad looking at the TV, looking up at me, and back again at
the TV.

He then turned and gave me the coldest stare he'd ever

given me, and said, "Bill Clinton is cleaning house."

I didn't ask him what he meant; I was scared.

It was after Foster's death that Dad became scared, worried, always walking around with a gun. He wouldn't walk to the mailbox without a gun.

> *"Jerry couldn't sleep at night. He had nearly pulled out all the hair in his eyebrows. There was a great amount of stress. He was afraid. He carried a gun. He carried a car phone, something he didn't normally carry, and he'd call me with it five or six times a day."*

Right after Foster's death our home was burglarized one afternoon. No one was home at the time. The telephone and power lines were cut, and the alarm was down. The only things the burglars took were Dad's files on Bill Clinton, which had been kept in the bottom drawer of his bedroom dresser. These files contained photos and notes and were several inches thick.

Dad never even told me about it; Mom told me after his death. They never reported it to the police either. As my mom said, "You can't call up the police and say someone just stole the investigative file on Bill Clinton."

> *"Someone had to get that file. What was in it could very well have been what cost Jerry his life; it was damaging. It could have unseated the President. Jerry took a lot of pictures. He documented everything. If you talk to the Little Rock police, they will tell you that Jerry taped conversations. He was a person who wrote everything down."*

The house was broken into again several weeks after my father's death. This time they picked the locks and got in, but took nothing.

After an article by Ambrose Evans-Pritchard appeared in the London *Sunday Telegraph*, which included an interview with my mother, the house was again burglarized. My mother's room was ransacked, but they only took a couple of pictures of her and some credit card receipts.

I know Dad was scared the night of our dinner after the Foster death because that was the first time he ever took the thirty mile detour to get home. But at the time I had no idea just how serious the situation was.

On the night of my father's murder, my phone rang at about 8:30 p.m. It was the Little Rock police. My dad, they said, had been in an accident. They then told me he'd been taken to Doctors Hospital.

As I drove down to the hospital, I spotted my father's Lumina sedan. I stopped right there in the middle of the road. I could see that the windows and doors of his car were riddled with bullet holes.

"This is what they call an accident?" I remember thinking as I began to cry.

My father's blood was all over the street. Nobody seemed to care about cleaning it up. It took me three days to get the fire department to come down and wash it off the road.

The investigation of Dad's death was headed up by the Little Rock Police Department. This is odd because Dad died just over the border of Little Rock in Pulaski County—in the jurisdiction of the Pulaski County Sheriff's Department.

The first thing the Little Rock police asked at the hospital was if Dad had any enemies. They also demanded that my mother and I not speak to the press. We honored their request.

We thought they were serious about the investigation because the day after Dad's death, FBI agents showed up at our home with sophisticated equipment and X-ray machines to search the walls and floors of the home. They conducted a similar search at his office. On the same day they also flew in an IRS computer expert from Miami who went through Dad's computers. They told us they were checking his case files for clues as to why he died. Yet later, the FBI and Little Rock police would deny they conducted these searches.

I am positive they were there for one reason: To find anything that might be incriminating against President Clinton.

The "official" police investigation was all a game. It seemed like the police busted their rear ends at the Little Rock Police Department for about a week. Mom would call the police and threaten to go to the media. They would tell her not to do it, and said it would jeopardize the case if we did.

> *"Tom James, who dealt with organized crime, was the detective originally working on Jerry's case. He told me he was really putting the pieces together. Then Clinton's name surfaced in the case, in newspapers and elsewhere. James told me he went to his police chief in February 1994, and said: 'This is getting hot. Clinton's name has been brought into it. When it gets political I can't work on it anymore.' James gave all his files, he told me, to another detective. Later he denied ever working on the case. He's a liar; I have his card. He was to my home maybe thirty times. He's the only one I talked to about the case."*

Each time we called the police, they would say they were only three to four weeks away from closing the case. They said that for ten months. A year after his murder, we still didn't have a ballistics or autopsy report.

The police told me recently that this will be just another one of "Arkansas' unsolved mysteries." My mother and I can't accept that; we won't. That's why we are speaking out.

I've been on hundreds of radio programs to tell my family's story, and thousands of calls from around the country have come into the Chief of Police's office. It hasn't had much effect yet, but it's good to know that people out there care. The *Arkansas Democrat-Gazette* had taken an interest in the case initially, but since Clinton's name has been linked to the murder, they now only write articles attacking me. I understand why so few people speak up and tell the truth here in Arkansas.

For several years Dad had prepared me for the death of my mother, who, doctors say, has about one more year to live. But now it's just us—my mother, my brother, my half-sister and me.

> *"One of Jerry's employees told me that just before Jerry died, he made the statement that while at church he had lifted up his arms and said: 'God, I have done all that I can do. I'm ready to come home. I feel it coming. Let it come quickly.'"*

All I have left of my father is the truth I know of him—that he didn't deserve to die. He was a good man. That's why I have given up everything to find out the truth about his death. I drive around in a heap. I've sold almost everything I have—everything.

But that doesn't matter, because I'm committed to making sure that the truth will come out. That's what's important to me.

PREFACE, CHAPTER 5

The sheriff handed me the thick, almost five-year-old case file. One of the detectives said at the time, "Now you have the stone."

"What do you mean?" I asked.

"This case is a stone that has hung around the neck of the department for a long time. It's just your turn to wear it now," he explained with a smirk.

John Brown's distinguished career as a law enforcement officer in Arkansas, gives him a respected platform from which to speak. His allegiance to law and order is ably represented by honors bestowed upon him such as the coveted Medal of Honor and numerous other commendations such as Officer of the Month. As a detective on the force, Brown's interest in upholding justice led him to seriously investigate the Henry-Ives death case, known locally as "The boys on the tracks."

Brown's tenacity at pursuing truth and his bravery in bucking corruption in law enforcement and political leaders in Arkansas have led to threats against his life which were serious enough to cause him to turn in his badge.

In the following pages, John Brown tells how this investigation has been stonewalled because of its ultimate connection with Bill Clinton.

CHAPTER 5

MURDER—THE BOYS ON THE TRACKS

by John Brown

As a police officer, I was sworn to uphold the law—to protect innocents, defend the weak, and bring criminals to justice.

A police officer is just part of a very thin line that divides civilized society from the thugs who would take advantage of innocent citizens. I learned in Arkansas that the thin blue line is very, very thin. I saw firsthand how this line could be used by the powerful and the corrupt to actually help the thugs.

I am afraid that some day—maybe it's already happening—our federal justice system will suffer the same fate. I have risked everything to make sure that doesn't happen. That's why I turned in my shield on August 16, 1994. I gave up being a police officer, my lifelong dream, because I was no longer allowed to do my sworn duty, to "uphold the law."

My resignation as a police detective from the Saline County Sheriff's Department took place on a hot August Arkansas day, just a week shy of the seventh anniversary of the night two Saline County teenage boys were murdered.

On summer nights like this in Arkansas, people generally stay out late to enjoy the cool breezes that come at the end of the sweltering days. Kids, especially, like to run around. It was no different for two kids in particular, Don Henry and Kevin Ives, both teenagers and the best of friends. Kevin was popular and loved to have fun, while Don was more of an adventurer.

Having only begun working as a police investigator in Saline County in 1992, I didn't have the opportunity of knowing Kevin and Don personally, but as a result of the investigation into their deaths, I feel like I know them very well. They were both nice kids and good sons.

It was a moonless Saturday night, August 22, 1987, when Don Henry and Kevin Ives left Don's trailer home to go deer hunting in the dense woods alongside the railroad tracks, about 300 yards from the Henrys' trailer. Don carried a .22 caliber rifle, while Kevin held a flashlight. They were out spotlight-hunting deer (a hunting method where deer become transfixed by the hunter's flashlight beam, making them easy prey).

We still don't know for sure what happened from the time the boys left the Henry home to the time their mutilated bodies were found on the railroad tracks early the next morning, but I have spent a great deal of time attempting to figure it out.

At approximately 4:45 a.m., a northbound train had just passed the Shobe Road crossing at Alexander and was roaring along at top speed through the dark night when the engineer saw two bodies lying across the tracks. The engineer slammed on the brakes, but it was too late. The train smashed into the bodies, which the engineer told the police were laid out as if they were "sunbathing on the beach."

The collision that took place that night was not just between a train and two dead boys, but was the beginning of an ongoing collision between a mother and the whole corrupt Arkansas establishment, embodied in Bill Clinton.

Let me give you a little insight into the devastation caused by these murders from the heart of Linda Ives, Kevin's mother:

> *"No words in the English language can describe how it makes you feel as a parent, or as a citizen of Arkansas, to see what our officials are capable of doing. We were kind of naive, common*

*ordinary people. We got up and went to work
every day, and came home and went to bed. We
assumed that everybody else did the same thing,
and tried to do what was right.*

*"I think Kevin's death has been the rudest
awakening that anybody could ever have. To see
what really goes on, and to see what's important
to elected and public officials; the fact that my
child's murder was not important in the overall
scheme of things, to anybody but me—there just
aren't any words in the English language that can
describe it. Anger. Rage. They are all inadequate.
That's one of the things that got me up every
morning, sitting on someone's doorstep raising
Cain. That is the only thing left that we could do
for Kevin."*

Linda Ives is one of the most loving, yet tough, people
I have ever met. Seven years after the murder of her son,
she still hasn't given up the fight to bring the murderers to
justice. In doing so, she has exposed a cover-up whose trail
leads to the doorstep of the White House.

I came into the picture rather late, having moved to
Saline County, a region just outside of Little Rock, in
September of 1992. My wife, whom I had recently married,
had taken a job in Little Rock, and I was still working as a
police officer in El Dorado, Arkansas, a hundred miles
away. After there were five shoot-outs (one in which I was
involved) in my shift alone at the police department in El
Dorado—a small city with a large crime problem—I decided
it was time for me to move on before my number was called.

I also realized, coming so close to death, that God has
a plan for each and every one of us. He's in control. Looking
back, I can see now why I ended up in Saline County.

I joined the Saline County Sheriff's Department in the
fall of 1992, and immediately I began to rub people the
wrong way.

The sheriff had assigned me as a detective to CID—the

Criminal Investigation Division—specializing in gang-related violence. Saline County, just ten miles from downtown Little Rock, has its share of crime, and is sometimes called "The Badlands" because of a history of harboring outlaws, as well as harboring a seamless web of official corruption.

Soon after joining the Sheriff's Department, I was asked to organize a town meeting for residents of the county's east end to discuss gang violence after a series of drive-by shootings had rocked the community. At the meeting, I outlined some steps private citizens could take to protect themselves. The crowd of over seven hundred people applauded warmly after I spoke. Then the Saline County Prosecuting Attorney, Dan Harmon, rose to speak. It was the first time I had met Harmon, who would become a constant thorn to me at the Sheriff's Department and an impediment in my search for truth.

Harmon told the gathering that the county needed more jail space, and he wanted them to support a sales tax increase.

I was incensed. The meeting was about the gang problem and how residents could help the police—not a forum to support a sales tax hike.

"Ladies and gentlemen," I responded, "I want you to know that I did not put together this meeting to increase your taxes or take your money." This comment brought applause. Then at the end of my speech the crowd gave me a standing ovation. Harmon looked enraged by my comments and the rousing response they received. This would not be the only time I angered this man.

On January 1, 1993, Judy Pridgen took office as the newly-elected sheriff. Pridgen was elected because of the Henry-Ives murder case, a long festering case I had only vaguely heard of. The murder of Don Henry and Kevin Ives had taken place years before, but because of the tenacity of Kevin Ives' mother, this unsolved case was still a political hot potato.

By February, I was moved off the gang detail and

assigned to the Henry-Ives case. I had heard through the grapevine that Judy Pridgen assigned me the case because I was considered objective—I was not from the area, I had no political ties, and I didn't know Linda Ives.

The sheriff handed me the thick, almost five-year-old case file. One of the detectives said at the time, "Now you have the stone."

"What do you mean?" I asked.

"This case is a stone that has hung around the neck of the department for a long time. It's just your turn to wear it now," he explained with a smirk.

Something was wrong. My first indication of this was when my boss, Lt. David Smith, head of CID, took me for an hour-long drive in a police car. During our drive to nowhere, he explained to me that there was nothing to this case. I just shouldn't look too deep; it's best left alone. It would do nothing but bring me and the department grief.

I met with Linda Ives and her husband, Larry, at their home. We spent several hours together; they both struck me as sincere and distraught. These were just two people whose only son had been murdered; two people who had discovered that for some inexplicable reason, the authorities had stonewalled any attempt to get to the bottom of the case.

Linda took me up to Kevin's room, which she had converted into an office. She called it her "war room," where she organized her effort to keep the memory of Kevin alive. She was also, by this time, heading the Arkansas chapter of Parents of Murdered Children.

Linda cooperated fully with me, although she didn't trust me completely. Why should she have, considering the agony she and Larry had been through? She even called and complained to Sheriff Pridgen, asking why a newcomer to Saline County had been placed in charge of such an important case. However, Linda soon realized that I wanted to do an honest job, and I quickly won her confidence.

As I left her home that first time, Linda handed me a six-inch stack of documents and news clippings which she had collected. "It's only a small part of what I have, but it'll help you get your feet wet," Linda told me as I put the papers under my arm.

As I pored over the case file and the news clippings, it didn't take long for me to realize that this whole thing stunk. This was obviously a cover-up, and the very thought of it sickened me.

The deception appeared to start almost from the time they found Don's and Kevin's bodies on the tracks that night. The next morning a Saline County sheriff's deputy showed up at Linda Ives' home to inform her that her son had committed suicide.

How could they know it was suicide? There was no note, no indication of psychological problems with either boy. The police investigators hadn't even conducted any forensic tests, let alone an autopsy. Police are never supposed to accept a suicide at face value. Yet, that's what they did, or tried to do here. (About six months later, when I read about the "suicide" case of Vincent Foster, I noted the many parallels of Foster's death and investigation to the Henry-Ives case. Arkansas technique, it seemed, had moved to Washington.)

When a sheriff's deputy met with Don's father to inform him of the "suicide," Curtis Henry told the sheriff, "You're crazy as h—." Linda and her husband were equally as astounded. There was no way that Kevin, "happy as could be" the day before his body was found, would have willingly sat down on those tracks.

Information leaked to the press indicated that the Arkansas State Medical Examiner, Dr. Fahmy Malak, was going to rule the deaths a double suicide. Linda met with then-Sheriff James Steed and raised a stink. Steed placed a call to Malak, telling him there was no way Linda Ives was going to accept a suicide ruling.

Malak eventually ruled the deaths "accidental," concluding that Don and Kevin were "unconscious and in a deep sleep on the railroad tracks, under the psychedelic influence of marijuana." Malak later claimed that the boys had smoked as many as twenty marijuana cigarettes each.

The ruling became the laughing joke of the sheriff's department as well as the state. Of course, Linda didn't take a liking to that decision either. She pushed to have a grand jury look into the case, and had them exhume the bodies of both boys for an independent review by Dr. Joseph Burton, chief medical examiner for Atlanta, Georgia.

The second autopsy found that Don had been stabbed in the back. Kevin had been bludgeoned, and his skull was crushed. Bloating of his facial tissues indicated the beating had taken place well before the train collided with their bodies.

Burton probably gave the families of these boys the only small consolation they might find in this mess: Don and Kevin were probably dead before the train ravaged their bodies.

The pathologist told Ives this was no simple mistake; the wounds were clearly evident. As for the marijuana, Burton indicated that the marijuana reading was totally invalid. Incredibly, Dr. Malak had used a urine drug test on the boys' blood instead of the necessary blood drug test. His choice to use this incorrect procedure produced Malak's incredible statement about the boys' marijuana use.

Dr. Malak had indeed engaged in a cover-up, but there was evidence indicating foul play well before any autopsy was performed.

The ambulance crew at the scene noted in their official report: "Blood from the bodies and on the body parts we observed was a dark color in nature. Due to our training, this would indicate a lack of oxygen present in the blood and could pose a question as to how long the victims had been dead."

Also, three members of the train's crew said they saw a "green tarp" made of cloth, which had partially covered the boys' bodies before impact. Another crew remembered seeing the tarp lying in the ditch beside the train tracks. But the tarp—evidence that someone may have covered the dead boys to ensure that the train engineer wouldn't see their bodies in time to stop the train—was never listed on the crime scene evidence sheets. It disappeared.

While reviewing case files, I found similar missing evidence. I realized later that "mistakes" made in the case were more planned than accidental. The case file had no transmittal sheets indicating where the existing crime scene evidence was preserved. Another major item missing from the file was the set of crime scene photos. There was a list detailing the photos in the file, but the photos themselves were gone. There were few actual witness statements, and the leads mentioned in the file had never been followed up.

At best, the police work that night was sloppy, making it impossible, among other things, to figure out exactly where the strewn bodies were found on the tracks. The deputy who completed the scene report used the train as a reference point to fix the location of the bodies and the other evidence found at the scene. When the train pulled away, the deputy's descriptions became useless.

Deputies had allegedly scoured the crime scene, but a relative visiting the scene days later found a foot of one of the boys the police had failed to recover. Dr. Malak never mentioned in his autopsy that one of the feet was missing. Other visitors found gold chains that the police had not collected either.

A tremendous breach in police work was to allow a second train to pass through the crime scene on parallel tracks, possibly destroying crucial evidence.

It's a basic policy in any death to note everyone present and anyone who enters the crime scene. Police at the scene failed to record the people who were present when they arrived at the site or the others who showed up that morning. Six months after the deaths, an ambulance driver testified seeing three men by a pickup truck in the woods who identified themselves as being with the Alexander Fire Department. Alexander didn't have a fire department.

Police only recovered one gun, which no one bothered to conduct a ballistics test on. A second gun was clearly seen on a news video as it was put in the back of the police pickup, yet that gun disappeared along with other evidence.

The police told Linda they would conduct a trace analysis test, which included suctioning the clothing of both boys, in search of unusual fibers and hairs—a standard practice for such homicide investigations, especially in this case where the source of the green tarp could be critical in finding the murderers. It was later determined that this crucial test was never performed.

Linda's outrage and attention had forced the empaneling of a second grand jury. The grand jury found not only that the deaths were obvious murders, but that they may have been related to Saline County's drug problem. The foreman of the grand jury explained, "We find that there is a tremendous drug problem that exists in Saline County."

Any homicide investigator worth his salt will tell you that staged murders of this type are frequently related to illegal drug trafficking. Traffickers are sophisticated, they wield a lot of money, and their influence in the political arena is increasing. What better way to commit a murder than to have the case closed as a suicide from the very beginning.

Looking through the police file and news clippings, it was evident that the deaths were linked to organized crime, what federal authorities have called the Dixie Mafia. The Dixie Mafia is a loosely knit group of thugs who are found throughout the South. They make their trade in drugs and are noted for being much more brutal than the ethnic Mafias in New York and Chicago.

Within three years of the deaths of Kevin and Don, at least six people known to be knowledgeable of the case were murdered or found dead under suspicious circumstances.

In the summer of 1988, Keith Coney was speeding on his motorcycle down Highway 40 when he crashed into a truck and died. Witnesses said he was being chased. Some police have said that Coney's throat had been cut before he fled on his motorcycle. There was no autopsy and his death was ruled a traffic accident.

Two days before his death, Coney told a friend, Boonie Bearden (who later mysteriously disappeared), that he knew that the police were involved in the deaths of the boys. Others have also testified that Coney was selling drugs for a man who had links to one of the "Alexander firemen" the ambulance crew encountered on the night of the deaths.

In November of 1988, another gruesome murder linked to the boys on the tracks took place. At that time the grand jury was still working on the case, and although Dan Harmon was not the prosecuting attorney during this investigation, he had offered to present the case to them as a special prosecutor, which they agreed to.

Keith McKaskle, manager of The Wagon Wheel—a bar not too far from where the boys were found—was a police informant and had been cooperating with the investigation of the boys' death. He told Deputy Kathy Pearson that the prosecuting attorney, Dan Harmon, was involved in drug trafficking; in fact, that Harmon "was one of our biggest suppliers."

McKaskle was murdered in his garage late one night while returning home. Five men, dressed in black and wearing hoods, stabbed McKaskle—known for his fighting prowess—one hundred thirteen times.

Police would later try to claim that a nineteen-year-old boy—who was five feet eleven inches tall—had overpowered McKaskle, who was three inches taller. Although the boy was convicted of the murder, the Arkansas Court of Appeals later threw out the case and overturned the conviction. Strong evidence clearing the boy had never even been presented at his trial. It was obvious the boy had been framed.

According to several witnesses, McKaskle said weeks before his death that his life was in jeopardy because of his knowledge of the Henry-Ives murders.

Months later, in January of 1989, Greg Collins, another young man wanted for questioning relating to the deaths, was murdered by shotgun. Just before Collins' death, his mother also died mysteriously. Police said she committed suicide by firing a revolver into her chest. There were no witnesses.

In March, Boonie Bearden, a friend of both Coney and Collins, disappeared. An anonymous caller told police he had been killed. Police found a piece of Bearden's clothing in the Arkansas River in the vicinity of where the caller said he had been murdered. Boonie's body was never found. He is officially listed as "missing."

April brought still another murder. Jeff Rhodes, a twenty-one-year-old Saline County resident, had been stabbed and shot in the head. His remains were found burned in a dump in Benton, the Saline County seat. Forensic evidence revealed that someone had attempted to cut off Rhodes' head, hands and feet. Rhodes' father told the press that his son had called him shortly before his death, explaining that he had to go into hiding because he had information about Kevin's and Don's murders as well as McKaskle's.

Another grand jury witness, Richard Winters, was killed in the summer of 1989. Winters was apparently murdered in a set-up.

And finally, in June of 1990, Jordan Ketelsen allegedly killed himself in his truck using a shotgun. His girlfriend was the only witness. The police did not conduct an investigation of the death despite the fact that Ketelsen was a known drug dealer widely believed to be linked to the murder of Keith McKaskle. No autopsy was conducted, and Ketelsen's body was quickly cremated.

Someone, somewhere, wanted the Henry-Ives case quashed. Each day beyond the date of an unsolved murder, the murder trail gets colder. In this case the trail had become deathly cold.

Here it was February 1993, and I was now on the trail. The first thing I did was to attempt to locate the clothes listed in evidence. It had been rumored they, too, were missing. I discovered they were still in the State Police "A" Troop Headquarters, sitting in a locker. I called to verify their existence.

When I arrived at work the next day, my phone was ringing off the hook. It was Barney Phillips, a former state police investigator who had worked on the Henry-Ives case.

"What the h— do you want with those clothes?" he shouted into the phone. He then informed me that I would need a court order from Dan Harmon to get the clothes. At every step of my investigation I would encounter this type of official obstruction of justice.

Through an arrested drug dealer I heard of a possible witness in the case, a girl known to him as "Sharlie." This potential informant had worked with the DEA; her actual name was Sharline Wilson.

While interviewing Sharline, I discovered that in 1990 she had been a star witness for the Saline County Drug Task Force, which at that time had been working with a federal grand jury looking into official corruption and drug trafficking in Saline County. The grand jury had gotten too close to the truth and was subsequently closed down. Jean Duffey, the head of the task force, had to go into hiding.

As former Deputy Pearson told the *Arkansas Times,* "I don't blame Jean Duffey a bit for getting out of here. That woman's life wouldn't be worth a flip if she were still around. Jean found out things on a lot of political officials, and that made her dangerous."

Sharline was now stuck, entrapped by her own testimony before the grand jury, and would later have to serve prison time. I located her in Malvern City Jail and went to visit her. She was brought into a back room, and when I began to question her, she moved into almost a fetal position, cowering in fear.

Between tears, Sharline incriminated Dan Harmon in the deaths of Kevin and Don. She said she knew Harmon from her days as a drug distributor in the late 1980s. She feared for her life. "He'll kill me," she said of Harmon.

Sharline implicated Harmon as having been present when the two boys were murdered, and that local police had committed the murder. She also indicated that high officials were involved, but they were too big, and therefore,

I would not be able to touch them.

I was skeptical of Sharline's testimony, although Gary Martin—assigned to the DEA with the Little Rock police—who was present at the interview, vouched for the quality of her information. I decided to return another day and have her take a polygraph test.

Shortly after my first meeting with Sharline, a state police investigator, Jim Howington, was assigned to work the case with me. Harmon had called Sheriff Pridgen and said he couldn't trust me and wanted a state police invest-igator to work with me. I had no objection.

Howington accompanied me on my next trip to see Sharline. We took her to the State Police "E" Troop Head-quarters in Pine Bluff to be polygraphed by Investigator John Howell. Howington told me Howell was a "darn good" polygrapher. The first thing Howell did was ask Sharline to write down her answers to his questions before he started the polygraph. Howell said this way he could analyze her handwriting as well.

When Sharline was finished writing her answers, Howell looked at them. One of the questions was about her first drug deal with Dan Harmon. Howell read her answer aloud to us. She had written that she had made her first drug deal by selling an "eight ball," or 3.5 grams of cocaine, with Harmon and Roger Clinton at a Little Rock nightclub.

Howell had no sooner finished reading Sharline's answer when he declared: "I'm not going to polygraph her. She's a crazy b—! I can tell by her handwriting that she's lying!"

I was fuming; I had wasted the whole day! Naively, I guess, I still didn't realize how big this whole thing was.

After that incident, I brought Sharline to see Bob Govar, an assistant U.S. Attorney in the U.S. Attorney's Office in Little Rock. He listened to her story and decided he would issue her a federal grand jury subpoena. This would give her added protection.

Harmon got wind of this by way of the Malvern Chief of Police. Harmon went nuts and called the sheriff, at which time—I am told—he threatened to kick me in the rear. Harmon later called Howington at home and said Sharline was "just a liar."

According to Howington, Harmon also offered to take a polygraph test to prove his innocence. I later found out from Howington that Harmon never took the polygraph because he had demanded that the polygrapher ask no questions about drugs or his knowledge of the Henry-Ives case.

Harmon obviously didn't want to do anything that might implicate him or connect him with drugs. I later learned that once before Harmon had avoided being implicated in drug use. In fact, Harmon had served nearly a month in jail for tax evasion because he had refused to take a drug test which would have allowed him to go free on bail.

By June of 1993, Howington had faded from the case. One day as I was leaving for the day, he leaned out his window and said, "All I know is that this Henry-Ives case creates more pressure at State Police Headquarters than any case I've ever seen. John, I'm real worried about how high up it goes."

Indeed, there were numerous allegations that it led right to the governor's family. Sharline, for one, knew of three men present at what she said was a drug drop near the tracks where the boys were found. During the course of the investigation, a number of people had claimed that drugs were regularly dropped by plane or train at a site near the tracks. Sharline also said her car had been used by Harmon to deliver a green tarp, which was, as she described it, just like the tarp that disappeared from the crime scene.

Early in my investigation, State Police Investigator Russell Welch, from Mena, Arkansas, had contacted me. Welch said that one of his informants, currently serving prison time, said the deaths of Don and Kevin were linked to the Mena drug smuggling operation.

Mena is an hour and a half drive from the site in

Saline County where the boys were found. But Welch explained that planes coming from Central America heading for the small airfield at Mena were also known to be making direct air-drops to other sites around Arkansas before landing.

If, in fact, Welch's allegations were true, then "higher-ups" in the state were linked to a major narcotics trafficking operation. I would later verify Welch's allegations during my investigation on the Henry-Ives case. The stonewalling by local and federal authorities of the investigation into drug trafficking at Mena has been well documented.

Don Henry and Kevin Ives, as fate would have it, probably stumbled into the wrong place one night, holding a flashlight and a rifle. How would the drug people know they were only out deer hunting? The boys evidently saw something that night which led to their untimely deaths.

The many "mistakes" in the original investigation were obviously becoming part of a well-orchestrated campaign to cover up the murders, and by the summer of 1993, I was evidently getting too close. Lt. Smith, in charge of CID, was constantly complaining to the sheriff about my activities. According to others in the unit, he would constantly be looking through my desk, reviewing notes and listening to any audio tapes of interviews I had conducted.

When Sheriff Pridgen left town for a trip in July, Lt. Smith took that as an opportunity to relieve me of the investigation, telling me he needed me on special projects. Smith also demanded the case file, which I obligingly handed over to him. He said Harmon needed to see it.

An hour later he came roaring back into my office, "There's nothing in there that you did! Not one interview!"

"That's right, you won't see a thing," I told him. I was thinking to myself, *There's no way I'm gonna hand my evidence over to you.* Having possession of that information was my protection; it still is.

Pridgen stood by me on that one, but assigned me to other duties instead of working on the Henry-Ives case. My home would be ransacked and burglarized three times after that; someone was obviously looking for something.

I had kept the sheriff updated on developments in the case. At first she strongly supported the investigation, but that support was dwindling fast.

By August 1993, Smith had swamped me with thirty CID cases. It was definitely a ploy to keep me too busy to follow up on the Henry-Ives case. By this time, Sheriff Pridgen was supporting Smith's obstruction of my work. I then decided it would be best to work the case during off hours.

The case began to break in November 1993 when a young man stated that he had been in the woods the night Kevin and Don were murdered. At that time he would have been twelve years old. Interestingly enough, Sharline Wilson had said that some kids were in the woods that night, but that they ran away before anyone could catch them.

By late 1993, the FBI office in Little Rock had taken an interest in the case, especially the testimony of the boy.

An FBI agent called me in February 1994 and explained, almost in a panicked way, that I was right—this case was much bigger than they had thought. With the FBI involved, Sheriff Pridgen decided that I should continue the investigation. But it was becoming dangerous working in CID, and I had received some threats. So we agreed I would work in the Warrants Division as a cover while working with the Bureau.

I found more evidence that the deaths were related to Mena. Through Larry Nichols, I met with a pilot who said he used to make drops at the site near where the bodies had been found—a drug drop location which the drug traffickers called "A-12."

I was very skeptical at first, but then the pilot intimately described the area and the specific spot where the drops were made. He also explained how he had his aircraft with a traffic signal that ran across the tracks.

Bingo! How would he know about those lights? The traffic lights were changed in 1988 or 1989. He was describing the lights as they were in 1987 at the time of the boys' deaths, when the drop had taken place. This information didn't prove his allegations, but his knowledge of the site made him very credible.

The pilot said that he understood the local sheriff, Jim Steed (known throughout the region for bootlegging), was involved in giving protection for the drops. He also alleged that Roger Clinton and Skeeter Ward (Seth Ward's son) participated in the pick-ups.

Despite these breakthroughs, I had committed the unpardonable sin in the eyes of my sheriff: I had spoken with Larry Nichols, the outspoken critic of Bill Clinton.

It was August 1994, and I had just returned from Washington after briefing some members of Congress about the whole scene of political corruption in Arkansas, including Clinton's involvement. The sheriff informed me that I would now be on the graveyard shift and could no longer work the Henry-Ives case or talk to the press about it. I was not only being shut up, but by changing to the night shift, I became a neon target for anyone who wanted me out of the picture permanently.

I realized the sheriff was not herself; she was scared to death and told me as much. After one meeting we had with Jean Duffey, Pridgen was followed all the way home.

At our last meeting in August, Sheriff Pridgen said: "We both know where this leads. Do you really want to take down the President of the United States?"

Eight o'clock the next morning I handed in my resignation letter. A sergeant drove by my house later that day to collect my case file on the Henry-Ives case. I told him that I had given the file to the FBI.

The cover-up of the murder of Kevin and Don continues to this day. It appears that many of the key players in this case have benefited as a result of their participation. For instance, Sheriff Jim Steed was appointed by Governor Clinton to a state job after losing the election of 1988.

Dr. Malak was even more fortunate. Despite his image as the Dr. Frankenstein of forensic pathology, Clinton stuck by him. Only after Clinton decided to run for President and it appeared Dr. Malak would become a liability did Clinton act. Unbelievably, Clinton's decisive action was to simply transfer the doctor to a different state job, paying him a salary of $70,000.

Clinton has steadfastly refused to even meet with Linda Ives and other families around the state who were victimized by Dr. Malak. A May 1992 front page story in the *Los Angeles Times* and a special edition on *20/20* laid out the relationship between Clinton and Malak: "Dr. Fahmy Malak was sort of protected by the governor and the state crime laboratory board," stated Rep. Bob Fairchild, a Democrat from Fayetteville to the *Times*."

The *Times* reported that one reason Clinton was so supportive of Malak was because of at least one favorable ruling Malak had made which benefited Clinton's mother, Virginia Kelley. In 1981, Kelley was working as a nurse-anesthesiologist at a hospital in Hot Springs. During minor surgery for a young woman who had been hit by a rock, nurse Kelley flubbed the anesthesia, and the young woman died. Malak ruled the death a negligent homicide by the young man who threw the rock. He was arrested and charged with homicide. He spent two and a half months in prison for Kelley's mistake. A month later Kelley's privileges as a nurse at the hospital were revoked, although no one saw fit to tell the public the real reason why the young lady had died.

Kelley was also being sued at the time by another family after a young mother had died during minor surgery due to problems relating to her anesthesia. Kelley's drinking problem was well known in Arkansas and was thought to have contributed to her ineptness.

The *Los Angeles Times* counted at least twenty other cases botched by Dr. Malak, including such cases as the 1985 murder of Raymond Albright, who was shot five times with a Colt .45. Malak ruled the death a suicide!

Malak also tried to have the deputy county coroner for Pulaski County arrested on murder charges after Malak misread a chart of a man whose life support was removed because he was brain dead.

In another murder case, Malak used the DNA material from the wrong corpse to ascertain at what distance a gun was fired. In still another case, one of his own technicians testified that Malak had him manipulate a photographic image of a rifle butt to fit the size of an injury to support Malak's faulty conclusions.

Malak outdid all of his other rulings when he ruled that James Milam died of natural causes when he had actually been decapitated.

Malak was well protected. The head of the State Medical Examiner Commission, Dr. Jocelyn Elders, refused to take action. She would later become the nation's Surgeon General. You see, cover-ups are like cancer. They just keep growing, involving more people, more payoffs, and sometimes more deaths.

If you ask anyone from Arkansas about "the boys on the tracks," they'll nod knowingly. Everyone knows about it. Seven years have now passed since the death of those two young boys, Don Henry and Kevin Ives—friends to the end. And seven years later Linda Ives is still fighting to find justice for her son. He deserved to live; Don Henry deserved to live.

The big and the powerful in Arkansas, by what they have done and by what they have failed to do, have shown that the deaths of these boys are not important. The callousness and obstinacy from those empowered to do something is both sad and frightening.

Why can't the people of Arkansas, and people across the country, find out who was involved in the murders of Don Henry and Kevin Ives? I'll continue to pray each night that the truth about their deaths will be made known.

PREFACE, CHAPTER 6

No fingerprints were found on the gun, even though the gun was found in his hand, lying neatly at his side.

Chairman Gonzales gaveled out all discussion concerning the death of Vincent Foster, saying everything was settled; there's no need for further discussion. He may have silenced the hearing, but the American people are still not satisfied. Citizens for Honest Government wants some questions answered. We want you to look at the evidence presented in this chapter and decide for yourself. Are powerful people in high places covering up a murder? If so, who committed the murder and why?

CHAPTER 6

VINCE FOSTER—THE SUICIDE THAT WON'T DIE

by Citizens for Honest Government

"All death investigations should be handled as homicide cases until the facts prove differently."

—Vernon J. Geberth, *Practical Homicide Investigation: Tactics, Procedures and Forensic Techniques*

Concerning the death of Vincent W. Foster, Jr., two vital questions leap out at judicious Americans, as stark and baffling as the strange position police found Foster's body in at Fort Marcy Park on July 20, 1993:

1. How did he *really* die?

2. What was the motivation for either Foster's suicide or homicide, especially since Foster, then Deputy White House Counsel and personal attorney for the Clintons, likely knew more than anyone else about the Clintons' personal dealings, including possible wrongdoing in the Whitewater matter?

Most Americans have been led by the major opinion makers into believing there's nothing worth occupying their time here, that we need to put this obscure death behind us and move on to "real" business.

They might not have been so easily swayed had they only borne in mind that Deputy White House Counsel Vincent W. Foster was the highest-ranking federal official to die under questionable circumstances since the assassination of President John F. Kennedy on November 22, 1963.

It is curious that almost all of the nation's prominent investigative reporters—whose credo concerning unexplained mischief in government is, "Follow the money trail"—have chosen not to pursue the overwhelming connection between Foster and the Whitewater affair, especially in light of the White House's highhanded, and possibly criminal, seizing of Foster's Whitewater files even before his corpse had turned cold.

In order to believe that Foster's demise was truly the routine suicide it has been officially declared to be, one must accept, among many other such doubtful premises, the following points:

- that Foster fired the supposed suicide gun—an antique 1913 Colt, which his family still can't positively identify (no matching bullets were found at his home)—with his right hand, *even though he was left-handed.*

- that the gun remained in that "opposite" hand despite the recoil of the gun.

- that although the gun's barrel was supposedly placed deep in his mouth, no teeth were even damaged, let alone broken.

- that no fingerprints were found on the gun, even though the gun was found in his hand, lying neatly at his side.

- that Foster, a devoted family man with three children, left no suicide note, bade no final goodbye and made no final arrangements.

- that he chose for his alleged suicide, a small, obscure Virginia park he was never known to have visited before.

- that he walked 600 feet through the wooded park without getting a trace of soil on his shoes or clothing.

- that his body fell into a stereotypical death position with arms arranged perfectly at his side, "as if he were ready for the coffin," as one paramedic put it.

- that the mysteriously small amount of blood on the front of his body was attributable to the almost instantaneous stopping of his heart—a highly dubious conclusion according to leading pathologists.

Conceivably, any one of these inconsistencies might have a plausible explanation; "freak" things can and do happen during suicides. But when there is a *prevalence* of such bizarre elements, which police refer to as "inconsistencies," the astute observer cannot accept the premise of chance occurrence. One player on a baseball team might happen to connect just right on a fast pitch and set a record-breaking home run without raising suspicions. Yet, if all of his teammates do likewise in the very same game, it's time for a thorough investigation of the team's bats.

"There's a preponderance of inconsistencies here," observed Gene Wheaton, a former Army Criminal Investigation Division agent whose quarter-century of experience in investigating homicides compels him to reject the official finding that Foster committed suicide. Let us examine some of the problems with the case, starting with the "missing blood."

At the spot where Foster's body was found in Fort Marcy Park in McLean, Virginia—one of a number of forts authorized by President Lincoln as a bulwark against Confederate attack—there was a decided lack of blood according to Kory Ashford, the emergency medical services technician who placed Foster's remains into a body bag. In fact, Ashford told investigators he didn't even bother using rubber gloves, nor did he wash his hands afterwards, as is customary when encountering blood.

But in wounds of the sort Foster suffered, "there should be pools of blood," a top New York City homicide detective said. "This is a head wound," he explained. "Usually there's tremendous amounts of blood—blood all over the place. It would be a mess."

"There should be pools of blood," he repeated. "Look at the gun—if it were the instrument of death, there would be blood on it. A .38 makes a powerful explosion. There's a backwash of blood and tissue."

Sergeant George Gonzalez, a paramedic for Fairfax County, Virginia, was the first emergency worker to reach the body. He told *New York Post* investigative reporter Christopher Ruddy that in his ten years as a paramedic he'd never seen a gunshot to the head resulting in so little blood. "Usually there's a mess," he noted.

The first Park Police officer on the scene corroborated Ashford's and Gonzalez' accounts. "There was little blood," he said, recalling Foster's clean, starched white shirt.

Faced with this curiosity, the pathology team chosen by Independent Counsel Robert Fiske explained that the bullet's track through Foster's head "contused the left side of the brain stem," disabling it and causing "instantaneous, complete incapacitation," including the stopping of the heart and the flow of blood therefrom.

But Dr. Richard Mason, a noted California pathologist who is considered an expert in analyzing gunshot wounds, disputes the premise that a shot through the brain stem would have to instantaneously disable the heart. "The heart has its own electrical impulse system," he noted.

He pointed out that a basic biology experiment involves removing an animal's heart and attaching it to a tube while providing it with glucose and oxygen—thereby demonstrating that it can beat for a relatively long period without the brain.

Mason explained that a gunshot to the brain ends heart activity because "the brain stem impairment should immediately end lung activity," and that "the heart is sensitive to oxygen—but certainly you can have heart activity for a minute or two." This, of course, would have been time for much more blood to have surfaced than the trickles emanating from Foster's nose and mouth.

Vernon Geberth, in his authoritative *Practical Homicide Investigation: Tactics, Procedures and Forensic Techniques* (2nd Edition), describes a death which is strikingly similar, anatomically speaking, to Foster's—one that vividly demonstrates how much blood can flow after a fatal wound of this sort.

The subject is the Pennsylvania official who, in an act that shocked the nation in 1987, committed suicide while holding a televised press conference. "The official," writes Geberth, "pulled a .357 magnum handgun from a manilla envelope and placed it into his mouth, pointing the barrel of the gun up toward his brain. He fired and effectively blew his brains out for the viewing audience."

The official was thrown against the wall behind him and slid into a sitting position. Though he was obviously dead, blood poured out of his mouth like a faucet—which a number of pathologists have said is normal. What happened in Foster's case?

Next we are faced with the problem of the strange-acting gun with which Foster supposedly killed himself.

"In my twenty-five years of investigating homicide, I have never seen a gun remain in the suicide's hand, and in that manner." So commented former Army CID agent Gene Wheaton of the circumstances of Foster's death that seem to have been accepted by the Fiske investigators.

Wheaton makes the grave charge that the gun was "put in [Foster's] hand" by someone; the event was "staged."

According to Geberth, "Under ordinary circumstances, after the firing, the gun is away from the person." Other homicide experts concur, noting that the gun can wind up many feet away from the body due to natural reflex actions of the individual committing suicide.

There's also the matter of the bizarre grip Foster supposedly used; his right thumb was found in the trigger guard, indicating that he fired the gun by pressing the trigger with that thumb, which was compressed into the guard when the trigger rebounded after the firing.

That, and other factors, led one of the nation's leading experts on the interaction of guns and the human body, Massad Ayoob of the highly respected Lethal Force Institute, to seriously doubt that Foster fired the Colt revolver said to be the suicide weapon.

In an analysis of the gun powder residue found on Foster's hands, Ayoob commented on the unorthodox way Foster supposedly wielded the suicide weapon: "This is an extremely unnatural and awkward grasp, totally inconsistent with what both experience and logic show us to expect of a suicidal person with a gun in his hand directed at himself.

"This person, committing a 'deliberate' suicide, will have a great fear of slipping or flinching on the gun and shooting himself in the wrong place, inflicting a wound that maims horribly instead of killing instantly."

Gunpowder residue was found on Foster's index fingers and the web area between his thumb and index finger, indicating that his four fingers would have been lying over the gun's cylinder and wrapped around the top of the gun's frame while his thumb remained on the trigger.

This awkward grip, Ayoob believes, would have put Foster's smallest finger in the way of the gun's hammer. None of this is consistent with Ayoob's belief that "deliberate" suicides use the strongest possible grip.

Considering the glaring inconsistencies of the case, the behavior of the U.S. Park Police and other officials involved is perplexing. Police procedure calls for treating all suicides as homicides until the facts prove differently.

For example, standard police procedure in cases such as this—even if the deceased is a vagrant, let alone a high United States official, and even in the absence of suspicious details like the paucity of blood and the strange position of the gun—is to conduct a door-to-door canvass of the area around a crime scene: Did you hear a shot? Did you notice strangers in the area? Anything out of the ordinary? etc.

The officials did none of this. Indeed, if anything, they seem to have gone out of their way *not* to conduct a proper investigation.

Within hours of Foster's death, even before an autopsy was conducted, Park Police were disposing of crucial crime-scene evidence. For example, Foster's White House-assigned pager was given back to the White House on that very night, leaving us to wonder: Who might have tried to call him that night? Were there any fingerprints other than his on the device? We will never know.

Moreover, according to testimony given to the Senate Banking Committee by John Rolla, the head investigator for the Park Police, he allowed the White House to have all of Foster's personal effects that were found on his body and in his car. Rolla had never before conducted a death investigation, yet he was allowed to head a case of this magnitude.

His bumbling might, by a stretch of logic, be attributed to gross incompetence, but no such charitable reading can be ascribed to what investigative reporter Chris Ruddy deems as an "out-and-out cover-up" by the Park Police of the circumstances of Foster's death.

Ruddy, in a special report he authored on the Fiske investigation of Foster's death, states: "There is powerful evidence that the Park Police lied in their official reports as to the location where Foster's body was found—changing its placement by a couple of hundred feet."

In order to fully understand this, it is useful to have a basic knowledge of Fort Marcy Park, a small parcel of land wedged between two north-south thoroughfares, the George Washington Parkway on the west and Chain Bridge Road on the east. Close to the latter, about midway between the northern and southern parameters of the park, the wooded land rises to form a roughly squarish plateau measuring a few hundred feet on a side; this was the original fort.

On two sides of this tiny fort the land falls away sharply, forming steep embankments, or berms. During the Civil War, numerous cannons overlooked the berms, giving the defenders maximum strategic advantage.

Just two of these cannons remain: one, which will be designated the "first cannon," on the west side near the southwest corner of the clearing; the other, the "second cannon," on the northern border of the fort, a short distance from the northeast corner of the clearing. This second cannon, unlike the first one, is hidden by brush and earthen mounds.

The location and description of these two cannons are critical to understanding the inconsistencies in the case.

George Gonzalez, a lead paramedic for the Fairfax County (Virginia) Fire & Rescue Station No. 1, was the first emergency worker to come upon Foster's body. In an unrehearsed account of that discovery given to reporter Chris Ruddy in January 1994, he said that he and two others, after entering the park's parking lot some 200 feet south of the original fort area, took a looping trail that moves northeast into the main clearing of the fort. Here he came upon the first cannon, on the western border of the clearing.

He remembers going by that first cannon. Then "at least twenty feet" beyond, he came upon Foster's body on the berm which that cannon overlooks.

Gonzalez told Ruddy he moved down the berm and checked Foster for life signs, closely examining his eyes and his fingers to see if they were cyanotic (pooling blood). They were; Foster was dead. Gonzalez emphasized—keep this detail in mind—that it's important never to assume death, but to carefully verify it.

The Park Police report, as well as the Fiske report into which it was incorporated, have a dramatically different version of events. These reports describe Gonzalez and his party reporting discovery of the body approximately ten feet in front of the *second* cannon.

Moreover, according to the Fiske report, Gonzalez testified to FBI investigators that he himself did not discover the body; rather, he arrived shortly after the two others in his team had come upon it. Further, according to the report, it was not Gonzalez who checked for signs of life, but Todd Hall, a fellow paramedic. Although Gonzalez admits he never *saw* Hall check for life signs, he, the lead paramedic, didn't personally check for them because he said—and remember how he'd emphasized the need for verification— Foster's condition was "obvious."

Gonzalez' flip-flop is even more stunning considering the accurate map he sketched in Ruddy's reporter's notebook at the time. The map correctly details the looping trail from the parking lot to the fort's main clearing; it also correctly positions the first, west cannon, which he recounted seeing just before discovery of the body.

Indeed, Gonzalez didn't even *know* of the second cannon at the time, nor did a Park Police officer who had been at the death scene.

Why should they know? That second, north cannon, as noted above, was hidden from view and was a couple of hundred feet away from where the body was discovered.

Other evidence corroborates the original account of Gonzalez and the police officer. Kory Ashford, who removed Foster's remains, claimed he didn't remember seeing a cannon at all, which is consistent with Foster's body being where Gonzalez originally had it; for the first, west cannon would have been out of Ashford's line of sight as he made his way up the path to the body.

If the body had been where the Fiske report placed it, Ashford could hardly have failed to notice that second, north cannon, since—although, again, it is hidden by vegetation from those approaching it from inside the park—it stands starkly and quite visibly over the relatively bare spot on the berm where the Fiske report had the body.

Then there's the matter of the missing photo evidence. No police procedure in death cases is more routine than photographing the entire crime scene. The Park Police don't have a single photo of the whole crime scene—the crucial "body against surroundings" type. Nor are there any critical pictures showing the body's relationship to any landmark, such as, say, a nearby cannon.

Indeed, the only photos we know of are thirteen Polaroids, showing only close-ups of parts of Foster's body and the ground around it.

Whether this was incompetence or a deliberate attempt to obscure the circumstances of Foster's death, at least one of these photos (which was leaked to ABC News) is incriminating in itself. It shows the body lying in *thick quantities of vegetation*—consistent only with the area near the *first* cannon.

The Polaroids, including the leaked one, offer other evidence that the Park Police changed the location of where they found the body. Directly in front of the second, north cannon the ground is clearly visible and devoid of vegetation, showing a well-worn pathway down the berm to where the body supposedly lay.

John Hanchette, a reporter for *USA Today*, visited the second-cannon site the day after the incident. He was later asked if the relatively bare pathway on the berm matched the photo he'd seen on ABC News. "No, it does not," he replied. "I thought [the photo] was fishy." The photo, he said, depicted an area "too verdant" to be the one he'd visited that day.

Hanchette and another reporter had conducted their own search for the death scene, since they had been given no precise information at that early stage. They quickly came upon the second-cannon site and found "a bloodstain on the dirt," indicating to them that this was the spot of Foster's demise.

But the truth is that Foster's body was on top of *vegetation*, on the berm by the first, west cannon. Not only do the Polaroids and eyewitnesses confirm this; the Fiske report itself notes the dense foliage around Foster's body.

Lt. Bill Bianchi of Fairfax Fire & Rescue was also on the scene that fateful July night. After the body was removed, he noted blood residue "*on the grass*," not on the dirt where Hanchette and his companion had seen one.

Bianchi, in a taped interview with Ruddy, also confirmed Gonzalez' original description of the body's location.

Obviously, someone wanted the media and the rest of the world to believe Foster's body had been found by that second cannon—enough so to create a second "crime scene," complete with bloodstain and rubber gloves used at a crime scene, which, Hanchette said, were rather gratuitously strewn around.

On July 18, 1994, Chris Ruddy released his *Special Report on the Fiske Investigation of the Death of Vincent W. Foster, Jr.*, which detailed the cover-up concerning the location of the body. Though the major media ignored it, Reed Irvine, chairman of the media watchdog group, Accuracy in Media, decided to explore some of the discrepancies and mysteries.

Noting that medical examiner Dr. Donald Haut (it was his deputy who conducted the autopsy on Foster) visited Fort Marcy Park the night of Foster's death, Irvine asked him about the body's location. Apparently no one had briefed Haut on the "official" version, and so he described the same area that Gonzalez and the Park Police officer had—that is, the area past the first cannon. Haut, too, was not even aware of a second cannon. Significantly, Haut sketched for Irvine a map of the crime scene near the first cannon which was strikingly similar to the one Gonzalez had drawn for Ruddy.

The astute reader is doubtlessly wondering, why would officials lie about one of the most elemental aspects of any death investigations: the placement and location of the body?

For the answer, we might look to Watergate. We still do not know for certain why this original burglary took place—only that it happened, and that a massive cover-up to hide the truth ensued.

Similarly here: We don't know yet why the death scene was changed in the official police reports; we just know that the location has been falsified, and that a concerted effort is being made to conceal this and other truths about the case.

Gene Wheaton, who investigated the case for several weeks, suggested that perhaps the Park Police recognized that Foster "did not commit suicide," and they may have wanted to move the official location in order to hide the real crime scene. "Maybe Foster's body, neatly arranged in the middle of knee-high brush, looked like a strange location to kill oneself," he speculated.

He also suggested that because the police did not find the bullet that went through Foster's head, they may have feared someone else would find it—a possible explanation for the ruse of the second cannon site, complete with rubber gloves and bloodstain.

And what about the so-called independent investigator, Robert Fiske? How did he, in the face of all the inconsistencies, substantiate something which has all the appearances of being the phony second-cannon site?

In his report, Fiske relies largely on a confidential witness identified only as "C.W.", who supposedly was the first to discover the body.

But, Wheaton thinks C.W.'s testimony strains credulity. For example, C.W. claims he stopped at the park because he had to urinate badly, and then walked several hundred yards through the heavily wooded park (which, it would seem, would be full of secluded spots) before coming upon the body.

In an off-air interview with talk host G. Gordon Liddy in May 1994, C.W. insisted that when he viewed the body he didn't see a gun in Foster's hand. The Fiske report, however, depicts him as backing off and saying he wasn't sure. C.W. says he then returned to his van and drove several miles to a park maintenance facility, where he informed a worker of the discovery before driving off. The worker called 911. A transcript of the call reveals that the worker said "this guy told me [there] was a body laying up there by the last cannon." The park worker repeated: "The last cannon gun."

Walking from the parking lot, the "last cannon" is, of course, the second cannon. That's the phony or *official* location—in direct contravention of all the evidence. C.W.'s placement of the body in the wrong location not only undermines his credibility, but makes him a suspect if foul play was involved in Foster's death.

A number of reporters have given credence to C.W.'s testimony, and have also been impressed by his seemingly significant testimony that no gun was in Foster's hand. But, as experts quoted above have noted, the gun shouldn't have been in Foster's hand in the first place. C.W.'s testimony, far from undermining the official line, helps buttress it. The fact that the gun might have been placed in Foster's hand after he committed suicide does not change the conclusion of suicide. However, the change of location of the body in official reports *does*, and could blow the investigation wide open.

There are other aspects of C.W.'s testimony that raise doubts about his credibility, in addition to the fact that the Fiske report uses him to corroborate the wrong location for the body. Nine months after the incident, C.W. reached out to Liddy with great trepidation. At this point he knew— assuming he didn't know all along—that the dead person he found was not just anybody, but a high-ranking government official, an official whom he indicated had been the victim of foul play. In fact, C.W. told Liddy not to reveal his identity because he feared he might end up like Foster.

No doubt C.W.'s credibility was enhanced by the fact that he turned first to Liddy, a staunch critic of the Clinton Administration.

Weeks later the unpredictable C.W. reluctantly agreed to speak to Fiske's FBI investigators—people who work for the same government that may be covering up for the death of this high-ranking official.

The Fiske report was issued on June 30, 1994. It clearly stated that C.W. said the gun *could* have been in Foster's hand, but hidden by the foliage (which again is inconsistent with the officially designated death location).

Further, C.W. agreed that Foster's head could have been tilted slightly to the right. His change in testimony supported FBI assertions which explained unusual blood drainage tracks found on Foster's head. Those tracks were not consistent with C.W.'s original testimony or the Polaroids, which indicated Foster's head was found straight up.

The maverick confidential witness now becomes the conforming and corroborating confidential witness.

Three weeks went by after the release of the Fiske report. Not a word of complaint was heard from C.W. concerning Fiske's representation of his testimony. The Ruddy Report on the Fiske investigation, critical of C.W. for his flip-flops, was issued on July 18. Only then did C.W. complain about the FBI badgering him to alter his testimony about the gun and head position. C.W. said the FBI asked as many as twenty-five times if the gun could have been in Foster's hand, but hidden by foliage. Indeed, C.W. told them that the foliage *could* have hidden the gun.

C.W. currently claims the FBI did not show him any photographs, especially the one leaked to ABC which showed Foster's hand palm-down, the gun underneath the hand. C.W. had said he found Foster's hands palm-up.

Despite wide publication of the photo through the Associated Press, C.W. claims never to have seen it. Presumably, he never took the interest to go, for example, to a library to review it in a magazine or newspaper.

Since Ruddy's report was issued, the so-called confidential witness has embarked on a seemingly fearless campaign, appearing on national television and radio shows to tell his version of events, still anonymously. He apparently believes—or wants us to believe he does—that those who might have conspired to kill Foster, or at least engineered the cover-up of his death, are incapable of establishing his identity.

But given that C.W. gave the wrong location of where Foster's body lay, it's no doubt important for him to keep his credibility by being as vocal as possible.

Reed Irvine met with C.W. at Fort Marcy Park in late August 1994 and confronted him with the fact that scant foliage exists at the second cannon site, and that the slope is not as steep as the Fiske report describes it. C.W. explained that the site had undergone major reconstruction, and that two or three feet of earth had been moved last year from the site. The skeptical Irvine called a park historian to verify C.W.'s claim of reconstruction work. The historian informed Irvine that no such reconstruction had taken place.

Shortly thereafter, Irvine received a call from C.W., who said that he really didn't think the body was directly in front of the second cannon, as the Fiske report quotes him as testifying, but somewhere to the right of the cannon. As for the discrepancy, he blamed that on the FBI's badgering him to corroborate the official account. Unfortunately, a number of journalists and other investigators have focused on the mercurial C.W. in hopes of breaking open this case. While his testimony about the missing gun may be tantalizing to some by zeroing in on that elusive point, critics of the Fiske report have allowed the focus to shift away from the *far more incriminating* inconsistencies of the case.

Syndicated columnist Robert Novak astutely observes that this case won't be resolved until C.W. is compelled to give his testimony under oath—a power that Fiske possessed all along, but chose not to exercise.

This begs the question of why wasn't *everyone* connected with the case put under oath? Given the strong likelihood that C.W. has been lying, who else might be? How can we be sure that a cover-up has not been underway from the time Foster's lifeless body was found at Fort Marcy Park?

The truth about this case is not that unattainable; over twenty Park Police and Fairfax Fire & Rescue personnel are aware of the location where Foster's body was found. It is inconceivable that, threatened with prison terms for perjury, they would all enter into a conspiracy to lie under oath—and trust that none of their colleagues would tell the truth. Why, then, wasn't this simple expedience of putting everyone under oath used by Mr. Fiske?

Fiske, in his report, tells of extensive interviews his office conducted with various witnesses. A footnote weakly tries to justify why he did not use the grand jury in the way veteran investigators like Vernon Geberth think it should have been used—that is, by putting everyone under oath: medical examiner, emergency medical workers, police, witnesses.

Fiske lamely noted that a grand jury wasn't necessary because anyone giving false answers to his staff investigators "would be prosecuted under Title 18, United States Code, Section 1001."

This is tantamount to saying that motorists in New York City need not be concerned about jaywalkers because the traffic code forbids such activity—which virtually every native New Yorker regularly engages in, secure in the knowledge that the last person to receive a jaywalking summons probably stuck it into the band of his stovepipe hat. "'Thousand and one' [Section 1001] is very, very, very, very seldom used," noted William F. Roemer, Jr., a thirty-five year FBI veteran who headed the Bureau's Organized Crime Strike Force in Chicago, and is its highest-decorated former agent. "I have never heard it applied. We never observed it. If Fiske had the power [of subpoena] and he didn't use it, something could be inferred from that," Roemer added weightily.

Yet, on three critical issues Fiske did not employ a grand jury: 1) on the death and its subsequent investigation; 2) on the matter of the removal of files from Foster's office, and later that same night from his office safe; and 3) the grave matter of whether justice was obstructed by keeping the FBI out of the Foster death probe.

Instead of the time-honored method of getting to the truth through a grand jury, Fiske's investigation, like the Park Police report, relied on a highly questionable autopsy report by a Virginia medical examiner, Dr. James Beyer.

Incredibly, ninety-one pages of Fiske's almost two hundred page report—of which only fifty-eight pages deal with Foster's death itself—are résumés trumpeting the qualifications of Fiske's medical and pathology team! Even more incredible, the one résumé that really counts is absent: that of Dr. Beyer himself.

Several Virginia newspapers, as well as the *New York Post* and *The Washington Times*, have seriously challenged Beyer's credentials and abilities.

Beyer, seventy-six, has been under fire for two "suicides" he ruled on. In one case, medical evidence suggested the deceased had been attacked, and in the other case someone later actually confessed to killing the deceased.

That confession came about after the family of twenty-one-year-old Tim Easley challenged Beyer's findings that the young man had taken his own life. At his funeral, the family noted and photographed a cut on Easley's hand that Beyer had not noted on the autopsy report.

"The cut on the hand is definitely *ante mortem* [before death], and I cannot understand how any competent forensic pathologist would miss it," said Dr. Harry Bonnell, chief deputy medical examiner of San Diego, California. "It is a classic 'defense' wound suffered while trying to avoid [a] knife attack."

Beyer admitted during an interview that he saw the cut, but that he failed to note it. He said it was "consistent with a needle mark." (Would, for example, a needle mark on Foster's body have been important enough to note?)

Bonnell also challenged Beyer's assertion that Easley could have stabbed himself, noting that the trajectory of the knife was "inconsistent" with a self-inflicted wound.

In the other case—one that has striking parallels to the Foster matter—Beyer ruled that twenty-year-old Tommy Burkett's death was "consistent with a suicide."

Burkett, like Foster, was found dead of an apparent gun shot through the mouth. After Burkett's survivors noticed that Beyer had failed to note a "bloody and disfigured ear" on his autopsy, they had the young man's body exhumed for a second autopsy, which was performed by Dr. Erik Mitchell, former chief of pathology for Syracuse, New York.

Mitchell found not only trauma to the ear, but other crucial evidence that Beyer had failed to note: a fractured lower jaw, which indicated the deceased may have been beaten first. The second autopsy also revealed that Burkett's lung had not been dissected, as Beyer claimed in his report.

Nevertheless, Beyer's report was the basis for Fiske's independent pathology report—signed off on by four prominent pathologists: "The postmortem findings demonstrated in this case are typical and characteristic of such findings in deaths due to intentional, self-inflicted intraoral gunshot wounds."

The pathologists determined certain critical findings *based solely on Beyer's notations*: that there was no sign of a struggle or injury on Foster's body; that the bullet path described by Beyer was accurate in that it passed through Foster's brain stem and out the upper-rear of Foster's head, disabling the brain stem and causing instantaneous death; and that toxicology tests were accurate, and no drugs had incapacitated Foster.

A number of noted homicide experts indicate that in this kind of death they would test the blood for many types of drugs, including exotic ones not normally tested for after an autopsy and not picked up using standard screens. Unless you make a concerted search for these drugs, you won't find them.

The Fiske report's blanket statement that no incapacitating drugs were found in Foster's blood only means that no such drugs were detected by *selected screens*. Interestingly, the FBI found traces of Valium and an anti-depressant in Foster's blood. Yet, the original blood work for Dr. Beyer's autopsy found not a trace of any drugs, including the two later found in the FBI analysis.

The nature of the toxicology tests assumes particular importance in light of the second major cover-up which officials engaged in. This, too, involved "location": that of the exit wound in Foster's head.

Where was that wound?

According to Dr. Beyer's original autopsy report, the bullet entered the back of Foster's mouth and then went "backward and upward, with exit from the back of the head." This path was also shown on a diagram drawn by Beyer, indicating that the bullet exited three inches from the crown of Foster's head.

The Park Police reinforced this theory over the course of the investigation, repeating in mantra-like fashion to anyone interested that the bullet track was "up and out," just as the autopsy report indicated. Indeed, the "up and out" track is typical of self-inflicted wounds of this kind, since the shooter wants to ensure death. To be graphic about it, to fire "up" more or less ensures that the brains will literally be blown out.

While such a wound does not, of course, *prove* that the shot was self-inflicted, it raises far fewer suspicions than, for example, a horizontal shot through the mouth and out the back of the neck—which, according to one extraordinarily credible witness, was the true nature of Foster's wound.

The witness—prominent Little Rock criminal attorney Joe Purvis—was a lifelong friend of Foster as well as a friend of President Clinton from their childhood days together in Arkansas. He, in fact, viewed Foster's body at Ruebel's Funeral Home in the University Heights section of Little Rock.

In a face-to-face interview with Chris Ruddy last March, Purvis related that his early statements that Foster's death couldn't have been a suicide (he says that he subsequently accepted that it was) led him to talk with a member of the mortuary staff. This employee confirmed to him that a "neat little" entrance wound was found deep in the back of Foster's mouth, and a similarly small-sized exit wound in the back of Foster's neck—wounds that are decidedly not consistent with the "up and out" line.

As Purvis related this encounter at the funeral home, he indicated the size of the exit wound with his thumb and index finger held about a half-inch apart, and then pointed to the base of his own skull to show the location of the exit wound.

Far more telling, Purvis said he was allowed to see the exit wound, which he described as a small hole *in the back of the neck.*

Several months after Ruddy met with Purvis, he was interviewed in a taped telephone conference by Accuracy In Media heads Reed Irvine and Joe Goulden. In that interview, Purvis acknowledged that he was permitted by the funeral home to actually see the exit wound. He confirmed that when Foster's head was lifted up, he found a neat exit wound "the size of a dime" at the hairline on the neck.

Bear in mind that Beyer located the wound at the upper back of Foster's head, a less suspicious location. Beyer also described the exit wound as being irregular, or jagged, at the spot where the bullet broke through the cranium, making a 1" by 1-1/4" hole—substantially larger than the "dime-sized" hole Purvis saw.

Who's to be believed here? It appears, again, that the officials have been lying.

EMS technician Kory Ashford, who (you may remember) saw little or no blood as he put Foster's body in a bag, said that he also couldn't remember seeing an exit wound—a circumstance hard to imagine if the wound was of the type described in the autopsy report.

Ashford's testimony is consistent with Purvis' location of the exit wound. Doubtless some blood drained out of the exit wound and—given that the body lay on the slanted berm with the head at the higher elevation—flowed into the single large pool that Fiske's investigators said was found on the back of Foster's shirt. Other circumstantial evidence supports the theory that this was not the real site.

Fiske's investigators excavated the site where the police said they found the body, but they found neither bone fragments from the exit wound nor the bullet fired through Foster's head.

The all-important matter of the exit wound could have been easily resolved were it not for the missing X-rays (redolent of the missing crime-scene photographs). Oddly, the autopsy report clearly states that X-rays were indeed made. The Park Police report confirms this: "Dr. Byer [sic] stated that X-rays indicated that there was no evidence of bullet fragments in the head."

Yet the Fiske report inexplicably states that no X-rays were made because the X-ray machine in Beyer's office was "inoperable."

Media critic Irvine didn't take that statement for fact either. He called the firm that services the (almost-new) X-ray machine in Beyer's office and discovered that no servicing was performed on that unit from June 1993 through October 1993. Did that machine, after supposedly becoming "inoperable" on that critical date of July 20, 1993, somehow manage to heal itself for the remainder of that period? No, it appears that those X-rays were indeed taken.

In any event, X-rays should not have been the only evidence of the exact nature of the exit wound. Beyer claimed to have taken at least twenty-seven photographs of the corpse, but a source close to the investigation believes that none were taken of that critical exit wound.

He said that a profile photo—one that can easily be dummied up to look real—supposedly does exist, which shows the trajectory of the bullet by way of metal rods coming out of the entrance and exit wounds.

All in all, there was certainly sufficient motivation for officials to not want the truth to be known about the exit wound.

Besides the matter of the "up and out" trajectory being less suspicious, there was the matter of the lack of blood—which, as we saw earlier, officials *tried* to attribute to cessation of brain activity. But even if the bullet followed the trajectory described by Beyer, much more blood should have been found at the crime scene. If the bullet took the path indicated by Purvis' observations, there would be even less reason to believe Foster's heart stopped beating immediately.

One conclusion that could be drawn from the lack of blood is that Foster's heart stopped *before* the shot was fired, meaning that the shot, obviously fired by someone other than Foster, was used to mask another *unknown* cause of death.

Fiske seems to have eagerly accepted all the anomalies of the case, farfetched as the explanations were. At the same time, he cavalierly dismissed any alternate explanations about Foster's death, including the not unlikely one that Foster's body was brought to the park.

Indeed, there is ample evidence that Foster never entered that park alive. For one thing, an FBI analysis found not a trace of the abundant park soil on Foster's shoes or clothing. The Fiske report has a simple explanation for this: the foliage in the park that July day was particularly dense, preventing Foster from encountering even a smidgeon of exposed soil.

Republican Congressman Dan Burton—of the same courageous and skeptical mold as Irvine—decided to check the park landscaping for himself. This is what he reported on the House floor on August 2, 1993:

"Foster would have had to walk a long way from his car to the second cannon. I walked all the way from the parking lot up to that second cannon; it was a dry day and I had dust *all over* my shoes. It is about 300 yards. For them to say there was no dirt on his shoes does not make any sense, unless possibly he had been moved to that position."

Burton's reaction was similar to that of the emergency workers at the time they discovered the body. In a March 7, 1993, article in the *New York Post*, Chris Ruddy reported that an emergency worker had noted that Foster's dress shoes were "very clean," an observation later confirmed by law-enforcement officials. The immaculate shoes were far from the only evidence that the body may have been moved. Consider the blood tracks on Foster's face, which indicated that his head assumed no less than four separate positions after his alleged instantaneous death!

Had Foster lain moaning and writhing on the ground after the supposed shot, that could conceivably have been the case. But it is the official position that he died *instantaneously.*

It must be one way or another, not an impossible combination of both. Those who claim instantaneous death are obligated to explain the four different positions of the head, as indicated by the blood tracks, to wit:

First, a blood stain on Foster's right cheek indicated his head had come into contact with his shirt, which was blood-soaked in the shoulder area.

Second, Fiske's report said Foster's head was tilted slightly to the right, based on the fact that blood tracks had run from the right side of his mouth and nose.

Third, Fiske's report also indicated that blood had run from the right nostril to where it was seen on the temple area above the ear. Given the way his body was sloped on the berm with the feet pointing down-slope, this could only come about with the head tipped backward.

Finally, the report notes the Polaroid photo, which shows the head to be looking generally "straight up."

Fiske accepted the possibility that Foster's head was touched by what he believes to be an early observer. But this hardly explains four different head positions.

Other unexplained evidence indicates Foster's body may have been elsewhere before it was found in the park. Blond hairs (Foster's hair was gray-black) were found on his clothing, including his underwear. Fiske's team didn't bother investigating this matter. The FBI also found carpet fibers of various colors all over Foster's expensive clothing. Yet Fiske's investigators didn't bother to check where they may have come from either.

Then there was the matter of the Park Police claiming they found Foster's eyeglasses thirteen feet down the berm from his body. The strange placement of the glasses, which Fiske says simply "bounced" down the berm through thick foliage, indicates someone meddled at the death scene before the police arrived.

Other evidence that the body might have been moved is admittedly circumstantial but, nonetheless, substantial. There are, for example, no eyewitnesses who saw Foster from the time he left his office in the West Wing of the White House at 1 p.m. until his body was found at 6 p.m. that evening. No one saw him drive his car. No one remembers spotting him alive around Washington or in the park—a highly unusual circumstance given that his photo was splashed for days across newspaper pages and television screens.

Leaving the circumstantial and returning to the substantive, a few other areas cry out for investigation. The most obvious is that of Foster's files and the unseemly haste and surreptitious circumstances under which they were removed. Just hours after Foster's death, three top White House officials—Bernard Nussbaum, then the White House Counsel; Maggie Williams, Hillary Clinton's chief of staff; and presidential assistant, Patsy Thomasson—rushed into Foster's office and took out files. They later admitted taking Whitewater files. What other files of the Clintons did they remove?

Later that very same night, even as the Foster family was trying to absorb the initial shock, one top White House aide thought, or was told, it was necessary to enter Foster's safe and remove more files.

This inappropriate haste to cover tracks before a close friend's body had been properly attended to might have backfired on them. After *The Washington Times* originally broke the story of the removal of the Whitewater files on December 20, 1993, calls for a special prosecutor came out from all quarters, including from close allies of the Clintons who were outraged by this callous, if not criminal, behavior.

These calls reached a fever pitch by mid-January during the President's trip to Eastern Europe. Over the apparent objections of his wife—who made the bizarre assertion that because they'd supposedly lost money in the sleaze-filled Whitewater investment, nothing could possibly be wrong; therefore, case closed—President Clinton finally relented and asked Attorney General Reno to appoint a special counsel.

That counsel, of course, turned out to be Robert B. Fiske, who promised to investigate not only the Whitewater matter, but also Foster's death and the unusual raid of his office. He also pledged that he would look into the serious charge that the White House had deliberately excluded the FBI from the investigation and had assigned the case instead to vastly less qualified Park Police. This is still another of those "substantive" areas which demand a full investigation. (The FBI was later brought in only after the head of the FBI had been fired by Clinton.)

Fiske, who curiously did not use the grand jury for this critical part of his investigation, devoted just little over half a page to explain why the FBI did not conduct the original investigation. While admitting that the circumstances of Foster's death came under FBI jurisdiction, Fiske explained that since "a preliminary inquiry by the FBI . . . failed to indicate any criminal activity, the FBI's inquiry into this matter was closed."

But in a two-page letter, Judge William Sessions, the former Director of the FBI, wrote that the FBI was kept off as the lead investigative agency because of a "power struggle [between] the FBI and the Department of Justice" at the time of Sessions' firing.

"The decision about the investigative role of the FBI in the Foster death was therefore compromised from the beginning," Sessions wrote, noting specifically that Foster's death took place "the day after my termination" and on the same day Judge Louis Freeh had been "proposed" as director. Freeh took office several weeks later.

The day of Sessions' firing, *The Wall Street Journal* ran a lead editorial called, "What's the Rush?" It began: "So the gang that pulled the great travel office caper is now hell-bent on firing the head of the FBI." The paper thought it strange that Sessions had to be fired—*when he had already offered to resign* once a replacement had been confirmed by the Senate.

Fiske didn't turn up any obstruction issues, yet there seems to be no explanation for charges, such as those published in *The Washington Times*, that "Mr. Sessions' statement corresponds with those of current and former FBI and Justice Department officials who told the *Times* of interference by the White House and Justice Department in the Bureau's work in the Foster investigation."

Similarly, ex-FBI notable, William Roemer, who said that "[Attorney General Janet] Reno and Clinton had undue influence. The FBI would normally be finding reasons to get involved in a high-profile case" like this.

Former CID agent Gene Wheaton concurs, describing the Park Police as being the "most pliable of federal law enforcement agencies." When the Park Police was asked for a breakdown of their approximately thirty-five death investigations last year, they could not provide even that basic information.

Often we hear plausible explanations for any of the unusual circumstances of this death. As noted above, such individual explanations may be credible, but the probability that *all* of this together adds up to the conclusion of suicide as set forth by the Park Police and Fiske is dim indeed.

The opening line to *Macbeth* resounds accusatorially over the official version of Foster's death: *Fair is foul and foul is fair.*

Without rendering judgment on the conclusion of suicide, Foster's death cries out to at least be investigated as a homicide—even as standard police practice dictates that far less suspicious apparent-suicides are; and even as such deaths involving far more obscure people than this top official are.

In retrospect, the results of Fiske's report were inevitable. Fiske accepted the Park Police testimony at face value, he chose not to use his subpoena power, and he accepted the autopsy report without question.

With the same type of acceptance, Fiske would have us

also believe that "there is no evidence that any issues related to Whitewater, Madison Guaranty or CMS played any part in [Foster's] suicide."

Perhaps he is right: Whitewater had no connection. Perhaps he is wrong. Perhaps even weightier reasons led to Foster's demise.

PREFACE, CHAPTER 7

"We in the press like to say we're honest brokers of information, and it's just not true. The press does have an agenda."
--Bernard Goldberg, CBS, "48 Hours".

Scott Wheeler's interest in knowing the truth about the vital issues concerning our country propelled him into investigative reporting. The thoroughness of his probes is reflected by the number of magazines and newspapers which publish his articles. His position as a nationally-syndicated talk show host enables him to feel the pulse of America.

Wheeler writes about the brazen bias and agenda of what once was an objective news media. He documents the media transition from reporting news to manipulating public knowledge and perceptions.

CHAPTER 7

MEDIA BIAS IN POLITICS—TRUTH "LEFT" OUT

by Scott Wheeler

Home at last! I grab my latest issue of Newsweek, *kick off my shoes and sink down in my favorite chair to catch up on the news.*

What's this? An article written about President Bill Clinton—"The Politics of Promiscuity." Well, it's about time. I've been wondering about him. Let's see what Newsweek *has to say . . .* "The national press has been restrained in its accounts of Bill Clinton's private life, and with good reason. Most of those who have made charges against him have been despicable people; jealous, stunted sorts." (*Newsweek,* May, 1994) *. . . Oh, great! Just another dose of "unbiased" journalism!*

The above magazine statement, describing those who criticize Bill Clinton as little more than Neanderthal low-lifes, typifies the attitude of the mainstream media—a perspective the press unceasingly strives to impose upon the American public.

There was a time in the United States when a newspaper was a piece of paper with news printed on it. Citizens were credited with enough intelligence to read the account of an event or the content of a speech and be able to arrive at a valid conclusion. Today, with the advent of radio and television as well as a plethora of printed matter, we can often see "the news as it happens." But is it all really "news?" Could some of this be engineered information?

Unfortunately, the potential for controlling public perception using these rapid and powerful methods of communication has tempted many in the media to utilize the "news" business to further personal agendas, rather than to just report the facts.

The obvious bias of today's media leans sharply toward liberal ideology. The fact that people in the media have personal biases is not in itself a problem. The problem arises when they allow those biases to obscure their objectivity; honesty is erased from their notebooks and everyone suffers. Honesty should *never* be a partisan issue.

Because the American public has been very slow to catch on to the onslaught of manipulated facts daily bathing their minds, a "darling" of the liberals (along with his "friends") has invaded the august rooms of the White House and, subsequently, has made many Americans not so "proud to be American."

The protectionist media has chosen to shelter the misdeeds of their darling—Bill Clinton—at any cost. They have demonstrated a willingness to ruthlessly discredit anyone who challenges their icon. This chapter recounts just a tiny sampling of the daily barrage of misinformation and twisting of truth coming from the mainline liberal media.

First, we see (in contrast to the ugly treatment of those who would dare criticize Clinton) a protest from George Bush about the media's scandalous handling of Quayle: "There was all this running around, yelling `Draft dodger!' and throwing names against the person. I don't happen to think that's fair."

In truth, many of the issues the press raised in determining Dan Quayle's fitness to serve as Vice-President during the 1988 presidential campaign were alarmingly similar to the allegations the media ignored while covering Bill Clinton during the 1992 presidential race.

The media made an issue of Dan Quayle's draft record, charging that Quayle served only in the National Guard during the Vietnam war. They then perpetuated unsubstantiated rumors that Quayle may have used family influence to obtain a spot in the Indiana National Guard.

This smear certainly appeared shallow considering there were openings in the unit to which he was admitted!

Conversely, when Cliff Jackson, an Arkansas attorney, raised questions about Bill Clinton's draft record, the media impugned Jackson's motives rather than investigating the charges or reviewing the evidence.

Whatever the reason for the media's reticence to criticize Bill Clinton's draft record, the press had a voracious appetite for "Quayle" concerning his military record—a record considerably more honorable than that of Bill Clinton.

Case in point: *Time* magazine writer David Beckwith, in an exclusive interview with presidential candidate George Bush, used the opportunity to concentrate on Dan Quayle's draft record. In fact, seven of the eleven questions published in the Bush interview related to Quayle and the draft. (*Time*, August 29, 1988)

Time's interest in candidate draft records was selective, as evidenced by its non-treatment of Clinton's draft dodging. Instead, typified by its September 21, 1992, issue, *Time* used its expertise in news reporting to gloss over Clinton's allergies to the truth. It referred to a host of lies told by presidential candidate Clinton during the campaign as "Clinton obfuscations."

The charges of womanizing, which surfaced in the last two presidential campaigns was another issue that received unbalanced treatment by the press.

On the one hand, we have Dan Quayle accused and indicted in the press for allegedly making a pass at Paula Parkinson in 1981. Parkinson, who had posed nude, was trying to get her book published in 1988, but the media, without questioning her motives or searching for corroboration, published articles claiming that Quayle's behavior was a serious detraction from his ability to serve as Vice-President.

On the other hand, we have Gennifer Flowers, who came forward telling about a twelve-year affair with Clinton, being given the "bimbo/gold-digger" treatment by not only the Clinton campaign staff, but also by the media covering the campaign—despite the existence of taped phone conversations between Flowers and Governor Clinton. After the disavowal of any more than a slight friendship with Gennifer, Clinton *denied the authenticity of the tapes*, then, unbelievably, he apologized to New York Governor Mario Cuomo *for derogatory remarks he had made about Cuomo on the Gennifer Flowers tapes!*

Classic Damage Control

In other pre-election coverage, we find *Time* magazine taking a defensive posture regarding the First-Lady-to-be. The need for defense resulted from Hillary Clinton's cutting remark, "I suppose I could have stayed home, baked cookies, and had teas." *Time* reporter Margaret Carlson defends Hillary in that article, stating that charges of conflict of interest "are easy to make, hard to refute, and can obscure a hidden intent to put an uppity woman in her place." (*Time*, March 30, 1992)

It is obvious, however, that Ms. Carlson's intent in writing the story, "When Spouses Earn Paychecks," was to exonerate Hillary Clinton of any wrongdoing in the Whitewater scandal, regardless of facts. According to Carlson, the allegation in question was that Hillary had "helped a savings and loan represented by her law firm to get a break from the state securities board." (This board was, by the way, appointed by her husband.)

Hillary quipped, "For goodness sake, you can't be a lawyer if you don't represent banks."

Carlson tried to cover Hillary's error. "Clinton was so rattled by the accusations that she forgot that she hardly ever represents banks."

It comes as no surprise that Carlson (in her feigned concern for objectivity), forgot to mention the name of the bank Hillary represented—the infamous Madison Guaranty Savings and Loan—whose president just happened to be the Clintons' business partner in the Whitewater Land

Development project. Despite the glaring aforementioned exception, Carlson assured her readers "that most legal experts agree that [Hillary] Clinton took the needed steps to avoid conflicts."

Actually, it could be said that the mainstream media avoided (and continues to avoid) *any serious investigation* into accusations of Clinton impropriety which occurred during their tenure as "governors" of Arkansas.

Continuing to examine pre-election press coverage of the Clinton era as governor of Arkansas, we see that *U.S. News & World Report* weighed in heavily on the Clinton side by doing what amounted to a public relations piece about what it considered to be "Bill Clinton's best program."

This piece by Paul Glastris refers, of course, to the Arkansas Development Finance Authority (ADFA). What is so astounding about this story entitled, "High Stakes in Little Rock," is that it credits ADFA for accomplishments it never achieved, and then defends charges against ADFA that were subsequently proven to be not only serious, but also accurate. (*U.S. News & World Report,* July 6, 1992)

Now that the truth about ADFA is unraveling, it is obvious that volumes could be written on the improprieties and illegal activities occurring at ADFA under the close supervision of then Governor Bill Clinton.

But Glastris had a mission. In his *U.S. News & World Report* story, he accused "an army of journalists" of producing a "barrage of stories, alleging shady business deals and conflicts of interest" surrounding its coverage of ADFA.

Glastris' list of what he contends were false allegations includes: 1) that "Clinton steered bond work to a political supporter later convicted of distributing cocaine" and 2) that the Rose Law Firm "unfairly gained state bond business." His article argues that "all the stories with ADFA ties turn out to be largely or wholly false."

However, Glastris' idealistic picture of ADFA could not be further from the truth. In fact, Dan Lasater of Lasater and Company *was* given 619 million dollars in ADFA bonds. He *did* contribute heavily to Governor Clinton's campaigns, and he *was convicted* of cocaine distribution in 1986.

In addition, the Rose Law Firm, where the governor's wife was a partner, did its share of legal work for ADFA. So it's difficult to discern exactly what was unfair about these ADFA stories that Glastris found objectionable.

Actually, the *U.S. News & World Report* story is not very accurate. It attempts to portray Bill Clinton as the heroic developer of ADFA, bent on helping the poor people of his state. But then, according to the article , along comes "big bad" Jack Stephens of Stephens, Inc., "who feared that the plan would hurt his dominance in the Arkansas bond business." The article painted Clinton as a hero for his determination in passing the legislation despite Stephens' objections.

The truth is Stephens Inc. had brought jobs and prosperity to Arkansas. With the inception of ADFA, Stephens lost their corner on the bond market which cost them a great deal of business. ADFA gave a portion of the lost bond transactions back to Stephens, but the amount was nothing compared to what had been lost. This is exactly what the company had feared would happen and amply demonstrated why they had previously fought against the ADFA legislation.

Clinton designed ADFA supposedly to create jobs for the needy of his state, but in reality he had taken business from the private sector and given it to a government agency, which in turn then parceled it back to the private sector with the piggy-back of bureaucracy.

As it turns out, what *U.S. News & World Report* called "Bill Clinton's best program"—ADFA—was in actuality a dismal failure. According to its own account, ADFA created a whopping 4,000 jobs. However insignificant that number is in relation to the hundreds of millions of dollars distributed by ADFA, it's still somewhat higher than L.J. Davis' tally, which totaled only 2,700 jobs created by ADFA (*The New Republic*, April 4, 1994).

Shifting now to post-election coverage, we find the President accused by yet another woman. Paula Jones' suit against Clinton is a very serious threat, not only because her case involves allegations of sexual harassment, but also because there are witnesses who can place both Paula Jones and Bill Clinton at the scene where the event took place, as well as people to whom she immediately told the story, visibly upset.

Media reaction to this situation was quite interesting. A sexual harassment charge had been made—a very politically correct allegation *if the accused is a conservative*. Whenever the accused is an ultra-liberal, as is the case with President Clinton, the liberal media instinctively begin to hound the accuser.

You may recall how the media savaged Supreme Court Justice Clarence Thomas—for charges far less serious, much further in the past, and far less substantiated than the charges against Clinton. But in typical form, instead of focusing on Paula's startling allegations, the reporters lost no time in going out and attempting to dig up some dirt on her.

The media had a mission, and it didn't include being fair to Paula Jones. Their goal was to protect the rapidly disintegrating image of their beleaguered favorite in the White House—Bill Clinton.

U.S. News & World Report sent out its first-string reporters. *U.S. News'* editor-in-chief responded to Jones' allegations with an editorial (*U.S. News & World Report*, May 23, 1994).

"It doesn't pass the smell test," remarked Mortimer B. Zuckerman. "What we have is the moral and legal equivalent of a late hit in football."

Mr. Zuckerman's resolution to the conflict at hand is to "oblige the plaintiffs to pay all or part of the legal costs for both sides if their claims are found wanting." (Perhaps Zuckerman is onto something. Why don't the taxpayers utilize his suggestion and send a bill to Anita Hill for the additional time the Senate Confirmation Committee spent listening to her capricious testimony?)

Again, in the name of honesty, how does the main-stream media justify being more willing to believe allegations made by Paula Parkinson against Quayle or by Anita Hill against Clarence Thomas, than those of Gennifer Flowers, Sally Perdue, Paula Jones and hosts of other women, all against the same man, Bill Clinton?

We see evidence in the liberal mainstream media that a completely different standard is applied to charges made against someone who shares their ideology (such as Ted Kennedy, Barney Frank, or Gerald Studds). The pleas when liberals get caught in a compromising situation become: Try to show some compassion—don't be judgmental—we must protect the dignity of the office.

The angle of pursuit taken by reporters in the Paula Jones case was: *Obviously she is a conservative*—a point that has never been established—*so whatever happens to her is of no consequence.*

All that is required is a whiff of conservatism or (perish the thought) a connection to the religious right and presto! The victim no longer has credibility with the press.

Another classic example of the media playing the role of the Clinton defense team is the *People* magazine story of January 10, 1994, entitled, "The Gadfly." As previously mentioned, rather than examining Arkansas attorney Cliff Jackson's testimony, this article questions Jackson's motives in bringing up Bill Clinton's draft record. The article then takes a shot at Arkansas state troopers and former Clinton bodyguards Larry Patterson and Roger Perry, calling their credibility into question.

James Carville, Clinton's campaign strategist, was sought out by the *People* magazine article's authors, Bill Hewitt and Margaret Nelson, for his pristine and unbiased view. "He's eaten with jealousy!" is the way Carville explained away Jackson's motives (Jackson's documentation, by the way, was completely ignored).

Attorney Jackson, the story implies, is especially suspect because he agreed to the personal interview with

People magazine "only after repeated requests." (Since when does a guarded response to an interview request make one's testimony invalid?)

Of course, the story would be remiss if it didn't reveal that Jackson is "politically conservative." That connection makes perfect sense to the media, because in their world-view no politically correct liberal would do anything to impede the progress of what they believe to be the most important presidency in the Western Hemisphere since Marxist Daniel Ortega (of Nicaraguan Sandinista fame).

The Bias Virus in Television

The print media have no exclusive on bias. The dominant television networks also show expertise in the practice of placing agenda over truth. In fact, in candid moments they even admit it.

CNN Environmental Director Barbara Pyle states, "I do have an axe to grind . . . I want to be the little subversive person in television." *(American Spectator,* quoted by Micah Morrison, July 1991)

Compare the lack of coverage and respect for the troopers' allegations to the treatment by ABC News of former California governor, Jerry Brown.

On the eve of the Democratic presidential primary in New York, April 9, 1992, Clinton and Jerry Brown were in a dead heat. The next day's election would be decisive.

The night before election day, ABC aired an investigative report followed by a story on *Nightline* about charges that Brown had "tolerated" the use of marijuana in his presence.

Based on *anonymous* testimony, ABC ran this politically damaging story, not even alleging that Brown ever smoked marijuana, only that he was present when it was smoked. It was later revealed that some of these anonymous sources had an axe to grind with Brown. Clearly, ABC News was out to do a hatchet job on him. (Even liberal politicians aren't safe from media attacks if they oppose Clinton.)

Also, it came as no surprise when ABC News aired a scurrilous story on Rush Limbaugh soon after Clinton had lost a procedural vote on the Crime Bill, which many believe was influenced by Limbaugh's opposition.

We see yet another example of ABC's bias in its treatment of Senator Al D'Amato of New York—a leader in the fight for open Whitewater hearings. He was targeted by ABC News in a detailed account about a stock deal in which D'Amato made $35,000. But when *The New York Times* revealed that Hillary Clinton made a suspicious $100,000 profit on cattle futures, *ABC did not even report on it for eleven days,* and then only in passing!

In March of 1994, ABC News with Peter Jennings ran a story on Vince Foster's death, airing a "leaked" photo showing a gun, supposedly in the hand of Vince Foster. ABC declared the death was in fact a suicide based on the specious logic that a Polaroid photo of "a gun" in "a hand" proved Foster killed himself. Yet the photo, a close-up, shows only one side of a man's upper body (which could have been anyone), not to mention the fact that the gun was in the wrong hand. Now that's prime investigative work!

ABC also gave misleading information, stating that it had reviewed "the complete set" of crime scene photographs. We know now that all of the key photos were conveniently "underexposed" in the Park Police labs.

As with *Time* and *U.S. News & World Report,* there appears to be the same old FOB problem with ABC also. Rick Kaplan, the executive producer of ABC's *World News Tonight* is—you guessed it—an FOB (so much so that he has even admitted to advising Clinton on how to downplay the Gennifer Flowers scandal).

By now you should begin to see how and why the media have covered for Clinton. You can also see that all of Clinton's critics will be subject to a hi-tech flogging by the likes of ABC News and other major media.

Returning to the print media coverage, we see biased coverage again in the reporting on Robert Fiske. Kenneth

Starr's being selected as the replacement for Fiske in the role of Whitewater independent counsel provoked a stinging reaction from the press. USA Today wasted no time at all in linking Starr to Senator Jesse Helms of North Carolina. However tenuous that link may be, writers Dennis Cauchon and Judy Keen were quick to point out that the investigation was now tainted because one of the judges on the three-judge panel that replaced Fiske with Starr was an ally of Helms and had been identified as a "former Republican activist."

The story points out that Fiske had "recruited a staff of a dozen young and talented lawyers to Little Rock," which supposedly should impress the readers concerning Fiske's dedication to finding truth. No mention is made of Fiske dragging his feet, skirting around Hale's testimony or the glossing over of major flaws in his Foster research. Conveniently ignored were *Fiske's own very close ties to the banks being investigated,* and the fact that Fiske had represented International Paper, a company involved in the Whitewater scandal.

Instead, the "objective" authors in USA Today conclude that because Starr is a Republican and has good friends who are conservative *(now there's incriminating evidence)*, the move by the panel to fire Fiske and install Starr could *only* have been motivated by politics.

The writers continue trying to establish a political motivation for firing Fiske by blaming "a handful of conservative Republicans who complained in a letter to the three-judge panel that Fiske wasn't aggressive enough."

In the USA Today story, the writers' anxiety over the possibility of the hearings being tainted is baseless when one considers that Starr can only investigate; he still needs a grand jury in order to indict anyone. But factoring in this detail would have ruined the opportunity for liberal reporters to take a free shot at some of their favorite political targets.

Why are the media suddenly concerned with Starr's connection to the Republican Party? They so widely reported that Fiske was a Republican, yet his ability to be fair was never called into question.

The clincher comes toward the end of the *USA Today* story with a quote from, of all people, Fiske's secretary, Michelle Corelli. Her "objective" opinion was used to rebut Representative Dan Burton's charge that "Fiske was doing some damage control work."

The magazine reported that "Corelli disagreed [with Burton's charge]. 'We were really into it, and making great progress.' " *USA Today* shows here its willingness to award credibility to anyone who happens to say the right thing.

The liberal media regularly imply that any negative news about the Clinton Administration emanates from a "conspiracy of conservatives" dedicated to making the President look bad. In contradiction, if anyone dares to suggest that Clinton or those around him may be involved in their own "conspiratorial" web of control, the media viciously lampoons them.

Satire Replaces Substance

Consider the treatment by the mainstream media of the video, *The Clinton Chronicles.* In almost lock-step formation, the media attacked everybody who has been a victim of, or a witness to, improper or criminal activity involving Bill Clinton or his associates.

From a satirical article in *U.S. News & World Report* we are told, "No episode seems beyond Clinton's reach in the world of conspiracy buffs." This story, written by Greg Ferguson and David Bowermaster, is entitled, "Whatever it is, Bill Clinton likely did it." The subheading reads: "Without proof, foes say he's tied to lurid crimes."

The writers of this silly piece of "investigative" journalism deemed themselves so capable that they were able to write their story based on a one-minute phone call to one witness in the film in which no information was exchanged. They ended up writing a piece in which they offered virtually no substantive proof of incorrect information in the video. Furthermore, when Greg Ferguson was invited to Arkansas to talk to the witnesses and review the evidence, he declined the invitation. At first breath, the *U.S. News* story refers to Citizens for Honest Government, the producer of *The Clinton Chronicles,* as a "conservative group." The tenor of their reference implies that all their accusations are motivated by politics and probably part of—here it is again—a conservative conspiracy!

All right, let's apply the same test to writers Ferguson and Bowermaster. If the motives of Citizens for Honest Government are relevant, aren't the motives of the *U.S. News* writers also relevant? Did they demonstrate a thirst for truth or a pre-packaged political protectionist bias?

The same article smugly portrays caricatures of President Clinton in "The Grassy Knoll" as well as asking where Clinton was on March 15, 44 B.C., the day that Julius Caesar was murdered. Of course, the comparison was made to cast aspersions on those who believe that Clinton could be connected to the deaths of certain people who may have had damaging information about him.

U.S. News & World Report suggests that it was the death of Deputy White House Counsel Vincent Foster that became the catalyst for rumors about Clinton's connection to a number of mysterious deaths.

The article also emphasizes a request by Foster's family to "end speculation" about whether or not he committed suicide. The writers state that the family fully accepts the conclusion of two "investigations" that rule Foster's death a suicide.

One of those reports, of course, is by Special Counsel Robert Fiske, Jr., who was later relieved of his duties. Notice, the proof the family chooses to accept is from the findings of Fiske, who was fired for his inadequate work!

Other deaths covered by the story include the so-called "suicide" of Kathy Ferguson, whose ex-husband Danny Ferguson is the co-defendant in the Paula Jones sexual harassment suit against Bill Clinton. Again, the writers use comments by a family member of the deceased to prove suicide—in this case the daughter of Kathy Ferguson, who told police her "mother had been upset." (That kind of conclusive proof would qualify nearly every death as suicide.)

Had she lived, Kathy Ferguson would have been one of the key witnesses in the Paula Jones trial. Her death occurred only four days after Jones file her suit—a "coincidence" which deserved headline coverage. Yet, while Paula Jones' picture was being splashed all over front pages, the sudden suicide of a key witness is hardly mentioned in the press.

In another instance of selective indifference on the part of the media concerns Herschel Friday. Herschel, a prominent Little Rock lawyer and ace pilot, recognized as the foremost bond expert in Arkansas, died in March of 1994 when his plane inexplicably crashed. The seventy-two-year-old Friday served on Clinton's presidential campaign finance committee. According to the *U.S. News & World Report* story, even though "the National Transportation Safety Board (had) not issued its final report," Friday's elderly widow, Beth, was confident that her husband's death was purely an accident. Again, a family member's testimony—a person who in no way qualifies to evaluate an aeronautical accident—was used to quell any speculation of foul play, even though the official report had not been released.

In the case of Luther "Jerry" Parks, who was brutally gunned down in his car on September 26, 1993, the family members were given different treatment by *U.S. News & World Report.* Writers Ferguson and Bowermaster responded to Parks' son, Gary, in a hostile manner, quite different from the response given the previously cited family members they quoted.

Gary Parks maintains that his father, a private detective whose security company had the contract to guard Bill Clinton's presidential campaign headquarters, kept a file on Bill Clinton's indiscretions. Gary Parks says that shortly before his father's murder, the file on Clinton was stolen from his father's home.

In an "about face" maneuver, the *U.S. News* story *discounts the family member's testimony* even though in this instance the family member, Gary, had first-hand knowledge of his father's files. The writers chose also to ignore the statement of Sergeant Clyde Steelman, the police detective who helped lead the murder probe, who publicly stated on March 20, 1994: "If they say that some files were missing, then I can tell you those files were missing. The Parks family isn't lying to you." Instead, this fine team from *U.S. News* quotes a Lieutenant Holladay as saying, "There is no evidence of such a file." What evidence were these super-sleuth authors looking for? Perhaps a note left behind by whoever stole the file saying, "We're taking the file on Clinton and leaving this note so you can prove that the file did exist!"

The information provided by Gary Parks was far more credible than statements provided by family members of the other victims; but because Parks did not support the writers' pre-conceived conclusions, they simply dismissed his eyewitness testimony.

"The Clinton Hater's Video Library" was the headline in *Time* magazine's August 1994 critique of *The Clinton Chronicles* video. Once again, an all-out attack on any person making allegations against Bill Clinton is the main thrust of writer George Church.

Church alleges that Paula Jones is "dressed in a little girl costume" and speaks in a "high-pitched voice" when she appears on the video accusing Bill Clinton of sexual harassment. Church accuses the producers of *The Clinton Chronicles* of using "ham-handed tricks" and having "little or no evidence" to support the accusations, yet he forgets that he has just made unsubstantiated charges of his own.

The message is clear: If you represent the mainstream press, it's all right to play fast and loose with the facts; but if you criticize someone whose political beliefs are in harmony with those of the major media, you will be accused of making unsubstantiated charges.

When attacking *The Clinton Chronicles* video, the issues are never addressed, investigated or disproved, yet the people telling the story are *always* attacked. It appears that the media are sending a more sinister message: If you are a victim of, or a witness to, government corruption involving the Clintons, then you better keep quiet or you'll be defending yourself against an unrelenting character assassination launched by the mainstream media.

The press denigrates any person or group of dissenters as "Clinton Haters." The media would have you believe some diabolical cult of "Clinton Haters" is obstructing the marvelous Clinton program by forcing the Administration to defend itself against "baseless" charges, thus detracting from the real issues.

As we saw, the same media were unforgiving regarding Ronald Reagan and Dan Quayle. It was the media themselves that pummeled Reagan and Quayle with insult after insult, yet members of the press would have you believe that Reagan and Quayle truly deserved the "day after day" shellacking they received. On the other hand, they want you to believe that Bill Clinton is merely an innocent victim.

Truth is anathema to the liberal media. In the media's belief system there is no ultimate truth, only relativity. Therefore, their idea of accuracy is to balance truth with liberalism.

No Honor Among Thieves

One of the highlights in *The Clinton Chronicles* video features an extraordinary confession from *60 Minutes* executive producer, Don Hewitt. On Super Bowl Sunday just prior to the New Hampshire primary, *60 Minutes* broadcast an interview with the Clintons which would forever alter America's future. Larry Nichols had just exposed Bill Clinton's affair with Gennifer Flowers, which in turn had all but destroyed Clinton's run for the presidency.

Conceding the campaign "needed a paramedic" in

order to salvage the nomination, Hewitt's television team blatantly ignored the veracity of Gennifer's testimony and "doctored" the Clinton interview. Hewitt states, "It was strong medicine the way I edited it, but he was a very sick candidate." He actually credits his own skillful editing for putting the Clinton's affair with Flowers to rest.

In spite of the fact that Clinton staffers (Nussbaum, Gergen and Cutler) unanimously agreed that the piece "got him the nomination," the Clintons were nevertheless outraged at Hewitt. Why? Because Hewitt had concentrated completely on denying the Flowers affair and had edited out Bill and Hillary's speech about their vision for America's future. Hewitt said he was now "persona-non-grata at the White House." He had single-handedly saved their campaign, and as a reward he got kicked in the head.

Despite all the overtime the major media put in to protect Clinton from his past, he still lashes out against his volunteer spin doctors. His inability to face even a modicum of truth is graphically demonstrated in this classic outburst: "I've fought more battles than any President in twenty years" and "have not received one d-- bit of credit from the knee-jerk liberal press."

It is revealing to see that Bill Clinton, who literally owes his political life to the mainstream media, will not hesitate to viciously turn on them when they make even the slightest gesture of objectivity.

Apparently, Hewitt recovered from the Clintons' thankless treatment back in 1992, evidenced by the *60 Minutes* program of September 25, 1994. This time Hewitt used a "praising by mildly damning" approach during an interview with Clinton cohort, Don Tyson. His superficial questions seemed inappropriate considering the availability of devastating information exposing Tyson's underworld activities—information which his staff could have easily obtained (and is included in our Appendices B and C).

In the same way that *60 Minutes* rescued Clinton's candidacy, were they now trying to salvage his presidency?

The spin doctoring continues . . .

PREFACE, CHAPTER 8

Clinton smoked marijuana regularly, pulling joints out of a cigarette case. Typically he would smoke two or three in the course of a three-hour stay. He always inhaled.

Clinton produced a bag of cocaine ... He had all the equipment laid out like a pro.

---Sally Perdue (former mistress of Bill Clinton)

British readers have been able to keep up with the Clinton scandals thanks to the news reporting of London's *Sunday Telegraph*. The *Telegraph* is no tabloid. It is one of the world's most prestigious newspapers and is Britain's largest circulating quality daily. This chapter includes highlights from the news reports of noted journalist, Ambrose Evans-Pritchard, who is the *Sunday Telegraph's* man in America.

CHAPTER 8

WHAT EUROPEANS KNOW
THAT AMERICANS DON'T

compiled by Citizens for Honest Government

March 13, 1994:

We were followed by a wine-red Chevrolet Lumina. It weaved in and out of the traffic on the main drag about 50 yards behind us, just too far back to make out the license plates. After a few blocks, the Lumina peeled away and a blue Mazda slid into place.

At the first turn, we were picked up by a cream-colored jeep. The Lumina, the Mazda, and the jeep, always the same trio, keeping watch all morning as we drove around the rural town of Conway, carrying out minor errands.

"They've been doing it pretty intensely for about a month," said Larry Nichols, in his gruff voice. "The way they rotate off like that, it makes me think it's Arkansas State Police."

Nichols no longer ventures out at night alone, and carries a loaded revolver at all times.

"What else can I do? It's getting real dangerous right now, and I don't want to end up another one of those mysterious 'suicides,'" Larry said.

Mr. Nichols claimed to have been a secret personal assistant to then-Governor Bill Clinton, alleging that he transferred state funds into special accounts used by Clinton to entertain his mistresses. He also investigated opponents and fixed things behind the scenes.

As a reward, Nichols said, he was appointed Marketing Director of the Arkansas Development Finance Authority (ADFA), an agency created by Mr. Clinton in 1985.

Officially ADFA was a simple development agency to help spur job growth in Arkansas. But as Nichols tells the story, ADFA allegedly became the instrument for a massive kickback scheme—infinitely greater than anything under investigation in the Whitewater scandal—for enriching Clinton's inner circle of friends and campaign contributors.

When Nichols became disenchanted and blew the whistle in 1988, he alleged he lost his job, his family was threatened, and the resources of Arkansas' one-party, one-media state were used, very successfully, to discredit his story.

The governor's supporters counterattacked that Nichols himself had misused the resources of his office. An embittered Nichols denies this, and has promised revenge ever since.

"I'm going to prove that everything I said about him is true," Nichols explained.

Nichols is unusual in his intimate knowledge of Clinton and his willingness to talk openly about the Arkansas political machine.

It was Nichols who first alleged that Clinton had an affair with Gennifer Flowers.

Nichols also charged that Clinton abused his office using state troopers and state funds to support his affairs. These allegations have been corroborated by four Arkansas state troopers who served on the governor's security detail.

Nichols' charges about ADFA, while not fully investigated by outside authorities, have also been corroborated by a number of published reports, including one in the liberal establishment magazine, *The New Republic*.

Nichols is more than just a "lone ranger." He, in fact, is part of an elaborate "underground" at work in Arkansas.

It is made up of people who feel that they have been injured or misused by the system, and they are eager to help journalists expose the chicanery of the last decade.

Many of their allegations are wild, but as more and more sources come out of the woodwork to corroborate past events, it is no longer possible to dismiss their stories so quickly.

A grizzled veteran of the underground revealed a list that he had put together on the mysterious deaths that had occurred in his home town. "The Arkansas State Police are nothing but a hit squad," he warned.

While it is hard to imagine that Third World police repression could be going on within the borders of the United States, a book by an Arkansas journalist says just that. *Conflict of Interests*, by Gene Wirges, tracked the history of a small Arkansas town where he was editor of the local newspaper.

Wirges makes a devastating case that the local Democratic machine, in power from time immemorial, was always allegedly corrupt and brutal.

January 2, 1994:

Those who have actually read the 11,000 word article by David Brock in *The American Spectator* will never be able to think of the President and the First Lady in quite the same way again.

Whether or not every detail is strictly accurate, the cumulative testimony of the four troopers who served Clinton from 1987 to 1993 is hard to dismiss as pure invention.

The little asides are so telling: the claims that the governor traveled coach on flights in and out of Little Rock, then bumped himself up to first class as soon as the coast was clear; the drafting of free prison labor to tend the garden of Hillary Clinton's parents; Bill Clinton comforting himself that fellatio outside marriage is not adultery because [according to Clinton's interpretation] nothing in the Bible proscribes it.

The central charge is that Clinton used the troopers to

facilitate trysts with six concurrent mistresses, to keep "Hillary Watch" with cellular phones and to solicit countless women for casual sex in hotels.

January 23, 1994:

It was 1983. Perdue was then a local radio talk show host, better known as a former Miss Arkansas.

"He had this little-boy quality that I found very attractive," Perdue reminisced of her affair, which she said began because she "was going through a second divorce; I was vulnerable."

According to Perdue, the affair lasted from August to December of 1983. State troopers regularly brought Clinton to her condominium at Andover Square.

"They'd pull up in a wooded area about thirty feet from the house and wait there," she recalled. Clinton would flick a patio light to summon the police car when he was leaving.

Perdue revealed Clinton's typical routine: he'd drink a few Budweiser beers, and then Clinton would begin playing the clown. She described Clinton as a "showman" and a "brilliant actor," who craved approval and needed the constant approval of women.

"When I see him now, President of the United States, meeting world leaders, I can't believe it . . . I still have this picture of him wearing my black nightgown, playing the sax badly; this guy, tiptoeing across the park and getting caught on the fence. How do you expect me to take him seriously?"

More serious, and more sinister are Perdue's alleged experiences during the 1992 presidential campaign after she tried to air details of her alleged affair. She tells how she sat through a three-and-a-half hour meeting at the Cheshire Inn in Clayton, Missouri, on August 19, 1992, with a man claiming to represent the Democratic Party. His name was Ron Tucker.

"He said that there were people in high places who

were anxious about me and they wanted me to know that keeping my mouth shut would be worthwhile . . . . If I was a good little girl, and didn't kill the messenger, I'd be set for life: a federal job, nothing fancy but a regular paycheck, Level 11 or 12 ($60,000 a year). I'd never have to worry again.

"But if I didn't take the offer, then they knew that I went jogging by myself and he couldn't guarantee what would happen to my pretty little legs. Things just wouldn't be so much fun for me anymore. Life would get hard."

A work colleague of Perdue's, Denison Diel, had positioned himself at the bar nearby and heard all of the alleged conversation. Diel wrote a report that was submitted to the FBI.

Tucker refused to talk to me about the Perdue conversation. But his former employer at Marion Mining, John Newcomb, said he overheard him talking about the subject in September 1992, on the telephone at work and confronted him about the matter.

"Ron Tucker told me that somebody from the Democratic Party in St. Louis had asked him through a friend to get to this woman and get her to shut up," claimed Newcomb.

Perdue did not heed Tucker's warnings, nor did she take the job offer.

Then things began to happen. She lost her job at the admissions office of Lindenwood College, Missouri, where she was also studying.

A Missouri lawyer, Paul Ground, said that a college official had admitted to him that she had been fired because of outside pressure.

Soon after the firing, Perdue began receiving threatening mail and calls. She produced one of the letters: "I'll pray you have a head-on collision and end up in a coma . . . Marilyn Monroe got snuffed."

Perdue found an unspent shotgun cartridge on the driver's seat of her Jeep. Later the back window of her vehicle was shattered, possibly by gunfire.

Both incidents were reported to the police.

These apparent attempts to silence Perdue fit a pattern of alleged dirty tricks that appear to have been undertaken by somebody to cover up for Clinton. Perdue's experience brings to mind the beating of Gary Johnson, a neighbor of Gennifer Flowers whose security camera captured videos of Clinton entering Flower's apartment.

And like others who have spoken out, Perdue has been ridiculed in the press.

"I've had it with the American press . . . The powers here are so strong. You know, they've protected Bill Clinton in a way they'd never protected anybody in the history of America," she said.

March 27, 1994:

An Arkansas woman filed a lawsuit accusing President Clinton of sexual harassment and misusing his powers while governor of Arkansas in "a flagrant abuse of workplace security."

Paula Corbin Jones, twenty-seven, has submitted a sworn affidavit alleging that while working the reception desk of a conference at the Excelsior Hotel in Little Rock on May 8, 1991, as a junior employee of the Arkansas Industrial Development Commission, she was approached by a state trooper, told that Mr. Clinton wished to speak to her, and escorted up to his room.

"The governor made a series of unwelcome sexual advances, each of which were unmistakably rebuffed," said the affidavit.

Mrs. Jones, daughter of a Nazarene lay minister, is now married and living in California. In an interview with the *Sunday Telegraph*, she said that she never had met the governor before the alleged incident and naively thought he had summoned her to talk about job prospects.

Instead, she alleges, he dropped his pants, and requested that she perform oral sex on him. She described his behavior as grotesque.

As she fled the room, Clinton let it be known that her boss was a personal friend of his. "I was really afraid of losing my job," Jones said.

Jones immediately told co-workers of the encounter. They have signed affidavits attesting to the facts as she remembers them. The White House has denied the story completely, and said Clinton never even met Jones.

April 10, 1994:

Efforts by the White House to weather a rising tide of scandal look doomed to suffer a new setback this week after it emerged that another Arkansas state trooper has made allegations against President Clinton.

The state trooper, L.D. Brown, has given a detailed account of what he claims were repeated abuses by Clinton of his office while governor of Arkansas.

Mr. Brown has been subpoenaed to give evidence to the Whitewater investigation.

Mr. Brown backs up the charges of other troopers by claiming that he, too, was involved in facilitating extra-marital affairs for Mr. Clinton while on the security detail of the governor's mansion from 1982 to 1985.

Brown alleged that he solicited over a hundred women on behalf of Clinton. Brown also said that he charged the cost of Clinton's visits to night clubs and resorts to a state police credit card.

Brown is currently part of the Special Investigations Unit at the state police headquarters in Little Rock.

His account is particularly damaging because he was said to be a close confidante of the governor, reportedly attending intimate social events with Mr. Clinton . . . Mr. Brown subsequently fell out with the Clintons in a dispute over a pay raise for the Arkansas police.

Some time after leaving the governor's detail, he said that Mr. Clinton's aides tried to ensure his silence on Mr.

Clinton's indiscretions with unspecified inducements and threats.

Subsequently, Mr. Brown said that he was the subject of an investigation for embezzling the funds of the Trooper's Association. The prosecuting attorney later found no basis for prosecution.

The fact the investigation took place raises serious questions because two state troopers have told the American Spectator that they overheard the Clintons discussing the need to neutralize Brown.

July 17, 1994:

When Bill Clinton was asked during the presidential election whether he had ever used drugs, he gave one of his carefully crafted, lawyerly answers.

Yes, he had smoked two or three "joints" of marijuana at Oxford, but had never inhaled. And he insisted that he never violated a drug law within the borders of the United States.

Evidence reveals that Mr. Clinton may have been more than a casual user of marijuana. A variety of witnesses present at the President's former Arkansas haunts claim his drug habit stretched well into his political career and included the use of cocaine. The pattern of behavior exhibited by Mr. Clinton, and attested to by these witnesses, goes far beyond questions of inappropriate personal conduct.

Consider that during the period of this abuse Clinton was either attorney-general or governor of Arkansas. From each position he was part of a law-enforcement system which gave stiff prison sentences to drug felons.

If these accusations that Mr. Clinton had a drug habit are true, when did the habit end? 1986? 1990? 1994? Perhaps the most compelling allegations revolve around Roger Clinton—rock musician, perennial ne'er-do-well, and the President's younger brother.

In the summer of 1984, Roger spent two months as a non-paying guest at Vantage Point, an upmarket apartment complex in Little Rock. At that time, Bill was in his second term as governor of Arkansas.

Until 1994, Mrs. Jane Parks, forty-one, former manager of Vantage Point apartments, had remained stubbornly silent about what she saw and heard during those two months that Roger was there. Mrs. Parks said she could hear the conversation in B107 very clearly, since her office was separated from the apartment by a thin wall.

Governor Clinton was a frequent visitor. There was drug use at these gatherings, she claimed, and she could clearly distinguish Bill's voice as he chatted with his brother. She said she could also hear them talking about the cocaine and marijuana as it was passed back and forth.

When Roger finally moved out, Parks found drug paraphernalia left in the kitchen drawer and cocaine spilt on the furniture.

Park's testimony is backed up by another resident of Vantage Point, who asked to remain anonymous. She said she saw Clinton enter the apartment on at least three occasions. She also heard some of the activity going on in the apartment while visiting Park's office, and backed up claims of drug parties.

Park's allegations would be outlandish if it were not for her reputation for straightforwardness and Christian devoutness. Her description of Roger Clinton's lifestyle fits with a police drug investigation in the mid-1980s in which Roger and his former boss, Dan Lasater, for whom he worked as a chauffeur and in his racehorse business, were both convicted on federal charges of distributing cocaine.

During the grand jury investigation into Lasater's activities, several women testified in secret that they were offered free cocaine by Lasater as a way of seducing them. The youngest girl was only sixteen, then a student at North Little Rock High School.

She also said in an interview with this writer that she also met Governor Clinton several times at Lasater's parties.

Another witness, a military sub-contractor who wished to remain anonymous, attended one of those Lasater parties in 1984 at which Bill Clinton was present.

The subcontractor said he saw Clinton smoke a marijuana joint. He also said cocaine use was rampant at the party, although he didn't see Clinton partake. "I was smoking a cigar and every time I tried to find an ashtray, the d--- thing was full of cocaine," he recalled.

Sally Perdue, a former Miss Arkansas who had an affair with Clinton, testified that in 1983 Clinton produced a bag of cocaine in her living room and prepared a "line" on the table. "He had all the equipment laid out, like a real pro," she said, noting Clinton's handling of the drug paraphernalia.

Perdue's claim of an affair with Clinton has been broadly confirmed by Arkansas State Trooper L.D. Brown.

During his visits, Perdue said Clinton smoked marijuana regularly, pulling joints ready-made out of a cigarette case. Typically, he would smoke two or three in the course of a three-hour stay. He always inhaled.

These claims suggest marijuana use may have been a feature of Clinton's life throughout his twenties and thirties.

A one-time reporter for *The Daily Texan*, who is now a prominent national journalist, said that he saw Clinton smoking a joint in Austin in 1972 at the headquarters of George McGovern's Texas campaign.

Drug use within Clinton's political circle in Arkansas was blatant during his first term as governor from 1978 to 1980.

"I can remember going into the governor's conference room once and it reeked of marijuana," said Democratic State Representative Jack McCoy, a Clinton supporter.

As late as 1986 Clinton was still smoking marijuana, according to Terry Reed, a former intelligence operative based in Arkansas who recently published a book about Clinton's involvement to help the Nicaraguan Contras during the 1980s.

Finally there is Sharline Wilson, a thirty-nine-year-old

who is serving a thirty-one year sentence for minor drug dealing at the women's prison at Tucker, Arkansas.

While her testimony as a convict must be looked at with caution, her story is compelling. Wilson is serving a long sentence for selling a half ounce of marijuana and $100 worth of an amphetamine. She argues that she was set up, because officials, including Clinton, wanted to discredit her testimony.

Wilson said she came to know Bill Clinton in the 1970s through her friendship with Roger Clinton. For a while she was a bartender at Le Bistro, a night club in Little Rock where Roger performed gigs with his rock band. Governor Clinton came frequently and would often snort cocaine, she alleged.

On one occasion in 1979, she said, she sold two grams of cocaine to Roger, who immediately gave some to his older brother.

Wilson also attended toga parties at the Coachman's Inn outside Little Rock, where she saw Governor Clinton using cocaine. Guests at these parties would wear sheets and share sexual partners.

In the 1980s Wilson began to help federal and state anti-drug agencies as she tried to break from drugs. Gary Martin, an officer with the Drug Enforcement Agency in Little Rock, said she proved very reliable: "I have no reason to doubt her word."

In 1990 Wilson testified as a star witness at a federal grand jury, held in secret, about her knowledge of cocaine use by Bill Clinton and others. This testimony, for a task force investigating drug involvement by Arkansas public officials, will remain secret forever.

According to Jean Duffey, who headed the drug task force, within days the investigation was in effect closed down. Wilson was subsequently entrapped.

"Sharline was my best informant," said Jean Duffey, who said she herself was hounded out of her job for being too diligent. She now lives in a secret location in Texas. "They couldn't silence her, so they locked her up in jail and threw the key away. That's Arkansas for you," Duffey said.

May 8, 1994:

Dennis Patrick was once a rising star in the Appalachian coal town of Williamsburg, Kentucky. He had made his mark as the youngest circuit court clerk in the nation.

The Republican Party was asking him to run for statewide office.

Now forty-two, Patrick digs ditches for a living. For the past seven and a half years, he has been in hiding with his wife and two children, afraid for his life. His friends do not know if he is dead or alive. He still does not know for sure what turned his life upside down. But he now suspects that it is related in some way to an investment banking firm in Arkansas called Lasater & Co.

The firm's owner, Dan Lasater, was the biggest contributor to the Arkansas campaign funds of Bill Clinton. The relationship between Lasater and Clinton, once intimate, has cooled over time. But the connection between Lasater's business dealings and Clinton lives on in the person of Patsy Thomasson, Special Assistant to the President for Administration.

Thomasson was Lasater's deputy and confidante throughout the 1980s. She was executive vice-president of Lasater & Co. Thomasson was in charge of operations, as well as acting as the liaison between Lasater & Co. and the Little Rock political establishment.

When Lasater was sent to prison in 1986 for drug distribution, it was Thomasson who managed his business empire.

Known as "the enforcer" among White House aides, she is said to be fiercely loyal to President Clinton.

Patrick was flabbergasted to learn that Thomasson works at the nation's highest office, the White House.

He first heard Thomasson's name mentioned on a radio talk show in February 1994. It brought back a flood of confused memories. He rummaged through a pile of documents at home and unearthed a wad of trading receipts from a brokerage account opened in his name at Lasater & Co.

According to the receipts, his account [reflected purchases of] tens of millions of dollars worth of bonds in late 1985. On a single day, August 21, his account showed purchases of 23.5 million dollars in Federal Home Loan Mortgage Corporation bonds.

At the time, Patrick said he was worth only about $60,000 total.

Patrick claims the trades took place without his knowledge, but admits he did become entangled with Lasater & Co. for a brief period in 1985.

In 1985 an old friend from college, Steve Love, took him fishing in the Gulf of Mexico and tried to persuade him to open an account with his firm, Lasater & Co.

Patrick refused.

The account was opened anyway, and credited with $21,000, as his friend showed him how easy it was to make money.

Unwisely, Patrick accepted the "profits." Over the next weeks he was wined and dined in Little Rock, and was even taken dove hunting in a party that included Clinton. Then Lasater & Co. suddenly dropped him.

Patrick's friend, Love, now lives in a small town in Pennsylvania. He was stunned when contacted by myself, saying that he too had been living underground for several years.

"I was used by Lasater, and flushed away, my whole life destroyed. I finished up sleeping on park benches."

Love said he was deeply sorry about what happened with Patrick, and denies having made the huge bond trades in the account. Those were done by a more senior broker, he said, for reasons he dared not talk about.

It appears that the account was used to move large sums of money, but the purpose of the transactions remains unclear.

What is clear is that while this irregular bond trading was going on, Thomasson was the "financial and operations principal" of Lasater & Co.

And Patrick believes Lasater & Co. is at the root of his troubles.

It was in late 1985 that Patrick's life began to fall apart. Someone sent pedophile literature to the court house as if he had ordered it. Rumors circulated that he was involved in drugs. His house was fire-bombed. According to federal law enforcement agencies, Patrick learned of three separate assassination attempts that were planned on his life.

"I never knew what was happening to me," he said in a melancholy voice, glancing nervously around the restaurant where we met.

"All of a sudden I was tainted and nobody wanted to go near me. People would walk out of the barber shop when I came in."

He went to the police for help, but they told him his problem was of his own making: he had gotten mixed up with drug dealers. Patrick bought a bullet-proof vest, booby-trapped his car, and turned his home into a fortress. He stayed awake each night, armed with a shotgun, as his pregnant wife slept.

Finally he packed up the family and vanished.

After each assassination attempt, the gunmen were arrested, prosecuted and served time in prison.

One assassin confessed to the police that he had been hired to kill Patrick for $20,000.

At that time, agents of the Bureau of Alcohol, Tobacco and Firearms believed Patrick was involved in drugs. One of the agents assigned to Patrick's case told the *Economist* magazine, he did not believe that Patrick was involved himself, but was merely a "victim."

Patrick wants the FBI to investigate whether the bond trading at Lasater & Co. had anything to do with attempts on his life.   The Patrick story, which raises questions about possible drug money-laundering, also has links with the S&L scandal of the eighties.

Lasater's company was sued by the Federal Savings and Loan Insurance Corp. for 3.3 million dollars because of reckless bond trading which churned bonds through several accounts, including Patrick's—to generate commissions. In the end, bonds were apparently dumped on an insured S&L, and the FSLIC contended that Lasater & Co. bond manipulations helped bring down an Illinois bank, First American Savings and Loan.

Interestingly, Rose Law Firm partners Hillary Clinton and the late Vincent Foster were hired by the government to pursue the $3.3 million suit against Lasater.

The Chicago Tribune has commented that their role in the suit was a flagrant case of conflict of interest, given the interlocking relationship between Lasater and the Clintons in Arkansas.

Hillary Clinton and Foster allowed the suit to be settled for a paltry $200,000, which the *Tribune* said was a surprisingly small sum.

Hillary and Foster also signed on to a secrecy agreement, with a strict ban on the dissemination of the facts of the case. As a result, it is difficult to establish exactly how or why the S&L collapsed. There are further grounds for disquiet.

October 9, 1994:

Once again there is talk of "Arkansas mores" in Washington. This time it is the Secretary of Agriculture. Mike Espy, who has seen his career destroyed by the curse of Bill Clinton's home state. Under investigation by a special prosecutor for accepting gifts from Arkansas poultry king Donald Tyson, Espy announced his resignation last week.

Don Tyson is one of Arkansas' great characters. Ensconced in a replica Oval Office with door handles in the shape of eggs, he presides over the biggest chicken processing operation in the world. He usually wears khaki overalls with "Don" stitched on his breast pocket and gets his hands dirty working side by side with his 54,000 employees.

It is said that half the American people get to eat a piece of Tyson's chicken every week. The family business, Tyson Foods, has grown at an explosive rate since the 1960s, swallowing up rival companies in a relentless quest for market domination. Annual turnover is now close to five billion dollars. "There's no second place. First place is the only place in the world," says Tyson.

With a base of operations in Sprindale, northwest Arkansas, Tyson is regarded with awe as the ultimate kingmaker in state politics. He sponsored Bill Clinton's early rise to prominence, then helped toss him out of the governor's mansion in 1982 when Clinton failed to deliver on a promise to relax trucking regulations. Clinton never made the mistake of crossing Tyson again.

According to claims made in a report by CBS television's *60 Minutes*, Tyson effectively vetted the appointment of Espy as Agriculture Secretary. Espy even went to Arkansas to have lunch with the chicken king in order to seek his blessing for the post.

Once in office, he proved to be a good friend of the poultry lobby. In March last year, his chief-of-staff at the Agriculture Department ordered bureaucrats to scuttle the implementation of tougher poultry inspections.

Business as usual, say most pundits in Washington. Just another case of money-men and politicians getting too cozy with each other. But there may be another dimension to this scandal.

Memoranda that circulated in the Criminal Intelligence Section of the Arkansas State Police show that Don Tyson was under suspicion of drug dealing from the early 1970s until the late 1980s.

A file note dated March 25, 1976, comments that Tyson "is an extremely wealthy man with much political influence and seems to be involved in almost every kind of shady operation, especially narcotics; however [he] has, to date, gone without implication in any specific crime. Tyson likes to think of himself as 'king of the hill' in northwest Arkansas."

The Federal Drug Enforcement Administration also had a file, "Tyson, Donald J. et al," including a document in which an informant reports on what is referred to as "Donald Tyson's drug trafficking organization."

A 1982 file from the DEA in Oklahoma refers to Tyson as the "Chicken Man" and talks of an allegation by an informant that "Tyson smuggles cocaine from Colombia, South America, inside race horses to Hot Springs, Arkansas."

None of these accusations led to prosecution.

One former state trooper who worked for eight years as an undercover narcotics agent, the last four in the Springdale region of Arkansas, told the *Sunday Telegraph* she had collected detailed intelligence that Tyson was smuggling cocaine stuffed inside chickens.

The state trooper is extremely bitter about what happened. She says she was the victim of a smear campaign from within the Arkansas State Police after she requested the Tyson files.

"They started passing out my photo on the streets, which put my life in danger," she said. By 1987, her position had become untenable. She resigned from the police, her career in ruins, and went into semi-hiding outside the U.S.

Using the intelligence she had gathered, another state trooper, J.N. "Doc" Delaughter, tried to start a second investigation of Tyson in 1988. He still has an internal memorandum showing that Federal Prosecutor Michael Fitzhugh expressed interest in pursuing a criminal conspiracy charge against Tyson, involving a "combined investigation team of the FBI, DEA, IRS and the state police."

Fitzhugh says that he does not know why the case fizzled out. "We're prosecutors, not investigators," he said.

Referring to the Arkansas State Police, he said that . . . "the ball was in their court. For whatever reason, I never head another word from them about the thing."

Ex-trooper Delaughter says that he was pulled off the case after being warned by his department not to hammer "the nails in his own coffin." Shortly afterwards, he was demoted to highway patrol, then sent off for a mental evaluation. The police psychologist deemed him a "danger to society" and recommended that he be suspended from service. Delaughter took early retirement.

"Trying to bring these guys down is not conducive to a good career," he said with a wry smile as we sat drinking a beer on the veranda of his remote lakeside cabin. "You develop leprosy. Fast."

The state police chief at the time, Col. Tommy Goodwin, said: "There was not enough information to start an investigation." He said the documents that have come to light recently "weren't in the Tyson file back then."

Calls from the *Sunday Telegraph* to Tyson's offices were not returned.

Meanwhile, the Whitewater prosecutor, Kenneth Starr, is investigating a $15,000 donation by Tyson to a secret political fund controlled by the then-Governor Clinton.

It was Jim Blair, a legal advisor to Tyson, who helped Hillary Clinton to turn $1,000 into $100,000 during her husband's first year as governor.

Asked by CBS if the money was a straight "pay-off" to the Clintons, Tyson gave a vehement denial.

Unless the precise trading records are subpoenaed from the Chicago Mercantile Exchange, Americans will never know for sure.

October 9, 1994:

It is engraved on the consciousness of the world by now that Arkansas is a corrupt one-party state. What is less known is that it is also a major point for trans-shipment of drugs coming from Latin America and the Caribbean. In the mid-1980s, it was perilously close to becoming a "narco-republic"—a sort of mini-Colombia within the borders of the United States.

Organized crime has long had a foothold in Arkansas, especially in the gambling town of Hot Springs, where Bill Clinton spent most of his childhood. And the geography is good for smuggling. Located in the hinterland, the state is safely removed from the microscopic surveillance of the U.S. Coast Guard.

Business exploded in the 1980s according to sources in state and federal law enforcement. Drugs were flown into airstrips all over Arkansas, and from there they were transported overland to cities such as St. Louis and Chicago.

Basil Abbott, a convicted drug pilot, says that he flew a Cessna 210 full of cocaine into Marianna, in eastern Arkansas, in the spring of 1982. The aircraft was welcomed by an Arkansas state trooper in a marked police car. "Arkansas was a very good place to load and unload," he said.

But the nerve center of the smuggling operation was at Mena, a small town in the Ouachita mountains of western Arkansas. Aircraft with modified cargo doors would drop their loads over prearranged sites, then fly empty into the Mena airport. The legendary smuggler Barry Seal had his base of operations there, storing aircraft at a retrofitting shop called Rich Mountain Aviation.

Seal was probably the biggest importer of cocaine in American history. Between 1980 and his assassination in 1986, his team of pilots smuggled in thirty-six metric tons of cocaine, 104 tons of marijuana and three tons of heroin, according to a close associate of Seal.

The sums of money involved were staggering. At his death, Seal left a number of operational bank accounts. One of them, at the Cayman Islands branch of the Fuji Bank, currently has an interest-earning balance of $1,645,433,000.

There were various attempts to investigate the Mena smuggling ring. All of them were obstructed. The first was a joint investigation by the Arkansas State Police and the U.S. Treasury's Internal Revenue Service. It lasted from 1985 to 1988. The IRS investigator, Bill Duncan, says that there was a cover-up in which crucial evidence was withheld from the federal grand jury. He resigned in disgust from the Treasury.

Russell Welch, the investigator for the state police, suffered a severe illness during the probe. He was hospitalized and diagnosed with anthrax poisoning. The *Sunday Telegraph* has a copy of his hand-written private notes for the full three years of the investigation, along with supporting documents from FBI and Drug Enforcement Administration (DEA) sources.

It is clear that Welch had stumbled on a complex operation in which narcotics trafficking and government covert operations had somehow got mixed up. On June 4, 1985, his diary says that an agent from the DEA "informed me in strictest confidence that it was believed, within his department, that Barry Seal is flying weapons to Central and South America. In return, he is allowed to smuggle what he wanted back into the United States."

In August 1987, he received a secret teletype from the FBI office in Chicago, advising him that "a CIA or DEA operation is taking place at the Mena airport." The *Sunday Telegraph* has a copy of the telex.

By late 1987, he was deeply disturbed. "I feel like I live in Russia, waiting for the secret police to pounce down. A government has gotten out of control. Men find themselves in positions of power, and suddenly crimes become legal. National Security?!"

In 1988, the Democratic whip in the U.S. Congress, Bill Alexander, started an investigation through the General Accounting Office. It went nowhere. Alexander then tried again with a joint investigation by the U.S. Congress and the Arkansas Attorney General's Office, but ran into endless obstruction.

Compromised: Clinton, Bush and the CIA, a best-selling book published this year, has helped to open up the mystery of what happened at Mena. The author, Terry Reed, has recounted his role in the drama, and since then other sources have come forward.

It appears that the CIA chose Barry Seal and his smuggling operation to be the sub-contractor for its covert scheme to supply arms to the Nicaraguan Contra rebels between 1984 and 1986. The CIA could not use government aircraft or pilots because of a Congressional prohibition on aid to the Contras. It was in a desperate hurry to get things started, and Seal was there with an infrastructure already in place—in Arkansas.

A big blunder? Undoubtedly. But it is probably going too far to accuse the CIA of complicity in narcotics trafficking. Seal had ostensibly turned over a new leaf by then. Facing indictment for smuggling, he had convinced Vice President Bush's drug task force that he could crack open the Medellin cartel as an undercover agent for the DEA, which he did in fact accomplish in a spectacular sting operation.

Big snag. He never stopped hauling cocaine for himself. In fact, he used the high-tech equipment given to him by the CIA and the DEA to perfect his smuggling skills.

"The CIA didn't realize that Seal had synergised their covert operation with the Dixie Mafia. They didn't figure it out until they were in the quicksand, and by then it was too late," said Seal's associate. "In the end you had a situation where the Dixie Mafia was blackmailing the CIA."

The result was a free-for-all in Arkansas. The regional drug cartel thought that it had acquired a sort of federal immunity for drug trafficking, and behaved accordingly. By 1986, there was an epidemic of cocaine, contaminating the political establishment from top to bottom.

The nightlife of the Clinton coterie was worthy of Caligula. Dan Lasater, a self-made restaurant tycoon and money-man for Governor Clinton, gave parties at which cocaine would be served like hors d'oeuvres and sex was rampant. Some of this is documented graphically in police records. Bill Clinton was in frequent attendance.

Lasater was eventually convicted on federal charges of distributing cocaine to friends. In 1986, he was sentenced to thirty months' jail.

In addition, there is a document from the Regional Organized Crime Center in Nashville, dated May 15, 1986, which shows a request for information on Lasater "in reference to narcotics trafficking via aircraft with possible organized crime ties." This was never followed up.

The DEA kept a file on Lasater. A memo from March 1984 names Patsy Thomasson, Lasater & Co. executive vice-president, as a designated passenger on private flights with Lasater to Latin America. Thomasson is now Director of Administration at the White House and a crucial figure in the inner circle of Bill and Hillary Clinton. (It was she who removed Whitewater files from the White House office of the late Vince Foster on the night of his death.) On February 8, 1984, she flew to Belize with Lasater to negotiate the purchase of a farm.

Lasater is now under investigation by the Whitewater prosecutor. The FBI is trying to determine whether Lasater's brokerage firm used client accounts to launder drug profits. In particular, they are looking at transactions worth $107 million that were put through the account of an unsuspecting court clerk in Kentucky.

Also under the microscope is the participation of Lasater & Co. in several hundred million dollars worth of bond issues by the Arkansas Development Finance Authority (ADFA), an agency created by Bill Clinton in 1985. There have been many allegations that ADFA served as a "laundromat" for dirty money. In December 1988 it wired fifty million dollars to the Fuji Bank in the Cayman Islands. Investigators will be looking for proof that the money—all of it—returned to Arkansas for its intended purpose of building family houses.

The more we learn about the circle of people who surrounded Bill Clinton in Arkansas, and the way they conducted business, the more alarming the picture becomes.

March 27, 1994:

Radio talk shows call me at a rate of about one a day to interview me. I stand by the window of the *Telegraph* offices at 13th Street and "F" Street, telephone in hand, and broadcast out in the hinterland.

Texas, Colorado, New England, California: huge audiences of people I know nothing about, all eager for the latest details about Whitewater. It is an eye-opener.

The callers talk about the President in a tone of undisguised contempt, and they want to know the answers to everything: who is sleeping with whom in the White House (no comment); whether it is true that Vince Foster, the deputy White House Counsel, was snuffed out with sodium mono-fluoride 10-80 in his office, and then shot later to make it look like a suicide (possible); and whether Bill Clinton really had his own counter-intelligence service in Arkansas (he did: it was called the Arkansas State Police Intelligence Division).

They discuss the minutiae of Whitewater with fluency, and often they tell me things about the affair that I never knew before. Clearly, there is a very effective grapevine out there beyond the capital, an underground network of tens of millions of people.

In many ways they are better informed than the opinion elite, cut off in the liberal-lawyer ghetto of the Washington Beltway.

Congressman Jim Leach, explaining the significance of Whitewater, summed up the underlying theme of every Clinton-related scandal so far uncovered: "In a nutshell, Whitewater is about the abuse of power."

How far things have come from the Democratic Convention in August 1992 when Clinton swept the nation to its feet with his moral fervor.

"We have seen the folks in Washington turn the American ethic on its head," he said.

"For too long, those who play by the rules and keep the faith have gotten the shaft. And those who cut corners and cut deals have been rewarded."

It makes you want to cry.

PREFACE, CHAPTER 9

*Bill Clinton selected for chief economic advisor his close friend, Derek Shearer, who has long proposed that **America's free enterprise system be dismantled and replaced with socialism**--The Wall Street Journal.*

How could we have a Commander in Chief of the U.S. Armed Forces who holds the military in contempt, who is anti-patriotic, who long ago embraced the dream of world socialism, and who, if he were not President, could not receive a security clearance?

Lieutenant Colonel Tom McKenney, U.S.M.C. (retired), served our country with honor in Korea and Vietnam. From his distinguished career in the military, he brings great insight and a keen grasp of Bill Clinton's ability to serve as Commander In Chief of The Armed Services of the United States of America.

McKenney's political expertise (including giving testimony to the Senate Select Committee), combined with his military background, equip him to warn Americans of the dangers of Clinton's foreign policy.

Exclusive interviews in this chapter reveal the cause of the debacles in Haiti and Somalia and expose an ominous political agenda for the compromise and dismantling of America's Armed Forces.

CHAPTER 9

BILL CLINTON—THE UNTHINKABLE COMMANDER IN CHIEF

by Lt. Col. Tom McKenney (retired)

In 1992, in the period following the swift Desert Storm victory in Iraq and Kuwait, morale in our armed forces was soaring, perhaps at an all-time high. The nation was unified as it had not been since World War II. Americans were proud to be Americans. Our warriors were proud to be American warriors, proud of their units, proud of their uniforms. We thrilled to Lee Greenwood singing "God Bless the USA." We couldn't get enough of it.

Since Bill Clinton's inauguration as President, morale has been at an all-time low. Many of our brightest, most highly motivated men and women, both officers and enlisted personnel, are leaving promising careers, resigning their commissions and declining to re-enlist. Many of those who are sticking with it are wondering how long they can.

Never in American history has military morale been so low. Never in our history has there been a comparable, radical plunge; and it has happened in only two years. How can we understand this sudden drastic decline?

Not since the terrible winter at Valley Forge has the morale of our armed forces even approached the abysmal nadir of today. In fact, a comparison of the condition of today's armed forces with that of the troops at Valley Forge is enlightening.

At Valley Forge, the men suffered terribly from cold and hunger. There was no money with which to pay them. They lacked adequate shelter and warm clothing; their makeshift huts provided little protection, even from the icy

183

wind. Many men had no shoes, their feet wrapped in rags against the zero temperatures. Some left bloody footprints as they moved about in the snow.

Many died in that miserable encampment outside Philadelphia while they could see and hear the British, living in luxurious comfort in the city from which the Continental Army had been driven. Yet the morale of the remaining soldiers was sustained, and eventually the war for independence was won.

Today, by comparison, our service men and women are well-fed, well-clothed, well-paid, living in air-conditioned comfort, and are surrounded with facilities for recreation and amusement. They are the best-trained and best-equipped fighting men and women in the world, representing the one remaining super power. Yet their morale is at an all-time low and is sinking fast. How can this be? How can we explain this remarkable contradiction?

I believe the answer can be expressed in two words: Bill Clinton.

At Valley Forge, those starving, freezing citizen soldiers, serving without pay or benefits, had a Commander in Chief, George Washington, who was one of them; a warrior who fought with them, who was cold and hungry as they were, who placed their safety and welfare above his own, who set for them an example of virtue and morality, and who was on his knees in the snow praying for them.

Today, the Commander in Chief is one who "loathes the military," who cravenly hid from hardship and danger when called upon by his country during time of war, and then lied about it. He also went to great lengths to give aid and comfort to the enemy with whom his country was locked in deadly combat.

The current Commander in Chief is one whose contempt for people and things military is common knowledge, one who is rapidly dismantling our military strength, forcing open acceptance of homosexuals in the military, and forcing assignment of women to combat units and Navy ships.

Bill Clinton is dedicated to forfeiture of our national sovereignty and is pushing the placement of our armed forces under command authority of the United Nations. As Commander in Chief, he seems determined to use the armed forces for social engineering.

Today our Commander in Chief is a man who has demonstrated his military incompetence and his willingness to sacrifice our fighting men to cheap political expedience, and who then seems unable to experience genuine remorse for their suffering and death.

Small wonder that the morale of our armed forces is at an all-time low and is continuing to decline.

ATTITUDES MATTER: SOME REVEALING GLIMPSES

During Bill Clinton's first year in office a minor incident occurred, one which was buried by the news media, but was common knowledge inside the Beltway (even though it is denied by the White House). It was in one sense trivial, a fleeting vignette on the First Family portrait; but in another sense it was powerfully revealing and terribly significant.

The occasion was the departure for a state function, a routine operation. Vehicles were lined up outside the White House, ready to transport the First Family and their entourage to the important event. Young Chelsea Clinton, like everyone else on such occasions, was assigned a specific sedan in which to ride. The driver held the door open for her, but as she got part of the way into the car she abruptly backed out as if she had seen a rattlesnake on the back seat.

She then turned and proclaimed to all within sound of her voice: "I won't ride in this car! There's a military man in here, and *I don't ride with military men!*"

The "military man" already seated in her sedan happened to be a senior officer. Being a gentleman, he said quietly that there was no problem, calmly got out of the sedan and found another vehicle in which to ride.

In a separate similar incident, also common knowledge (but denied by the White House and unreported by the protective media), young Chelsea asked the Marine who was escorting her to school to wear civilian clothes in the future, not his uniform, explaining, *"My family doesn't like military people."*

Think about this for a moment; think of what it means. I suggest to you that this innocent little girl didn't learn to despise "military men" at Sunday School or in the Brownie Scouts. I suggest that she would not have committed such acts of flagrant rudeness and presumption had she known that her parents would have disapproved; nor would she have so ingenuously expressed herself. No, it seems apparent that she learned this at home from her mother and father and that she learned it well.

In another incident that was actually reported briefly by the media (and then buried), highly decorated Lieutenant General Barry R. McCaffrey was summoned to the White House early one morning. As he was leaving he encountered a young woman, a member of the White House staff who had just arrived for work. Being a gentleman, the general smiled, saluted informally and pleasantly said, "Good morning."

She snapped back, her voice harsh and cold, *"I don't speak to the military,"* stuck up her nose and stomped by.1

No White House staffer would dare commit such an act of deliberate rudeness if it were not understood that such behavior is in keeping with White House values. There is no record that she was ever reprimanded, and the incident vanished suddenly and permanently from the news.

White House military aides are outstanding young officers assigned primarily to greet guests, discuss military matters, and answer questions at social events. These handpicked aides are sharp and well informed, and most are career professionals. In another gross breach of custom and violation of the dignity of their position, four of these outstanding young officers assigned to the Clinton White House found themselves pressed into service as waiters. At a White House dinner for the Democratic National Committee, these officers, in their dress uniforms, were forced to work in the kitchen, carrying trays of hors d'oeuvres to the guests. This uniquely Clintonesque insult to the armed services was a first; it had never, ever been done before.

After the story became known, at least two of the four aides were contacted by the White House and told not to say anything about it. One of them did speak, however, and told *The Washington Times*: "When is this White House going to learn to think before acting? Little things like this make big impressions." Yes they do, Lieutenant; they also tell us a great deal about the Commander in Chief's attitude toward the military.[2]

Marine Helicopter Squadron One at Quantico, Virginia, is a highly specialized elite unit, responsible for transporting the President on short trips in the same way that Air Force One flies him on long trips. These are the helicopters you see landing on and taking off from the White House lawn. Far from ordinary, these helicopters are the very best: specially manned and equipped to function as the President's flying office, particularly during emergencies. They are very expensive, with handpicked pilots and crews, and they must be in a constant state of perfected readiness. National security could literally depend on this readiness and "at any moment" availability .

Yet, the use of the President's helicopters by the White House staffers for a golf outing was apparently not considered inappropriate until the story leaked out and angry members of Congress made an issue of it.[3]

The cost alone of the round trip to the golf course was estimated at more than $13,000 (taken from your taxes). Beyond the cost, however, a disturbing attitude toward things military is revealed here, as well as a frightening failure to understand military realities.

These small incidents speak volumes about Bill

Clinton's fitness to serve as Commander in Chief of the Armed Forces of the United States when the welfare, the support, and the very life of every military man and woman in this nation's armed forces is his direct responsibility. What are his true feelings about the military? What are his priorities, his values and his commitments? Is he actually anti-military? Does he truly "loathe the military?" Let's examine the evidence. What is his record in terms of patriotism, sacrifice and military service?

CLINTON, THE DRAFT DODGER

Bill Clinton's anti-military, anti-patriotic attitudes and beliefs can be traced back at least to the 1960s during his college days at Georgetown University. While an undergraduate, he had an automatic student deferment and was thus safe from the draft. During his undergraduate years he became involved in the pro-communist, anti-war movement and worked as an aide to Senator J. William Fulbright on the Senate Foreign Relations Committee.

In March 1968, three months before his June graduation from Georgetown, he was reclassified "1-A" (most likely to be drafted), and became a prime candidate for the draft. He had also been selected for a three-year Rhodes Scholarship to Oxford University in England.

Politically influential friends, including Senator Fulbright, went to work for Clinton. Opal Ellis, who was at the time executive secretary of Clinton's draft board, remarked that he told her he "was too well educated to go to Vietnam," and that he "would pull every string" he could think of. He did.4

One of his closest friends at Oxford, Cliff Jackson, recalled, "I aided Bill Clinton in implementing a plan, concocted by him, to avoid the draft notice issued to him." Jackson had also written in a letter in July 1969 that Clinton "was feverishly trying to find a way to avoid entering the Army," and that he, Jackson, had friends in influential positions pulling strings for Clinton.[5]

The next step was supposed to be a pre-induction physical examination, normally completed within sixty days of being classified 1-A. Without bothering to take this physical, Bill went off to Oxford for the fall term of 1968. Strings had indeed been pulled, and the draft board had "been handled" in order to give him time to get to Oxford.[6]

In February 1969, the situation finally caught up with him; he was ordered to report for his pre-induction physical in England. He passed it and, in April 1969, was ordered to report for induction; he had been drafted. However, once again the draft board was "handled," and Bill was given a "quasi-official" deferment until July 28.

Searching for a place to hide, Clinton used all the influence he could muster, including intervention by Senator Fulbright again,[7] and promising to enter the University of Arkansas Law School, was accepted into the University of Arkansas ROTC program in spite of the fact that the program had no openings.[8] Bill signed a letter of intent, a written contract to complete the ROTC program and accept an Army commission. On August 7, 1969, Clinton received an ROTC deferment from his draft board and was reclassified 1-D (deferment status, undraftable).

With his deferment safe in hand, Clinton left Arkansas. Without so much as a wave good-bye, without even enrolling at the University of Arkansas, let alone reporting to the ROTC program (which had, under political pressure, just rescued him from the draft), Bill returned to England and re-enrolled at Oxford.

In the fall of 1969, combat units were beginning to be pulled out of Vietnam and the U.S. commitment there was winding down. The last American units weren't withdrawn until 1973 (and our men continued to die there until 1975), but from the fall of 1969 on, fewer men would be needed for the draft.

On September 19, President Nixon cancelled further draft calls for 1969 and spread out existing call-ups to the end of the year. The lottery system was established by which potential draftees were given randomly assigned numbers. The lowest numbers would be called up first, and at that time the highest numbers would not be called up at all. Although Clinton had his phony 1-D classification, he was still in the system.

On December 1, Clinton's draft lottery number was announced. He had drawn number 311, a number high enough to assure that he would never be called. Two days later, safe from the draft at last, he wrote his now-famous letter to Colonel Eugene Holmes, ROTC commander at the University of Arkansas, announcing that he would not live up to his ROTC commitment.

Clinton's letter to Colonel Holmes is a remarkable document (included in its entirety in Appendix A). In this letter, written in December 1969 (which coincided with a trip Clinton made behind the Iron Curtain), he admitted his deliberate deception and the fact that his motivation in avoiding military service was a combination of his philosophical opposition to military service and his fear of suffering or dying. (It is important to keep in mind here that many hundreds of thousands of other young Americans had the same fears Clinton did, but—out of loyalty to their country—entered the military service anyway; 58,000 of them died.)

The thing that makes Bill Clinton's lying and maneuvering to dodge the draft particularly despicable is his determination not merely to avoid the hardships and dangers of military service, but also to dodge the draft in such a way that it would not hinder his overriding political ambitions for the future.

Rather than be an honest, "out in the open" draft resister and face the consequences, he decided to lie and outmaneuver the draft—to use his own words, "for one reason: to maintain my (future) political viability within the system." He wanted not only to avoid military service, staying safe and comfortable, but he wanted to do it in such a way that it wouldn't hinder his intense political ambitions for the future. This is world-class dishonesty.

Perhaps we can have an even more revealing grasp of Bill Clinton's selfish arrogance and inability to understand sacrifice if we know something of the man to whom he wrote that letter. Colonel Eugene Holmes—the ROTC commander to whom Clinton had lied and then explained that he didn't want to suffer, die or even be inconvenienced, yet wanted to cover up his selfishness so he could fool the voters in future elections—was a man who knew real sacrifice.

This man, whom Clinton expected to feel sorry for him for losing sleep, was a soldier who had fought for hopeless days and nights without sleep before being overrun and captured by the Japanese. He was a survivor of the Bataan Death March in 1941. After four years of torture and starvation in prison camps, Colonel Holmes went on to fight willingly and bravely in Korea. It was to this man, a paragon of sacrifice, courage and selfless service, that Bill Clinton wrote his infamous letter.

CLINTON, THE PRO-COMMUNIST, ANTI-AMERICAN "PEACE" ACTIVIST

Quite typically, during the 1992 presidential campaign, Bill Clinton denied any connection with the "anti-war" movement which had occurred during the Vietnam War. When confronted with evidence that he had indeed participated in demonstrations where coffins were carried and the American flag burned, he admitted that he may have attended one or two, but only as a spectator on the fringes to see what they were like.

The truth is quite different, although difficult to obtain. Clinton, of course, simply denies it—this being his modus operandi when confronted with unflattering truth. Now that he is President, sources for the truth are even more reluctant to speak out, making the facts more difficult to obtain. But, his old friend, pro-communist priest Richard McSorley, has been quite candid about Bill's activism in the '60s and '70s. While disclosing that Clinton organized and led demonstrations in England in 1969, Father McSorley still said that Bill would be foolish to admit all that he had done.[9]

Although it is difficult to unearth facts about Clinton's pro-communist activism during that time, enough can be documented to paint a clear picture of a zealous young socialist with dreams of "*rapid* social progress," driven by a desire to radically change his country[10] along Marxist lines. We see this from his participation in Group 68 (a Soviet-sponsored, pro-communist group in London)[11], his planning and leading of demonstrations and moratoriums in the United States and England, and his disappearance behind the Iron Curtain at a time when the Soviet bloc was funding and directing the North Vietnamese/Viet Cong enemy with which his country was locked in deadly combat.

A clear picture of a young leftist zealot emerges, one who moved in radical circles and whose closest friends were leftist activists and draft dodgers.

The Demonstrations Were Anti-American—Not Anti-war

One key matter that must be clarified at this point, one deliberately clouded by the major American news media, is that those *anti-war* demonstrations were actually *anti-American* demonstrations. While many of the participants were sincerely working for peace and an end to the war, the events themselves were clearly anti-American and treasonous, and became progressively so as the war wore on. These demonstrators weren't simply urging a quick end to the war—they were screaming for communist victory and American defeat.

For example, whose buildings did they blockade and throw red paint and pig blood on? It was always the American buildings, never communist-bloc embassies or consulates. Whose flag did they invariably burn? The American flag. Yet, whose flag did they wave triumphantly and carry proudly and defiantly in their parades and demonstrations? You guessed it—*the enemy's flag!*

In the early days the "peace" activists chanted such foolish, misguided slogans as, "Make love, not war," but as time went on their chants and speeches became increasingly anti-American and pro-North Vietnam. The most familiar cry by the late '60s and early '70s was "Ho Ho, Ho Chi Minh, the NVA are gonna win!" Their speeches screamed for defeat of the American forces and for the triumph of the enemy.

I think it should be obvious to even the most skeptical person that this was not an anti-war movement; it was an anti-American one, and it was unquestionably treasonous. Had Bill Clinton, Jane Fonda, Tom Hayden, Abbie Hoffman and their friends done these things during World War II, they would, at the very least, have been imprisoned.

The Martha's Vineyard Meeting, Moratorium and March on Washington, 1969

In early 1969, John Gardner (later the founder of Common Cause) organized a closed-door weekend retreat on Martha's Vineyard (an island off the Massachusetts coast) for forty handpicked, young, leftist zealots, all of whom had worked in the Robert Kennedy and Eugene McCarthy presidential campaigns. During the weekend, plans were made for the National Moratorium of October 15 and the March on Washington of November 15, the largest ever held.

When asked during his presidential campaign about his involvement in these activities, Clinton said that he had taken no part in them; yet the facts say otherwise.[12] His old friend and fellow radical, homosexual activist David Mixner (who from homosexual sources raised $3.5 million for Clinton's presidential campaign) said that Clinton was present at the Martha's Vineyard planning session, and that during the summer of 1969 Bill "volunteered his time and effort to assist us in planning for the moratorium and the March on Washington."[13] Another long-time friend of Bill's, leftist Sam Brown, agreed with Mixner.[14]

Radio Hanoi enthusiastically praised both the moratorium and the Washington march. The direct and close relationship between the communist enemy and the American activists is clearly illustrated by the fact that on October 14, 1969, the day before the October moratorium, the activists received a personal message from North Vietnamese Premier Pham Van Dong, praising them and encouraging them for their work in "our people's patriotic struggle."[15]

Then, during the March on Washington, the American flag flying in front of the Justice Department was torn down and the enemy's flag was raised in its place. Is this just anti-war? No, it is clearly anti-American.

Demonstrations in London, Fall 1969

In a very real sense, Bill Clinton played a key role in the weakening of the American negotiating position which led to the abandonment of the American POWs in 1973 and the eventual defeat of free South Vietnam. During the fall of 1969, after participating in the planning and preparations for the moratorium and the Washington march, Clinton returned to England, avoiding the draft and leaving his ROTC commitment behind. Thanks to a false ROTC deferment from a university he never attended, he was able to organize demonstrations in London to coincide with the two in Washington, D.C.

For the November 15 demonstration in London, Clinton organized a "March of Death" involving 1,200 demonstrators.

Vietnam veteran Colonel George Jatras attended this parade on his way home from the war. He angrily stated in a 1993 interview on the *Larry King Live* television show: "I was there. I just returned from Vietnam and I saw papier maché skulls with the photographs of POWs in the eyeballs."

Little did Jatras know that the organizer of the parade, who also marched carrying a coffin, and who led the demonstrators to the U.S. Embassy, would later become his Commander in Chief! Clinton has, of course, denied he carried the coffin (on the *Phil Donahue Show*).16 However, his old friend from Georgetown, Father Richard McSorley, recalled vividly that Clinton helped carry a coffin to the American Embassy in London, and that when police stopped the group from entering the embassy compound, it was Clinton who acted as spokesman for the marchers.17

On another occasion, McSorley said that Clinton introduced him to some of his activist friends in London after a demonstration led by Bill, and that together they carried crosses over to the American Embassy, which they left there in protest.18

Michael Kelly of *The New York Times* reported that Clinton became "a figure within the anti-war movement, helping to organize one of the largest marches on Washington that the movement ever produced." Clinton also served as "chief organizer of two small demonstrations in London" and "took a trip through the Scandinavian countries to Russia and Czechoslovakia," according to this article.19

Into the "Workers' Paradise": Clinton's Trip Behind the Iron Curtain

In December 1969, after writing his now-famous letter to Colonel Holmes admitting that he never intended to keep his ROTC commitment, Clinton took a forty-day "vacation."

He traveled to Norway and Finland, then disappeared behind the Iron Curtain for a while, emerging in late January or early February 1970. Like his draft and ROTC files in Arkansas, records of this trip seem to have "vanished." However, enough pieces of the puzzle still exist to establish the overall picture, which isn't pretty.

At a time when no one could go behind the Iron Curtain—let alone to Moscow—without KGB approval, Clinton simply got on a train and went. Apparently without so much as a "by your leave" to American authorities, but with an "open arms" invitation and warm welcome from the Soviets, Bill went on a pilgrimage to the "workers' paradise" making a significant stop in Scandinavia, where he participated in a number of important anti-American "peace" conferences.

On December 4, one day after Clinton wrote the letter to Colonel Holmes, American activist leaders met in Hanoi with the enemy's top leaders to plan an international conference-demonstration for January 1970 in Stockholm, Sweden.

Later that month Clinton left London for a "tour" of Scandinavia, his trip apparently coinciding with the conference in Stockholm and activist meetings in Oslo, Norway. During his presidential campaign, Clinton denied the Oslo meetings and said he had only seen Father McSorley there for a few minutes, having run into him "by accident in the train station." McSorley, however, said that *at Clinton's request,* Bill and he spent an entire day together meeting with activists in Oslo.

After visiting the Institute for Peace Studies and activist groups there, Clinton left Oslo.[20] Traveling to Helsinki, Finland, in late December, he spent Christmas there with a friend. In Helsinki he boarded a train for Moscow by way of Leningrad.

Clinton's version of his trip to Scandinavia, Russia and Czechoslovakia is that he was just a member of a group of students on an educational trip. The facts say otherwise. Except for his KGB escort, Clinton traveled alone. Dee Dee Myers, spokeswoman for the Clinton campaign and later Clinton's White House Press Secretary, was quoted in *The Washington Times* as stating that Clinton "rode *alone* from Helsinki, Finland, to Moscow."[21]

Clinton arrived in Moscow on New Year's Eve and stayed for seven days. What he did in Moscow is difficult to establish. From there, Clinton journeyed to Prague, Czechoslovakia, a center for important meetings between communist leaders (including Viet Cong/NVA) and American sympathizers. It was in Prague after meeting with

Viet Cong leaders that Tom Hayden (Jane Fonda's husband of that era) raised his arms, fists clenched, and shouted, "I am a Viet Cong—we are all Viet Cong!"

Little is known about what Clinton did during his stay in Prague except that he stayed at the home of one Bedrich Kopold, identified by the Czech Federal Security and Intelligence Service as a communist official and an agent of the Czech equivalent of the KGB. Comrade Kopold was also the father of Jan Kopold, a friend of Clinton's at Oxford.[22] (Americans got a chance to see Mr. Kopold on television in January 1994 when Clinton, as President of the United States, visited Prague and had a nostalgic reunion with his host of January 1970.)

After forty days, Clinton emerged from behind the Iron Curtain and returned to London.

BILL CLINTON IS GUILTY OF TREASON

In happily joining with his Soviet and communist Vietnamese friends in a massive anti-American propaganda effort, one which strengthened the enemy's resolve while weakening American resolve, Bill Clinton was clearly giving aid and comfort to the enemy in time of war. This is still the definition of treason.

In addition to being treasonous, Clinton's activities caused many more to die. By the summer of 1969, the Viet Cong were virtually extinct, and the once-powerful North Vietnamese army was a shattered remnant, no longer capable of conducting large-scale operations. In spite of all the political limitations imposed on our troops, our enemy was broken and spent, on the ropes. The actions of Clinton and other "peace" activists encouraged the enemy[23]—who had taken such horrendous losses—to continue to fight, *causing many more people to die,* both American and Vietnamese. Yes, Bill Clinton and his pro-communist friends added many names to the Vietnam Veterans' Memorial (commonly known as "The Wall").

Congressional Medal of Honor winner, retired Admiral James Stockdale, who survived seven years as a POW in Vietnam, estimates that as many as 20,000 *additional* American serviceman died because of the demonstrators. "Their blood is on your hands, you war protesters!" he said in 1992. "You strung it out. You didn't stop it one minute."[24]

Clinton's actions bewildered and demoralized our troops and significantly weakened President Nixon's hand in conducting the war and pursuing a just peace. The moratorium of October 1969 and the subsequent March on Washington so significantly weakened Nixon's resolve that his decision made in July 1969—to deal from strength and to force an end to the war on American terms—was abandoned, and by early 1970 Nixon began secretly negotiating for peace on Hanoi's terms.[25] It is irrefutable that this eventually led to the abandonment of eighty-six percent of the American POWs Nixon had expected to repatriate.[26]

In 1970, safe at last from the draft, Clinton abandoned the pursuit of his Rhodes Scholarship. To this day, most Americans (including virtually everyone in Arkansas) believe that Clinton finished his Rhodes Scholarship and took his Oxford degree; but he didn't even come close. After his first year there, he returned in the fall of 1969 but didn't pursue his courses. He spent most of his time traveling and organizing anti-American demonstrations, and after that term returned to the U.S. and enrolled in Yale Law School. So much for Oxford and his Rhodes Scholarship.

UGLY FACTS OF CLINTON'S "ANTI-WAR" MOVEMENT

Before leaving this significant period in Bill Clinton's life, permit me to clarify the true ugliness of the movement of which he was such a significant part. Then, as now, the major news media moguls protected their own; thus, most Americans don't know what Clinton's "peace" movement was really like. The movement was portrayed as spontaneous, idealistic and innocent—just multitudes of college students rising up in groups and pleading for everyone to be "nice," to stop the war.

Many of the participants, themselves being used and manipulated, did view what they were doing in this way, especially in the early days. But from its inception, the movement was actually orchestrated from Moscow and Hanoi. Aided enormously by leftist university professors, it became a propaganda, espionage and sabotage arm of the enemy. In its darkest expressions it was violent, unthinkably cruel, and fueled by hate.

Cruelty by the "Peace" Crowd

Let me briefly cite some examples of the clearly treasonous and horribly cruel aspects of the "peace" movement.

There is a fundamental fact of life which deserves clarification here: wars are not fought by those who create them; wars are created by safe and comfortable politicians and wealthy businessmen—for their own, often selfish, purposes. However, once undertaken, wars are mostly fought by eighteen-year-old boys who don't want to be there. Remember this.

During Vietnam our returning soldiers were often treated cruelly. Being lifted out of Vietnam and flown directly to the U.S. as they typically were—having been in the horrors of combat only hours before—would have been a difficult enough adjustment had they been welcomed home with appreciation. Too often, however, "peace" activists met them with verbal and physical abuse, calling them baby killers, spitting, and throwing pig blood on their uniforms. These "protests" were deliberate and vicious.

These returning soldiers, most of them still in their teens, had not wanted to go, but had obeyed their country's call anyway. They didn't create the war, they only fought it, suffering things those protected demonstrators would never pay the price to know. Then, returning home with their minds reeling, bodies aching, their hearts sick, they were treated as villains. Small wonder that so many of them, now men in their forties, are alcoholics, sleeping under bridges, wandering hopelessly through their persistent nightmares.

An activity much less known, but even more cruel and inexcusable than the abuse of our returning servicemen, was the deliberate abuse of the wives, children and parents of those killed and captured in Vietnam. The activists of the "peace" movement had ways of finding out when casualties occurred, and it was not uncommon for the wives to immediately begin receiving obscene phone calls and threats to themselves and their children. These "peace activists" called them filthy names and said that their "pig" husbands (fathers/sons) deserved what had happened. When these innocent families—already making the sacrifice of separation—were suddenly shattered with death and made pitifully vulnerable, desperately needing the comfort and support of those around them, they were instead terrified by vicious attacks. In some cases their homes were vandalized and their tires slashed by the "peace lovers." Yes, it really happened.

Think, if you will, of World War II, of the American POWs who fought until overwhelmed and then suffered the nightmares of captivity in Japanese POW camps. There they were tortured, starved, denied medical care, and worked like animals until they dropped, struggling to be faithful to their country and fighting to survive. Then imagine, if you can, American citizens, including celebrities and politicians, living comfortably and safely in the U.S., working on behalf of the Japanese enemy. Imagine such people sending supplies to the enemy, making speeches on their behalf, traveling to Tokyo, visiting the camps, posing for enemy propaganda photos, praising the guards and heaping more abuse and torture on the American prisoners. Then try to imagine other Americans back in the U.S., dodging the draft, conducting background studies of the POWs and providing this information to the Japanese so as to better break the POWs.

This scenario is indeed difficult to imagine because it just couldn't have happened. During World War II anyone even attempting such things would have gone to prison and probably have been executed if they weren't first lynched from the nearest tree. Yet that is exactly what happened during the Vietnam War (a war in which 58,000 Americans died, hundreds of thousands were crippled and 25,000 disappeared into the limbo of the Missing in Action), and those who committed these horrendous deeds go unpunished today, prospering in a freedom they never paid for.

The Betrayal of Nick Rowe, POW

Yes, you probably knew about these treasonous practices already—except for one. Most of us in this country have never heard that Americans acted as spies for the enemy during the Vietnam War, providing personal information about the POWs and their families to their captors. Such detailed information would in turn be used during interrogation of the POW in the form of threats upon his family in order to entrap him and break him, thus reducing his chances of resistance and survival. This information always caused mental and physical anguish, sometimes even causing the death of the POW being reported on. I'll give you a verified example.

Special Forces Lieutenant Nick Rowe was the only long-term POW to escape from the communists during the Vietnam War. Marine PFC Bobby Garwood managed to escape six years after the prisoner return of 1973, but Nick

Rowe was the only one to escape successfully during the war. Many tried, but only Nick succeeded. Interestingly, his opportunity to escape came about because he was being taken out for execution. Let me explain.

Nick Rowe was captured when his Special Forces camp was overrun. He survived imprisonment for five years because he had convinced his captors that he was a civilian engineer, not a soldier. Realizing that if they knew his true identity they might be able to torture information out of him that would endanger his friends, he chose and successfully maintained his false identity.

This ploy worked for five years until "peace" activists in the U.S. conducted a background study on him and sent it to his captors. As a result, Nick was condemned to death. As he was being taken to the place of execution, an American helicopter appeared overhead; the guards scattered and Nick escaped.

Had he not escaped, he would have died on the spot, and his blood would have been on the hands of those American traitors. Other American POWs, similarly betrayed, did not escape; their blood remains on the treacherous hands of these American spies.[27]

What Does all This Have to do with Bill Clinton?

All of these deeds done by Americans in the "peace" movement are terrible, some quite unthinkable. But what, you may ask, do these awful things have to do with Bill Clinton? Am I saying that he personally abused returning soldiers, terrorized and abused wives and children of those killed and captured, or that he worked as an enemy agent, providing information on our POWs to the enemy? No, we have no evidence to suggest that he did.

But what we do know is that Clinton was a totally committed activist-leader in a "peace" movement that proudly included all these activities, and that he indeed embraced the movement overall.

We also know that since entering politics, Clinton has

lied about his participation in the "peace" movement. However, now that his involvement has become known, he has yet to show remorse for his actions; nor has he renounced even the foulest of deeds committed by his fellow activists. In fact, Bill Clinton said to the world on the *Phil Donahue Show* that he wished that he could have been more deeply involved than he was, and wished that he had done more.

He did plenty, thank you! No, if Bill Clinton disapproves of any of the despicable actions of any part of his beloved "peace" movement, he has never said so.

BILL CLINTON AS PRESIDENT-ELECT

Clinton's election in 1992 was a massive body blow to the veterans of America. For the Vietnam veterans it was an even more devastating blow, a final kick to the teeth. A pampered draft dodger who had despised them and their sacrifice, and who had actually given aid and comfort to the enemy they had fought against in his place, was going to be President of the United States.

The very crowd who had praised and encouraged the enemy they had fought, the enemy who had tortured and killed their friends, those people who had waved the enemy's flag and burned the one for which the veterans had fought, would be running the country.

For many Vietnam veterans, it was a final form of rejection. The election returns proclaimed to them: "You are trash; what you did was wrong. Remember how you were treated when you came home? Remember being called an imperialist pig? Well, it was all true. You deserved it—the election proves it."

But they still had each other, and they still had their "Wall." There, with their 58,000 dead and missing friends, they belonged. There they were understood and accepted. There on that sacred ground, where memories lived and where voices were never raised, they were all right. There, where family members came for much the same reasons, there on that sacred spot they were brothers and sisters, surrounded by an indifferent world which had suddenly become hostile. Their aching hearts asked, how could such a person be elected President? At that time they had not yet begun to learn just how hostile a President they would soon have.

The election was held on Tuesday, November 2, 1992. Veterans Day, nine gloomy days later, was the occasion for President-elect Bill Clinton's first public utterance about the Vietnam Veterans' Memorial. He revealed his abysmal lack of understanding and his colossal insensitivity by expressing pleasure that the Wall was "the number one tourist attraction in Washington." A tourist attraction? Yes, that is exactly what he called it. The collective veterans' community groaned deep within itself.

Veterans Day is one of the two most important days of the year at the Wall. The mood that November day in 1992 was somber and subdued. Old unpleasant feelings stirred, yet went unspoken. An unusual cloud of heaviness hung over the area and the people. By afternoon actual clouds settled in, heavy and gray. A light, cold rain began to fall, misty, like most of the eyes there that day.

The people seemed not to notice the rain except to cover some of the mementos and gifts they were leaving, as they always do, at the base of the Wall—gifts for the friends and loved ones they remembered. The aching, solemn silence was broken only by the soft sounds of shuffling feet and muted voices. In the chilly gloom, raindrops sparkled like diamonds on the plastic bags and cling wrap.

A Question From a Daughter's Aching Heart

At the west end of the Wall at the entrance, a young woman stood for hours, holding a piece of poster board. With felt-tip markers, she had written on it a public message in words I shall never forget: "BILL CLINTON: WHERE WERE YOU FEBRUARY 7, 1969, WHEN MY

FATHER, LT. RUSSELL MOKE, USMC, GAVE HIS LIFE FOR HIS COUNTRY AT [the village of] AN HOA, VIETNAM?" Diagonally across the lower right corner, she had added a personal note: "I love you, Daddy."

Just an unknown casualty, a little girl from the '60s remembering the father she never had gotten the chance to know, trying to find him there, and speaking out of the heavy aching in her heart a question many of us asked.

After dark she placed the sign below her father's name and disappeared into the night. As the rain continued, her sign sagged progressively down on the cobblestones, the mist slowly washing the letters into spreading smears of pale pastels. Clinton, of course, was nowhere near, in body or in spirit.

The veterans weren't the only ones for whom the election was a kick in the face.

BILL CLINTON AS COMMANDER IN CHIEF

The Constitution provides that the President of the United States is automatically the Commander in Chief of our armed forces. Clinton's visceral contempt for military matters and military people, combined with his abysmal lack of knowledge and understanding of things military, make him singularly unqualified for the position. To make matters much worse, he has surrounded himself entirely with others of like mind and like inexperience.

This situation, fraught with dangers, is not without precedent. King Rehoboam, son of King Solomon of old, was young and inexperienced when he assumed the throne of Israel. Instead of surrounding himself with the older, wiser, experienced men who had been his father's counselors, he rejected them and surrounded himself with his friends, all as young, inexperienced and unwise as himself. The results were disastrous, leaving a weakened, vulnerable remnant of the mighty kingdom he had inherited. The outlook for our country under Bill Clinton is not better.

Bill Clinton has been in office now since January 1993. How has he done in his role as Commander in Chief of the Armed Forces so far? Let's examine his dismal record to this point with some revealing examples.

Memorial Day at the Wall

Three months after becoming President, Bill Clinton performed his first significant act as Commander in Chief—one he *shouldn't* have performed. In order to "polish his image" with veterans (words from the official White House statement), Clinton decided to appear at the Vietnam Veterans' Memorial to make a speech on Memorial Day, May 1993. Characteristically, he had changed his mind several times about coming. Just the possibility of this tarnished draft dodger's appearing to speak on that sacred ground had touched off a firestorm of angry opposition from veterans and families of the casualties.

North Carolina attorney Richard Kania, a veteran deeply offended at the very thought of Clinton's attendance, composed a post card asking Clinton to have the good taste and consideration to stay away. Then he asked his friend, Special Forces veteran John Roberts, to make copies and send them to his friends. Those friends asked other friends, and soon this private little protest spread in all directions, like a crackling firebrand thrown onto a dry prairie in a high wind. It was definitely an idea whose time had come,

The idea then spread to a friend of Richard's in Raleigh, retired Special Forces officer Rolf Kreuscher. Rolf called me. I, in turn, made hundreds of copies and put them on the counter of Kathy Roberts' flower shop up the street. Once people found out what they were, they snatched them up faster than I could make them, so my wife and my secretary started helping to turn them out. No ads, no promotion, just one fed up American telling another. From our one little town of 3,500 people, more than 1,000 cards were mailed out.

From individuals having one or two cards made up on

photocopy machines to veterans' groups printing large quantities, copies of this card were distributed. With no plan, no central direction, no headquarters and no funding, this idea, once loosed, started to blaze its way through the deep, dry tinder of anger and frustration in ordinary American hearts, and quickly raced from coast to coast—a pure and powerful grassroots reaction. It was evident that Clinton's planned appearance was just one outrage too many.

These post cards were all exact copies of that very first card that Richard Kania had made for himself.

The cards began to flood the White House mail room. Even the media took an interest and asked about those unusual cards. Dee Dee Myers, Clinton's press secretary, reluctantly admitted that "a few hundred" had come in. Only God and the White House staff really know how many cards actually arrived (and the White House staff certainly isn't going to tell), but a conservative estimate of the total number of cards Clinton received before Memorial Day is between two and four million.

May 1, 1993

Dear President Clinton:

Please, in view of your activities during the War in Vietnam, let's not see you engage in any hypocrisy by attending ceremonies either at the Vietnam Wall or the Tomb of the Unknown Soldier.

While your "esteemed" conscience led you to organize events that provided aid and comfort to the enemy, American soldiers were maimed and killed obeying the legal processes of representative government.

Sincerely,

REPLICA OF KANIA'S POST CARD

A few days before Memorial Day, Clinton finally made up his mind to appear at the Wall despite the massive public outcry. CBS News asked me to fly to Washington to appear on its morning news hour to explain why so many felt so strongly that the President should stay away. The rationale of the White House and the political friends of Clinton who control the Memorial was that as Commander in Chief, Clinton had an obligation to come. The question of why we couldn't forgive him was asked rhetorically; it was contended that the Wall was for "bringing healing" to the nation.

I pointed out that all these positions were spurious, and that I personally had already forgiven the man (as a Christian I had no choice). But in the seven minutes I was given that morning at the Wall, I attempted to answer CBS's question.

First, speaking for the multitudes of Vietnam War veterans and their families, the question of forgiving Clinton was not only irrelevant, it was moot—moot for the simple reason that Clinton had never asked for forgiveness, never expressed any regret, and never admitted any wrongdoing. He didn't on that Memorial Day, and he hasn't since.

Second, as President, Clinton is Commander in Chief of both active duty and reserve forces, but he is not Commander in Chief of dead men and women, their survivors, or veterans. In that capacity, he had no obligation to speak there. Although by virtue of the office every President (since the building of the Wall) has received an invitation to speak, no President before Clinton had ever done so. There was no precedent for his attendance.

Finally, the purpose of a war memorial is to memorialize warriors, not to provide a platform for self-serving politicians to "polish" their images with veterans and their family members, nor to make draft dodgers feel justified in what they've done.

The Shameful Treatment of the Veterans

You didn't see this on network TV, but on this somber Memorial Day the chairs down front with the smiling faces were filled by invitation only, and were enclosed with a fence. (In the months following, complaints surfaced that front row seats were sold for $500.)

Behind this handpicked, approving crowd was an open grassy area about 200 yards deep, followed by another fence. Behind this second fence, at a safe distance from the Memorial and the platform, was the real crowd—10,000 veterans, family members and patriotic citizens kept back like animals by mounted Park Police, District of Columbia Police, Secret Service agents and, I swear to you, a SWAT team! It was a disgrace!

Within this crowd, 1,000 uniformed veterans standing in formation executed an "about face" and "parade rest" and then hung their heads in silent protest when Clinton appeared. The cameras were kept on the "politically correct" few down front, and even though the microphones were turned away from the real crowd to mute their protests, the deafening sounds of the angry veterans objecting to Clinton's presence were still heard.

This treatment of the veterans and their family members was outrageous. The Vietnam Veterans' Memorial is, after all, *their* memorial, *their* sacred place. Here they can quietly come to make contact with their memories, confront their grief and find some peace in silent, supportive fellowship. They purchased this memorial with their blood and tears and built it with their own money. Their hearts have been kicked and stepped on for more than twenty years now, and they deserve much better.

Those of us who spoke for them then were simply saying, "Please, don't step on them one more time; don't politicize this precious place to 'polish your image.' If you don't appreciate them, if you can't understand their sacrifice, then, for God's sake, just leave them alone!"

Bill Clinton didn't appreciate the military, he didn't

understand their sacrifice, and, characteristically, he didn't leave them alone. For his own selfish reasons, he just kicked them one more time.

As Clinton was about to begin his speech, the outcry from the veterans kept behind the fence increased to the point that Clinton's voice coming over the loudspeaker was barely heard. He began his speech: "To all of you who are shouting: I have heard you. I ask you now to hear me."

During most of Clinton's speech, the unhappy sounds of the protesters could be heard above the sporadic applause of the front row VIP section. Twice, however, the crowd responded warmly. Clinton managed to strike a hopeful cord even with most of the angry vets. People cheered when he promised to declassify all Department of Defense documents concerning POW-MIAs. The vets, overjoyed to at last hear a promise of help concerning their missing comrades, never suspected Clinton's duplicity. You see, he neglected to mention that George Bush had already issued such an executive order *the previous year!*

The other statement drawing applause had been carefully crafted to impress the vets—those who had fought in a frustrating war with a no-win policy dictated by politicians influenced by the protest movement. Clinton assured those gathered: *"If the day shall come when our service men and women must again go into combat, they will go with the training and support necessary to win; and most of all with a clear mission to win."* The promises were good, but the keeper of the promise was not.

In scarcely more than a year, two of Clinton's pledges rang hollow in two *different* combat situations. The first, his reversal on "a clear mission," was seen both in the poorly designed mission in Somalia, and vividly illustrated on the "D-day" in Haiti by the words of a young Marine. In combat clothes, rifle in hand, he said to a news reporter, "I don't know why we're here; I only know they told us not to shoot anybody."

The second betrayal—which the world watched in horror on television—was the Ranger massacre in Somalia.

These unnecessary deaths demonstrated Clinton's broken promise to the veterans that in any future combat, our service personnel would go in with the "support necessary to win." Yet again, after the Ranger fiasco, the potential for disaster caused by sending our troops to Haiti without necessary support shows that Clinton's promises have no meaning. The paratroopers of the 82nd Airborne Division landed with only fifteen rounds each for their rifles (1/2 magazine)—after one burst, they would have been out of ammunition and defenseless. They received no opposition, so were mercifully spared.

Bill Clinton and the Abandoned POWs

Clinton's election gave many POW family members and activists fresh hope. During the campaign, he had promised to go beyond anything any previous Presidents had done by seeing that bringing home the POWs was not just "*a* matter of highest national priority," but "*the* matter of highest national priority." He promised that before normalizing relations with Vietnam, he would require full disclosure of all files and records by Vietnam and demand their active assistance in resolving the issue once and for all. Until then, he promised us, he would provide no assistance to any of the captor nations. He also said that "America must never leave its warriors on the battlefield."[28]

And so, many hoped we had a President who would bring our POWs home at last; it was a vain hope.

Within his first year in office, Clinton was given the opportunity to bring home a number of living American POWs, in captivity in Southeast Asia since the Vietnam War. Private citizens had located them, made the contacts and all the arrangements; the skids were greased. It would not cost the government one cent; it was all privately funded. All that was needed was, literally, a stroke of the presidential pen for authority, and protection once they crossed the border.

A message was sent to Clinton informing him of this.

People of the highest credibility guaranteed its validity. It was made clear that this operation, although he had nothing to do with it, would make him a hero, would cover a multitude of sins, and probably guarantee reelection. His response? He didn't even bother to reply.

As has been his way, after saying all the right things in order to deceive the voters and achieve election, Clinton has left his promises behind in the ankle-deep litter of the November victory celebrations and has gone about doing whatever serves his selfish purposes.

On Thursday, February 3, 1994, he drove a decisive nail in the POWs' coffins. While his Commerce Secretary, Ron Brown, was being investigated by the FBI for taking a $750,000 bribe from the Vietnamese to get the trade embargo lifted, Bill Clinton lifted the nineteen-year-old embargo, signing the death warrant for the surviving POWs, and then *blithely went jogging past the Vietnam Veterans' Memorial.*[29]

So much for his compassion, his moral responsibility, and his command responsibility to brave, brutalized American fighting men. So much for his words about never leaving our warriors on the battlefield. Bill Clinton has demonstrated his readiness to deal them all away in a political poker game, like so much trash left behind on the battlefield.

Clinton's Disastrous Bungling in Somalia

Clinton's visionless, unprincipled foreign policy took Marines, already in Somalia, on a humanitarian mission to deliver food to the hungry, and sent them into ever-widening combat with a fleeting enemy. While having to operate on enemy turf and on the enemy's terms, the hands of our Marines were tied by "rules of engagement." The "policy" evolved, and soon their mission was broadened to disarming bandit bands. In the growing confusion over those rules of engagement, over who the enemy was and what the objective was, Marines died; more were disabled.

As the quagmire widened, it developed into a bizarre attempt to capture a bandit leader. Although network news teams could easily locate this man and interview him on camera, the Clinton Administration, with its massive, sophisticated intelligence assets, couldn't find the guy.

Army Rangers were deployed to Somalia with specially trained Special Forces units. Highly motivated, the best in the world at Special Operations, they were sent after the outlaw.

In classic Ranger style, they conducted a raid on what they had been assured was the warlord's headquarters. They executed the raid perfectly, but there was an embarrassing problem: instead of capturing the bandit headquarters, they had actually captured a U.N. headquarters. *Under U.N. command,* the Rangers had been sent to the wrong place! Rangers and U.N. leaders could have died, but they didn't.

What could have been a tragedy then became a joke. As bandit morale soared, the mighty U.S.A. was ridiculed the world over.

The next time, however, wasn't funny at all. Clinton's military incompetence produced a great American tragedy.

On October 3, 1993, sent to capture a bandit chief and rescue the crew of a downed Black Hawk helicopter, our Rangers were ambushed and surrounded by a howling mob, which outnumbered them one hundred to one and was better armed. Our soldiers suddenly found themselves not rescuing the helicopter crew and capturing the bandit, but fighting for their lives. Over a period of twelve hours of intense combat, the Rangers fought on with what they had. While they begged for tanks to support them in the battle and armored personnel carriers to evacuate their casualties, their men were being slaughtered.

No tanks came. No armored personnel carriers arrived to evacuate the wounded. One of those who died there, Corporal Jamie Smith, bled to death over a period of three hours. Had he been evacuated, his life could easily have been saved.

This disaster ended in the death of eighteen of our best soldiers, and the wounding of seventy-six more. Incredibly, the naked bodies of some of the dead were dragged around the streets for their families to see on television. The entire Somalia fiasco was ill-conceived and without clear purpose or end-point. This tragedy need not have occurred at all; it was completely unnecessary.

It was cheap politics that decimated our troops. An AC-130 support aircraft, with its devastating firepower, had previously been withdrawn, labeled by civilian policy makers as being "too warlike." The small helicopter gunships which had been allowed to remain were not given full freedom to fire in support.

General Colin Powell, Chairman of the Joint Chiefs of Staff, had recommended armored vehicle support; the Marine general in overall command had requested armored vehicle support; the Army general in local command had requested armored vehicle support; and the Rangers and Special Forces men dying there had begged for armored vehicle support. It was, unbelievably, denied. Would you care to know why?

A Deadly Ignorance Of Military Realities

When the Clinton Administration was planning for the raid, the need for armored vehicle support was pointed out. Secretary of State Warren Christopher said "no" to the use of armored vehicles. His rationale? "We don't want to escalate the situation."

Bill Clinton concurred, and there in the air-conditioned safety of the White House, the doom of those Rangers in the stifling, stinking, bloody heat of Mogadishu, was sealed.

One question immediately comes to mind: What do tactical military decisions have to do with the Secretary of State anyway? Shouldn't he have been across town settling matters of protocol or telling the U.N. there would be "serious consequences" if those antisocial Somalis didn't stop killing our troops?

Unbelievably, two spokesmen representing Secretary of Defense Les Aspin, and the acting Chairman of the Joint Chiefs of Staff (both of whom *should* have participated in the decision), reported that they had no knowledge of the request for armored vehicles. However, Aspin later admitted having personally received the request and acknowledged denying it. In fact, Aspin *emphatically* denied the armored vehicle request, stating: "It's just not going to happen."[30]

Any one of those Rangers could have told that gathering of politicians that armored vehicle support in such an operation is a must; but the politicians didn't know that, and refused to listen to those who did.

Retired Army Captain James H. Smith (a veteran disabled in Vietnam combat), father of Corporal Jamie Smith, told a May 27 press conference in Washington that the disaster was the result not only of Clinton's ignorance of military matters, but also of the same ignorance shared by his top advisors.

The late Colonel Charlie Beckwith, perhaps the leading authority on such military operations, agreed, saying that the deadly failures to properly utilize and support the Rangers were all inflicted "by civilian leadership."[31]

An Ominous Déjà Vu

It is significant that the man Clinton turns to for military advice—who argued against the tanks and APCs for the raid in Mogadishu—is the same Warren Christopher (then a high official in Jimmy Carter's National Security Council) who helped plan the disastrous raid to rescue the hostages in Iran.

At a planning session for the Tehran rescue, the man selected to lead the raid, the late Colonel Charlie Beckwith, was asked what he would do about the Iranian guards. Beckwith, a no-nonsense veteran of special operations, replied that as they came out the door they would be shot in the head—twice—to be sure they couldn't do any harm.

Warren Christopher gasped, grimaced, viscerally shocked, and asked, "Couldn't you just shoot them in the hand?"

Had Charlie Beckwith been allowed to plan the Iranian raid as it should have been done and left alone to carry it out, it would have succeeded.

Concerning the Mogadishu disaster, Beckwith wrote in *The Wall Street Journal* that the raid was bungled by committing the Rangers and Delta Force without giving them the freedom and the support they needed.[32]

Captain James H. Smith lays the blame for the death of his son directly at the door of the White House. In summarizing the disaster, he bluntly states that his son's death had served no purpose, and that "the Rangers had been betrayed—denied proper combat support, and, with unreliable U.N. allies, disaster was preordained."

Retired Army Lieutenant Colonel Larry Joyce, also a veteran of combat in Vietnam and father of slain Sergeant Casey Joyce, agreed with Captain Smith, saying that the dead soldiers were "betrayed by an Administration that gave them a no-win mission and didn't provide them with the resources and the support they desperately needed."

Major General Garrison, commander of the Ranger Task Force, when asked by Senator William S. Cohen (R-Maine) whether lives would have been saved if the armored vehicles had been provided, answered, "I am absolutely certain that would have been the case."[33]

The Soldiers And Families Were Not Deceived

The Rangers and Special Forces troopers who survived know exactly what caused the disaster in Mogadishu, and they know who is responsible. When Clinton visited the survivors at Walter Reed Hospital, he offered to have his picture taken with them. Ordinarily, any soldier would be honored to have his picture taken with the President of the United States, his Commander in Chief; it would have been an heirloom for his children and grandchildren. But this

Commander in Chief was different. At least four of the wounded Rangers refused to be photographed with Clinton, deciding individually that they wouldn't lower themselves, nor would they dishonor their uniforms and their fallen comrades.[34]

In the predictable political maneuvering to smooth over Clinton's disastrous bungling in Somalia, aided by the silence of the Clinton-friendly media, the American people are already forgetting what little they've been allowed to know. Two of the most important stories, which the major media knew about, were deliberately ignored; they simply were never reported. On these pages, you will almost certainly be reading them for the very first time. You and I must not allow them to be forgotten.

Soon after the slaughter of the Rangers, the parents of Corporal Smith received the obligatory letter of condolence from Bill Clinton. The letter itself is a remarkable document: instead of simply expressing regret and condolence, Clinton took the occasion to pat himself on the back for what he had accomplished there.

Corporal Smith's father replied by mail, refusing to accept Clinton's condolences, and told him plainly that he was directly responsible for his son's death.

His letter is classic, concluding with: "Until you as President and Commander in Chief are either willing or able to formulate a clear foreign policy, establish specific objectives and, most importantly, support the men and women in uniform, I will 'lead the way' in insuring that you no longer send America's finest to a needless death. When you are capable of meeting these criteria, then I will accept your letter of condolence." (Both letters are included in toto in Appendix A.)

Eventually, after Clinton had sat on the paper work for eight weeks, two of the slain soldiers, Master Sergeant Gary Gordon and Sergeant First Class Randall Shughart, were posthumously awarded the Medal of Honor. As usual in such cases, the medals were presented to the next of kin.

Following the May 23 presentation at the White House,

the families of the two men were invited into the Oval Office for a private visit with Clinton. Inside the office, the father of Sergeant Shughart refused to shake Clinton's hand, then looked him in the face and calmly told him that he was responsible for his son's death, that it was for no purpose, and that Clinton was not fit to be President *or* Commander in Chief.

Clinton was visibly shocked and momentarily speechless. It is revealing that he was surprised that the man should feel that way. (Clinton really doesn't think the way most people do, seeming to lack any sense of personal responsibility.) After a brief, awkward silence, Clinton caught his breath. Becoming angry, he turned to the mother of the dead hero and said: "What's he jumping on me for? I didn't kill the kid!"

He actually said that—to the bereaved mother— he really did! It was an eloquent demonstration of Clinton's insensitivity, and of his absolute inability to understand sacrifice and responsibility.[35]

Shedding Responsibility

After the botched raid, Clinton, in typical form, tried to shed any responsibility for the tragedy. After it was learned that the parents of some of the dead soldiers were in Washington to testify before the Senate Foreign Relations Committee, a White House meeting was hastily arranged.

Speaking to some of the parents, Clinton assured them that his approach to resolving the warlord problem in Somalia had always been to use diplomacy, and that he had not authorized the raid. He went on to say that he "was as dismayed as you are," and that "when reports came in on October 3, my reaction was, 'Why did they do that?'"

In complete contradiction, on another occasion he said that he approved of the decision and had found no evidence of disobedience or incompetence in the conduct of the raid, but never clearly accepted responsibility for the debacle. In classic Clinton form, he claimed that it was someone else's fault.

But in speaking to the parents he outdid himself by placing at least part of the blame on the sacrificed soldiers themselves. *In perhaps the most unbelievably insensitive, outrageous thing a President ever said, Clinton told those grieving parents of the fallen Rangers that the Rangers themselves may have been responsible for their own deaths by being "too aggressive."*[36]

In eloquent contrast was the response of Ronald Reagan—a Commander in Chief who was loved and respected by his service men and women—when 241 Marines were killed in the car-bombing of their barracks in Lebanon in 1983. In a situation where his subordinate commanders really were at fault and should have been relieved, Reagan instead shouldered all the blame immediately, and genuinely grieved with the families for their dead.

Many politicians today tend to file away as mere statistics those who are killed and mutilated while serving their country. In sweeping Mogadishu under the White House rug, Clinton dismissed the casualties as "unfortunate losses." Friends who fought with them can't think of them that way; neither can their families.

The father of sacrificed Ranger Sergeant Casey Joyce, in an eloquent *Newsweek* article, takes exception, pointing out that "'Unfortunate losses' have names. And they have families and friends who remember their smiles."[37]

Yes, those "unfortunate losses" do have names and families and friends. In sending these men into harm's way with no valid national interest, no clear-cut goal or exit strategy, Bill Clinton, as President, *was doing the very same thing he had so passionately opposed in the '60s.*

Bill Clinton and His Haiti Policy

In the first eighteen months of his presidency, Bill Clinton clearly demonstrated his remarkable ineptness in foreign policy matters, and in military matters in particular.

His contempt for things and people military, his stunning lack of principle, and his lack of purpose beyond immediate political expediency have combined to produce a confused foreign policy that is the laughing stock of the world.

Haiti is a perfect example. Clinton has had more than six Haiti "policies" in eighteen months. This confusion and his constant vacillation have led directly to the drowning death of hundreds of Haitian refugees trying to reach Florida.

While trade embargoes against communist Vietnam have been lifted by Clinton, thus dooming surviving American prisoners, similar embargoes against anti-communist Haiti were being maintained. These embargoes, supposedly imposed to force the Haitians to take Aristide back, didn't hurt the rich rulers at all.   The poor people, on the other hand, suffered terribly from inflated prices. They literally starved; many died. By conservative estimate at least *one thousand additional* children died of malnutrition during each month of Clinton's embargo. This figure does not include the additional adults who died.[38] If this makes sense, then reason has no meaning.

Even *The New York Times*—one of Clinton's most friendly apologists—in its lead editorial of September 2, 1994, eloquently skewered his plan to enlist 266 soldiers from tiny Caribbean countries to legitimize his invasion of Haiti as "multinational." Pointing out the transparent phoniness of Clinton's plan, the *Times* observed that he was fooling no one, that he was merely squeezing "another droplet from the Administration's almost empty vial of foreign policy credibility."[39]

In his determination to invade Haiti in order to buy votes from the Congressional Black Caucus for his legislative programs and to prop up his sagging image as a leader, he was not only willing, but anxious, to sacrifice the lives of American Marines and sailors (to say nothing of the thousands of Haitian lives that were involved).

And what did he claim to be the driving, compelling motivation for all this madness? It was the moral "rightness" of forcing the return to power of deposed Marxist Jean Bertrand Aristide, an ex-Catholic priest who was defrocked for his commitment to violent Marxist revolution, who calls free enterprise "a mortal sin."

Aristide takes pleasure in watching "necklacing," a practice he introduced to Haiti in which an old tire is placed around the neck of the helpless victim, filled with gasoline and set afire. These tortured victims die horribly, screaming out their last breaths. Expressing his perverted enjoyment in watching this, Aristide has said, "It's cute, it's pretty, and it smells good."[40]

And so, in the face of overwhelming opposition by the American people, against vocal bipartisan objection by Congress, Clinton pressed on with this madness, taking the chance of spilling innocent blood and sacrificing still more American fighting men (the bloody fiasco in Somalia taught him nothing) in order to replace one dictator with another whose record was even worse. All this happened in a tiny, starving nation still living in the 19th century, which couldn't possibly have threatened the U.S. or its interests.

The official reason given for the "invasion" was "to restore democracy." This motive fails to compute when we examine Clinton's previous attempt to establish democracy in Somalia. *U.S. News & World Report* commented on the unheralded pull-out of troops from Somalia in an article headlined, "SOMALIA AFTERMATH: A LESSON FOR HAITI." We see this as summary and a warning: "U.N. and U.S. attempts to install a democratic government have come to nothing—in what some see as a lesson for Haiti."

Bill Clinton's own words, from his infamous 1968 letter to Colonel Holmes, condemn his determination to meddle in the internal affairs of another nation in which there is no valid American interest.

Let's allow him to speak for himself concerning the rightness of his plan: *"No government really rooted in limited, parliamentary democracy, should have the power to make its citizens fight and kill and die in a war they may oppose, a war which even possibly may be wrong, a war which, in any case, does not involve immediately the peace and freedom of the nation."*

Should we dismiss Clinton's statements because they were made so long ago? Let's compare his past position with his current ideology as expressed in his speech on Memorial Day, 1994. *"We cannot dispatch our troops to solve every problem where our values are offended by human misery, and we should not. We are prepared to defend ourselves and our fundamental interests when they are threatened."*

Clinton's intervention in Haiti is also in direct conflict with the provision of his official policy decision as stated in Presidential Decision Directive (PDD)-25, that before U.S. troops may be committed to combat action it must be determined that "domestic and Congressional support exist." For the invasion of Haiti, he had neither.[41]

LENS CAPS, PEBBLES ON THE BEACH AND OTHER "PHOTO OPS"

Bill Clinton, a basically sociable, pleasant guy—but a pathological liar—loves photo ops (photo opportunities). Whenever photographers are in his presence, he is generally accommodating and loves posturing before them, taking advantage of every chance for valuable propagandizing. Sometimes, if the news cameras don't happen to be there, he takes his own cameras along. A consummate actor, he can appear to be what he thinks people want to see.

Sometimes Clinton and his image makers see an opportunity in advance and set it up, as in Italy and Normandy during June 1994 when he went to Europe for the 50th anniversary of the Normandy invasion. At other times, he poses for the retinue of working cameramen that follows him around. Because of his tendency toward insincerity, either situation can turn on him, revealing the shameless opportunism which dominates so much of his public life. Let's look closely at a few "spontaneous" glimpses of the private Bill Clinton pretending to be emotionally moved.

You probably saw the moving footage in June 1994 as Clinton walked "alone," reflectively, among the thousands of white crosses in the American military cemetery in Italy. Strolling toward the cameraman, looking lost in thoughts of the sacrifice of those Americans buried there, he stopped suddenly and looked down; something on the ground had caught his eye. Why, it was a miniature American flag, just one in a sea of thousands of other little American flags which were stuck neatly in the ground beside every grave marker. But, oh dear, this one had fallen over. The only decent thing for a patriotic guy to do, deeply moved by the sacrifice made by the soldier buried there, would be to pick it up and replant it by the grave. He looked down at the flag and, moved by a noble "spontaneous" thought, stooped down, picked the flag up and replanted it. Wow! This guy has a heart after all; he must really love his flag and respect that dead soldier.

But wait a minute, something was peculiar there. Was there something strange about that flag he "found" fallen over in the grass? Indeed there was: *he had to unroll it first!* That flag hadn't "blown over;" it was still tightly rolled up, purposely placed there for Clinton to "find" it while being filmed. Could this whole situation have been a typical Clinton-staged photo op?

Later during that same trip, having arrived at the beaches of Normandy, a deeply reflective Bill Clinton strolled "alone" on the beach, supposedly being photo-graphed with a long-range lens. Lost in thoughts of patriotism, he walked, completely alone, on the beach where so many had fought and died fifty years earlier. He was likely having religious thoughts too: profound ponderings of life, death and eternity.

Suddenly, like before, he looked down. There at his feet was a small pile of rocks. Moved by the feelings surging deeply within him, he stooped and looked intently at the little rocks. Then, quite spontaneously, all alone with his thoughts, he arranged the rocks into a simple cross in the sand.

Wow! A powerfully candid moment—a scene to live forever in American memory, like little John Kennedy saluting at his father's funeral.

But wait—something didn't seem quite right. Ah yes. If you looked carefully, you may have noticed shadows in the edge of the picture, shadows of other people. He wasn't alone! And, now that I think of it, that beach he was walking on was pure sand as far as the eye could see—no rocks at all, let alone piles of rocks! Could it be that those rocks had been planted there for Clinton to "find," that those shadows in the background were White House public relations people, staging and directing the entire "spontaneous" event? It appears that way.

But the Clinton photo op that most merits placement in the Phony Photo Op Hall of Fame took place in Korea.

While bravely standing on the green, neatly mowed grass slopes of the American positions along the DMZ in South Korea, President Clinton, ascribing to himself exceptional courage, boasted that he was standing closer to the North Korean enemy than any other American President ever had.

Facing those evil enemy soldiers, he looked unflinchingly through large binoculars, studying their positions on the other side of the Demarcation Line fence, 1,000 yards away. By golly, those commies don't scare *this* American President! Wow, that's inspiring! Maybe some of those stories about his running from danger and dodging the draft aren't true.

But wait a minute . . . something was wrong. Did you notice something strange about those binoculars? They were just the ordinary military 7X50 binoculars like we used in World War II, Korea and Vietnam—but something was different. What was it? Oh, I know! Those binoculars with which Clinton was bravely and thoughtfully studying the North Korean positions and staring down those commie soldiers still *had the lens caps on!* He wasn't seeing a thing through those binoculars, and news cameras caught the faux pas!

As usual, Bill Clinton was just pretending. For a minute there, we had thought there was hope for the guy.

BILL CLINTON AND THE GAY AGENDA

Bill Clinton's campaign for the presidency was built on one issue—the economy. We heard it over and over: "Worst economy in fifty years!" and "It's the economy, stupid!" George Bush was characterized as a President who cared only about foreign affairs, one constantly rushing around the world concerning himself with the problems in other nations while neglecting domestic problems, especially the economy.

One would expect that Clinton's first days in office would have been devoted to what he had been telling us was our number one problem. But it didn't happen that way. His first days in office were devoted, not to the economy, but to injecting his moral values in the lives of the American public, particularly the military people.

Once inaugurated, Bill Clinton took up the presidential pen and immediately began a frontal assault on the national morality, especially in areas important to the gay and feminist agendas. With his old friend David Mixner busily filling quotas for homosexuals in the Administration, Clinton immediately issued executive orders removing remaining barriers to abortion. Eventually he ordered overseas military hospitals to perform abortions, something which had never been done before. Why would he do this?

After we were told throughout Clinton's campaign that the number one national problem was the economy, how can we explain the contradiction represented by his actions? In fact, it was over a year before he even pretended to do something about the economy, during which time he busied himself with pushing the gay/feminist agenda on all fronts. One can only conclude that the priorities reflected in his first executive acts reveal his true priorities.

He obviously didn't mean the things which he'd said during the campaign.

The Priorities of the Gay Agenda

The ultimate goal of the homosexual movement is the total acceptance of homosexual behavior as normal and healthy. Specific steps toward that goal are clearly spelled out in the demands of the Gay Rights Platform of 1972. Of seventeen demands, number one on the list is special rights for them as a protected minority under all civil rights legislation. Number two is "Issuance by the President of an executive order prohibiting the military from excluding (men or women) for reasons of their sexual orientation."[42] In the 200 year history of our nation, there has never been a President who would issue such an executive order—until the inauguration of Bill Clinton.

The Priorities of Bill Clinton

During the presidential campaign, Bill Clinton made his pro-homosexual position clear. Gays were featured at the national convention and were prominent at the November victory celebrations. During the inauguration festivities, there was a precedent-setting homosexual dance called the "The Gay Inauguration Ball," which Clinton honored by his attendance by way of a personalized message on closed circuit television.

Homosexual activist David Mixner, a long time friend of Clinton and a fellow "peace" movement radical, was an important part of Clinton's transition team. Mixner was responsible for filling a quota of jobs earmarked for homosexuals in the Clinton Administration, which he did. In January, Mixner moved with Clinton to Washington.

At least thirty "out of the closet" gays and lesbians were appointed to Clinton's staff, including Secretary of Health and Human Services, Donna Shalala, Undersecretary of Housing and Urban Development, Roberta Achtenberg, and AIDS Czarina, Kristine Gebbie.[43]

Since Clinton has taken office, he has pushed to force acceptance of homosexuals by the armed forces. Very significantly, he has done this against every precedent in American history, against the nation's first principles, against the clear positions of our Founding Fathers, against the judgment of virtually all experienced military authorities and against the will and beliefs of the vast majority of the American people.

What Could His Motivation Be?

To persist in this radical, destructive program, in the face of all reason, Clinton must have a powerful motivation. What could that motivation be?

Surely part of his motivation is his political indebtedness to the homosexual community for their support in his election. As mentioned before, David Mixner raised at least $3.5 million from gay donors for the Clinton campaign, and in Washington $3.5 million will still buy a lot of influence. But could that explain his determination to homosexualize the armed forces?

If paying a political debt were his only motivation, it wouldn't explain his passion and persistence in forcing gays and lesbians on the military. Only God knows his heart, but the possibilities for motivation here are even deeper than paying a debt. Could he be driven by a more sinister motivation than simply advancing the "gay rights" agenda? Military leaders tried to make Clinton understand that full and open inclusion of gays and lesbians in our armed forces would surely lead to their weakening and, ultimately, their destruction as effective fighting forces.

Could he possibly want that?

A DREAM OF GLOBALISM

Bill Clinton's dream, and that of those around him,

seems to be for a New World Order, a socialist world government with a world police force, a world currency and a world army, all under United Nations control. This world government would control every aspect of the lives of the people; that's what socialism meant in Hitler's Germany and in Stalin's USSR, and that's what it would mean in Bill Clinton's New World Order.

You may remember that Adolf Hitler called his national socialist government—of which "Nazi" is an abbreviation in German—"Die Neue Ordnung" (The New Order). He predicted that National Socialism would use its own revolution for the establishing of a "New World Order," which would last for 1,000 years.

It goes without saying that a dream of world government (no matter who the dreamer may be) cannot be realized without surrender of the sovereignty of all the individual nations and forfeiture of the personal freedoms of the citizens of those nations.

Even though the vast majority of Americans would never *choose* to give up national sovereignty—let alone their personal freedoms—these precious liberties are slowly and quietly being taken away from them—in such a way that it's hardly noticed.

One by one, the institutions in this nation which stand in the way of these fundamental changes in our unique American system—which include the surrender of our national sovereignty and a takeover by a New World Order—have been infiltrated and subverted.

Our system of government, which was carefully designed to serve and protect the American people, is now rapidly becoming subverted to the point of being an oppressive master of the people, placing us in increasing bondage. The traditional churches, the prestigious theological seminaries, the universities, the news media, the public school system and related educational institutions—all of which once were strongholds of American tradition, godly values, moral standards, patriotism and truth—have slowly been converted into fountainheads of revisionism, relativism, situation ethics, Marxist globalism, and socialist propaganda.

What Stands in the Way?

Only one such institution in America remains traditional and patriotic, and, as such, stands solidly in the way of our national surrender to global government: The United States Armed Forces. Incidentally, this institution is also the only one with the size, organization, will and weaponry to resist all others. If globalism and the New World Order are to succeed, the U.S. Armed Forces must be infiltrated, subverted and weakened so as to lose the ability and the will to resist. Our fighting forces would have to be weakened to the extent that the American people would accept the protection (and thus the control) of the United Nations.

Significant "change agents" for bringing this about are the inclusion of homosexuals, the placing of men and women together in the same units (already done), the assignment of women to combat roles (being pushed hard by Clinton and friends) and the weakening of standards of discipline (under way since the "demilitarization" program at the end of World War II).

David Horowitz, editor of *Heterodoxy,* is a recognized expert on subversion of American culture. He believes the purpose behind the push for allowing open homosexuals in the armed forces and the assignment of women to combat roles is to weaken the one remaining American institution that stands in the way of the collapse of America as a strong and independent nation. And he should know.

Horowitz grew up in anti-American radicalism and revolution. He was born into it: both his parents were zealous American communists, dedicated to the overthrow of the American government and culture and the creation of a global socialist "paradise." In the '60s and '70s, David became a prominent leader in the "New Left" and played a central role in the revolutionary radicalism of the day.

He said that by the '70s the radical movement had subverted all major American institutions except the armed forces, and that its plan for subverting the military was through the inclusion of open homosexuals and the assignment of women to combat roles.[44]

In combat, men must know and completely trust one another; it is for one another that warriors are willing to die, even more so than the flag.

By far the most destructive "change agent," the one with the most immediate effect on our armed forces, would be the inclusion of homosexuals.

Homosexual men desire sex with "straight hunks," especially strong virile men like those in the armed services. This homosexual "everyman's fantasy" is graphically illustrated by a 1993 Christmas card published for homosexuals. It featured a photograph of muscular, sweaty Marines running toward the camera. The lurid inscription inside the card made plain their intentions.

Imagine the disastrous effects of mutual suspicion, jealousy and lovers' quarrels in the rifle platoons; of unit commanders falling in love with subordinates; of lusting, sexual harassment and rape. *Those things would happen;* they would be inevitable, along with the proliferation of AIDS and other sexually transmitted diseases.[45] The only questions would be of time and degree.

Remember the ultimate goals of the homosexual agenda, and remember that their pattern is to move toward those goals progressively, one bite at a time. What they demand today, once surrendered to, is only the prelude to a more outrageous demand tomorrow. Once madness is embraced, it has no end point.

If I were Bill Clinton, and if my goal were to weaken the will and effectiveness of the armed forces to the point where they would not resist a national takeover by the U.N., that is the change I would push. He does push it, and I believe this is why. Speaking of that, have you noticed Clinton's inclination to place our armed forces under U.N. control?

CLINTON'S LOVE AFFAIR WITH U.N. CONTROL OF U.S. TROOPS

One consistent feature of Clinton's otherwise inconsistent military and foreign policy is his determination to place American troops under United Nations control. This, of course, is entirely consistent with his basically globalist agenda and his New World Order dream.

Such placement of our armed forces under foreign command goes completely against the nation's first principles (including the Constitution), against every precedent of American history beginning with the transcendent wisdom of George Washington's Farewell Address, and against the will of the overwhelming majority of the American people.

But these things don't seem to bother Bill Clinton. He is, after all, a product of the '60s, and his liberal/leftist education, a man remembered by a long time friend as a young man "driven by a desire to remake his country."46

Bill Clinton is a member of the Council on Foreign Relations, the Trilateral Commission and the Bildebergers, organizations hostile to national patriotism and dedicated to global government.

He is friendly with the World Federalist Association, *an organization dedicated to the creation of world government.* This association presented its 1993 Norman Cousins Global Governance Award to Strobe Talbott, Clinton's old Marxist friend and fellow "peace" activist, who is now Clinton's Ambassador at Large to the former USSR. In a letter to the World Federalist Association, Clinton wrote approvingly that "Norman Cousins worked for world peace and world government," and wished the association "future success."47

The First Time in American History: A Globalism Milestone

In October 1993, during Clinton's disastrous, bungling intervention in Somalia which cost the lives and limbs of so many of our very best fighting men, he did something terribly significant, something which had never before been done. (This incident went virtually unreported and is, therefore, largely unknown to the American people.)

For the very first time in history, American troops were put under direct command of a foreign general in combat. Under U.N. auspices, Bill Clinton, as Commander in Chief, gladly relinquished control of American combat units and placed them directly under the command of Turkish General Bir. Politically speaking, it was a highly significant relinquishment of American sovereignty.

On a level closer to home, it placed the lives of our fighting men in the hands of a commander who neither understood them and their capabilities, nor cared for their welfare as would one of their own. Apparently, both of these circumstances are not only acceptable to Clinton as Commander in Chief, but desirable.

Colonel Charlie Beckwith, known both for his expertise in special military operations and his candor, laid the blame for our disaster in Somalia on two things: unwise political decisions by incompetent civilians, and placement of our troops under U.N. control. Writing for *The Wall Street Journal,* he said that what happened in Somalia was "just another case of U.S. troops [operating] under U.N. command, and suffering for it."[48]

The danger to U.S. troops in being under U.N. command, or fighting alongside U.N. "allies," was vividly illustrated in the Mogadishu tragedy of October 3, 1993. The Rangers' reaction force, urgently needing to break through and rescue its surviving members, had no armored vehicles.

Their Malaysian U.N. "allies" had the needed armored personnel carrier, but were not willing to help. With the delay causing more to die, a Ranger officer put his pistol to the head of a Malaysian leader and forced him to go with them to the rescue.49 No explanation needed here.

More Behind-Their-Backs Sellout of American Servicemen and Our National Sovereignty: PDD 13 and PDD 25

Something else you may not know, which affects you and your loved ones in uniform—a project dear to Bill Clinton's heart—is the secret program to legitimize and normalize the control of the American armed forces by the United Nations.

This is something profoundly important to the welfare of our armed forces and to our nation's continued independence and freedom, yet it has never been mentioned in network news. In the briefest possible form, let me explain what I mean.

Presidential Decision Directives carry the authority of law without being enacted or approved by Congress. In this case the result would be to give the President authority to place any and all U.S. Armed Forces under U.N. command. In August 1993, this concept was formalized as PDD-13, but it was apparently consigned to the "pending" basket by the disaster in Somalia in October of that year.

However, the interruption was only temporary; this globalist dream of Clinton's has been resurrected as PDD-25, and has rolled through the bureaucratic policy mill on the fast track. Clinton signed it on May 3, 1994.

According to Congressman Jim Lightfoot of Iowa, General Colin Powell had inserted language in PDD-25 to protect U.S. troops to some extent by limiting the authority of U.N. commanders.50 Powell's exceptions were: (1) when orders were outside the scope of the mission; (2) when orders would be illegal under U.S. law; (3) when orders were militarily imprudent or unsound.

Now, with Powell in retirement, and a new Chairman of the Joint Chiefs, General John Shalikashvili, who apparently has no such objections to foreign control, the

Administration has subsequently removed Powell's safeguards. PDD-25 will now surrender command of our armed forces to any U.N. commander, who can then send them to do anything, wise or unwise; U.S. law will be meaningless and impotent.

Incidentally, you, the American taxpayer, will foot the bill for this surrender of our national sovereignty and the placing of your sons and daughters under foreign commanders. Under PDD-25, money appropriated for operation of the American Department of Defense will be simply and quietly sent over to the U.N. to pay for all of this.

Your Commander in Chief, Bill Clinton, not only agrees to this, but demands it!

As soon as PDD-25 was completed, Bill Clinton classified it. That means, without the proper security clearance no one is allowed to see the contents of this disastrous directive, not even members of the U.S. Congress. Clinton has published a fifteen-page unclassified summary, but even that is very hard to come by. So forget about seeing the real thing.

It is interesting to note that the person who holds the office of the President is not required to pass a security investigation, yet is able to design secret directives that can only be read by people with high level security clearances.

This brings us to yet another distressing subject . . .

A COMMANDER IN CHIEF WHO IS A SECURITY RISK

Bill Clinton has been sympathetic with communism most of his adult life. Many of his closest friends have been associated with the pro-communist left, and he himself has been involved with pro-communist and communist-related organizations. Group 68, with which he was associated in London, was sponsored by the British Peace Council, which was sponsored by the Soviet Peace Council in Moscow.

As mentioned previously, Clinton disappeared behind

the Iron Curtain during the Vietnam War when our enemy was being supplied and controlled by the Soviets.

You may find this hard to believe, but in 1987, Governor Bill Clinton traveled to Italy to study communism. At Legga (Province of Florence), he studied the communist cooperative there. He also became acquainted with a number of communist leaders in the Florence area. He so admired what he saw there that he said he returned to Arkansas and "put together about seventy youth cooperatives." In an interview with Italian journalist, Antonio Socci, of "Il Sabato," Clinton said that the *communist model is his economic prescription for the United States.*51

The IPS Connection

Bill Clinton has also had a long-time involvement with IPS (the Institute for Policy Studies), a Marxist think tank in Washington identified by the FBI as a dangerous communist front.52 The IPS is intent on creating a Marxist society in America by "reshaping public sector institutions in ways that give political power to the leftist movement thus far denied by the electoral process."53 IPS was founded in 1963 with funding from the Samuel Rubin Foundation. (Soviet Samuel Rubin, a friend of Lenin's, was an original member of the elite Comintern—the Soviet leaders' council.)

The FBI has an extensive file on IPS, documenting it as being anti-United States, pro-communist, violent and dangerous. The FBI warned that it posed a threat of infiltrating revolutionaries into government agencies. The file links IPS programs and personnel to kidnappings, murders, espionage and terrorist bombings.54

Bill Clinton has appointed at least a dozen IPS activists to high government posts, including his chief economic advisor, Derek Shearer. Shearer, who has long proposed that America's free enterprise system be dismantled and replaced with socialism, is perhaps Clinton's closest friend.55 Shearer has written approvingly that communism "humanizes" societies: "Marxist economic and social philosophy . . . was and is an attempt to humanize economic and social life."[55] (Note: Shearer's sister, Brooke, is Hillary's traveling companion.)

Top Clinton officials with close and long-term ties to Derek Shearer and IPS include Les Aspin, Leon Panetta, Timothy Wirth, Morton Halperin, Edward Feighan, Clinton's old friend and fellow pro-communist activist, Strobe Talbott (Derek Shearer's brother-in-law), and homosexual activist David Mixner.

If he were not the President, Bill Clinton couldn't qualify for the lowest level security clearance; yet, as President, he has access to, and control of, *every secret our nation possesses.*

Security Problems at the White House

Loose security standards at the White House are notorious. Even the Clinton-friendly major news media have raised their eyebrows at it. According to *The Wall Street Journal*, after more than a year of the Clinton Administration, White House spokesmen admitted that there were still more than 100 staffers who had not yet been cleared for security passes; yet they functioned as freely as if they had been.

Among those still not cleared after nearly two years were: Chief of Staff Mac McLarty, Press Secretary Dee Dee Myers, and key staffers Patsy Thomason, Paul Begala, James Carville and Mandy Grunwald. Many of them had simply not filled out the questionnaire necessary for the FBI to conduct a background investigation, reportedly because they knew they couldn't pass it (because of drug convictions, drug addiction, alcoholism and tax problems).

The routine was to continue to issue temporary passes—which require no investigation—and renewing them indefinitely with no questions asked. Congressman Frank Wolf, attempting to learn how many staffers were still operating with temporary passes, reported getting "zero cooperation." He also said that many visiting "friends of Bill," who don't even work for the government, get temporary passes with no investigation, giving them free access.57

Some Interesting Choices

The records of some of Clinton's other friends and associates he has chosen for high office are revealing.

Until he failed to be reelected in 1992, Stephen Solarz was a powerful congressman. Before the voters rejected him, Solarz was the leading enemy of open investigation of the POWs abandoned after the Vietnam War, and was nasty and hostile to POW family members. Solarz has very close IPS ties. After considering Solarz for Secretary of State and Ambassador to the U.N., Clinton appointed him Ambassador to India; but he had to withdraw the nomination because Solarz flunked the FBI security investigation.58

Clinton wanted to appoint Congresswoman Patsy Schroeder *as Secretary of Defense*, but she turned him down.59 Schroeder, like Solarz, has very strong IPS ties. And, like Solarz, Schroeder's responses were rude, even hostile to the sincere questions of the POW families.

Clinton's old friend and fellow pro-communist radical from the '60s, Sam Brown, was appointed Ambassador to the Conference on Security and Cooperation in Europe (CSCE). This permanent organization oversees non-nuclear treaties in Europe and settles disputes within the former Soviet Union. Because of his communist background and alleged conversion of funds and workers from VISTA (a federal program) to a Clinton political campaign, he was not confirmed by the Senate. That didn't stop Clinton or Brown; Clinton sent him to Vienna anyway—*without confirmation.*

Clinton appointed Jane Fonda as his Ambassador (without credentials) to the left-dominated World Conference on Population Control in Cairo. Perhaps Fonda's most outrageous statement during the Vietnam

War was to an audience at Michigan State University: "I would think that if you understood what communism was, you would hope, you would pray on your knees that we would become communist."[60] Jane Fonda's pro-communist history is well established.

The Company Clinton Keeps

The company one keeps is always significant. So are one's actions. If I act like a duck, talk like a duck, look like a duck, and consistently choose ducks as my closest friends and associates, one may fairly conclude that there is a high probability that I am a duck. Bill Clinton is far too smart to state his agenda plainly. But can there be much doubt about where his heart is?

Unthinkable Indeed . . .

How could this be? How could we have a Commander in Chief of the U.S. Armed Forces who holds the military in contempt, who is anti-patriotic, who long ago embraced the dream of world socialism, and who, if he were not President, could not receive a security clearance?

It is, indeed, unthinkable. But it is apparently true.

CONCLUSION

Our integrity as a nation is based on absolutes—principles established by our Creator and recognized by our Founding Fathers in the Declaration of Independence. America has gradually been departing from these principles to the point where we now have a man in the Office of the President of the United States who is the epitome of immorality and dishonesty. Even more unsettling than this is the reality that many Americans don't seem to care.

Ironically, in our nation "of the people, by the people and for the people," we have been so preoccupied with enjoying "for the people" that we've neglected the very important "*of* the people" and "*by* the people" aspects. If we, the people, relinquish our responsibilities, the government will gladly take up the slack, growing in the process by feeding on the freedoms of the unsuspecting populace. The quality of government we experience is relative to the amount of effort we put into "taming" it. We get the kind of government we deserve; we have only ourselves to blame if it's not what we want.

We can and we must become involved. Every American citizen has a responsibility to see that the laws and principles on which this nation was founded are upheld. Part of that responsibility is to recognize, expose and remove corruption at every level of government, ranging from local school boards and city seats all the way up to the executive branch of the federal government. In addition, we need to elect and support representatives who embrace honesty, integrity and the intent of the U.S. Constitution.

However, the expectations of our leaders cannot exceed the expectations we have for our own lives. We will

239

not be able to find honorable people to represent us in government unless we first demand morality and integrity in ourselves and in our families, where character is first developed. This country will only change as its people change.

The United States may be in a state of moral neglect and disrepair, but with hard work and dedication to time-honored principles, the beauty and integrity of this nation can be restored.

Citizens for Honest Government was founded by ordinary citizens who are fed up with the direction our national leaders are taking us. As Citizens grows, we plan to establish chapters in every state to function as "watch-dogs," promoting honesty and exposing dishonesty in government and serving as a conduit to worthy citizens groups throughout the nation.

People are imperfect—that is why we as a nation must never give up our sovereignty, nor allow ourselves to be controlled by an elite group that can, and will, undermine the U.S. Constitution. Concentration of power breeds corruption; it's been happening in our beloved country and we want it to stop.

Let's act *now*, while we're still able.

ENDNOTES, CHAPTER 9

1. "Clinton's Warrior Woes," *U.S. News & World Report*, March 15, 1993, p. 23; *Sunday Telegraph* of London, April 1, 1993; *The Buffalo News*, April 14, 1993, p. 3
2. John McCaslin, "Inside the Beltway," *The Washington Times*, June 24, 27, 28 and July 1, 1994
3. *AP Bulletin*, May 26, 1994; *Washington Post*, May 27, 1994
4. *Washington Enquirer*, February 14, 1992
5. *Raleigh News & Observer*, September 8, 1992
6. *Raleigh News & Observer*, September 2, 1992
7. July 1969 Fulbright Memo with phone numbers of Clinton and Col. Holmes: "Must have first year ROTC def. (deferment), Holmes to call me Wed., 16th." *New York Post*, March 6, 1992; Accuracy in Media Report, June 1992
8. Letter from Fulbright aide, Lee Williams to Col. Eugene Holmes, thanking him for making room for Clinton in his "already filled" ROTC unit, *L.A. Times* story reported by *Raleigh News & Observer*, September 26, 1992. Clinton signed a letter of intent, a written contract to complete the ROTC program and accept an Army commission. On August 7, 1969, Clinton received an ROTC deferment from his draft board and was reclassified 1-D (deferment status undraftable)
9. *Insight*, November 9, 1992, pp. 20, 21
10. Bill Clinton letter to Col. Eugene Holmes, December 3, 1969; Michael Kelly, *The New York Times Service*, reported in *Raleigh News & Observer*, October 9, 1992
11. Meredith Oakley: "On the Make (The Rise of Bill Clinton)," Regnery Pub., Inc., Washington, D.C., 1994, pp. 65, 66, 80; Father Richard McSorley: "Peace Eyes," Center for Peace Studies, Washington, D.C., 1978, p. 22
12. *Human Events*, October 24, 1992
13. *Ibid*
14. *The Washington Times*, July 5, 1994, p. A4
15. Nancy Zaroulis & Gerald Sullivan: *Who Spoke Up?* Holt, Rinehart & Winston, New York, 1984, p. 275
16. *Human Events*, October 24, 1992, *op. cit.*; *Insight*, November 9, 1992, p. 20
17. *Raleigh News & Observer*, October 8, 1992; *Human Events*, October 24, 1992
18. *Raleigh News & Observer*, October 8, 1992, Father Richard McSorley, "Peace Eyes,", p. 23, *op. cit.*
19. *Raleigh News & Observer*, October 9, 1992
20. *Insight*, November 9, 1992, p. 20; Father Richard McSorley: "Peace Eyes," *op. cit.*, Foreword, p. 59
21. *Insight*, November 9, 1992, p. 20
22. *Reuters*, *The Washington Times*, "92 Election Czech-up," July 22, 1994
23. Robert Davis, *USA Today*, October 28, 1992
24. *USA Today*, October 28, 1992
25. Zaroulis and Sullivan: *Who Spoke Up?*, p. 275, Holt, Rinehart & Winston, New York, 1984
26. U.S. Senate Committee on Foreign Relations (Rep. Staff): "An Examination of U.S. Policy Toward POW/MIAs," May 23, 1991; Testimony of Roger Shields and Henry Kissinger before the Senate Select Committee on POW/MIA Affairs, *Report of the Select Committee on POW/MIA Affairs*, January 13, 1993, pp. 95-103, 120; Evans and Novak, *Washington Post*, September 16, 1992, p. A19;

September 23, 1992, p. A21

27. James N. Rowe: *Five Years to Freedom*, Ballantine Books Division, Random House, Inc., New York, 1984 pp. 404-406

28. Clinton policy statement on normalizing relations with Vietnam, April 27, 1992; and Clinton letter of October 13, 1992, written to Chris Maile

29. UPI/Reuters, *Washington Times*, February 4, 1994

30. *Raleigh News & Observer*, November 1, 1993

31. *The Wall Street Journal*, November 1, 1993

32. *Ibid*

33. *The Washington Times*, May 13, 1994

34. Phone interview with Captain James H. Smith, September 20, 1994

35. "Dead Hero's Father Tears into Clinton," *Sunday Times of London*, May 29, 1994

36. Telephone interview with Captain James H. Smith, September 20, 1994, *op.cit.*

37. *Newsweek*, April 11, 1994, p. 12

38. Personal interview with J.B. McKenney, M.D., missionary to Haiti, October 5, 1994

39. *The New York Times*, September 2, 1994, p. A24

40. *Paul Harvey News*, July 8, 1994

41. *The Washington Times*, May 11, 1994

42. Enrique Rueda: "The Homosexual Network," Devin Adair Co, Old Greenwich, Connecticut, 1982, pp. 197-203

43. "Clinton Lauded by Openly Homosexual Appointees," *The Washington Times*, November 3, 1993, p. 3

44. David Horowitz: "The Feminist Assault on the Military," Center for the Study of Popular Culture, Los Angeles, p. 29

45. Retired Marine Col. Ronald D. Ray: "Military Necessity and Homosexuality," First Principles, Inc., Louisville, Kentucky, 1993, pp. 55-68

46. *Raleigh News & Observer*, October 9, 1992

47. Letter from President Bill Clinton to the World Federalist Association (on White House stationery), dated June 27, 1993

48. *The Wall Street Journal*, November 1, 1993

49. Testimony of battle survivors, related in phone interview with Captain James H. Smith, September 24, 1994

50. *The Liberty Standard*, Louisville, Kentucky, July 94, p. 1

51. William F. Jasper: "Whom Have We Elected?", *The New American*, February 22, 1993, p. 24

52. FBI File 100-447935, Vol. 6, Atlanta Field Office Report, May 31, 1973, pp. 3-6

53. Dr. Steven Powell, *Covert Cadre: Inside the Institute for Policy Studies*, Green Hill Pub., Ottawa, Illinois, 1987, p. 15

54. FBI File #100-447935, *op. cit.*

55. *The Wall Street Journal*, September 11, 1992

56. Derek Shearer and Martin Carnoy, *Economic Democracy: The Challenge of the 1980s*, M.E. Sharp Co., White Plains, New York, 1980

57. *The Wall Street Journal*, March 16, 23, 24, 1994; *Human Events*, June 16, 1994

58. Dr. Charles A. Provan, *American Freedom Movement Newsletter*, December 1993, p.4

59. Reuters News Service Dispatch, November 5, 1992

60. *Detroit Free Press*, November 1970; quoted in *The Summit Journal*, Manitou Springs, Colorado, September 1985, p. 6

APPENDIX A

LUTHER GERALD "JERRY" PARKS

Died September 26, 1993

Murdered Private Investigator from Chapter 4,
"Hit and Run Execution"

JOHN BROWN

Arkansas policeman investigating Henry-Ives murder case
as outlined in Chapter 5,
"Murder—The Boys on the Tracks"

LETTERS FROM CHAPTER 9

University College
Oxford, England

December 3, 1969

Dear Colonel Holmes:

I am sorry to be so long in writing. I know I promised to let you hear from me at least once a month and from now on you will. But I have had to have some time to think about this first letter. Almost daily since my return to England I have thought about writing, about what I want to and ought to say. First, I want to thank you, not just for saving me from the draft, but for being so kind and decent to me last summer, when I was as low as I have ever been. One thing which made the bond we struck in good faith somewhat palatable to me was my high (kind?) regard for you personally. In retrospect, it seems that the admiration might not have been mutual had you known a little more about me, about my political beliefs and activities. At least you might have thought me more fit for the draft than for ROTC.

Let me try to explain. As you know, I worked for two years in a very minor position on the Senate Foreign Relations Committee. I did it for the experience and the salary but also for the opportunity, however small, of working every day against a war which I opposed and despised with a depth of feeling I had reserved solely for racism in America before Vietnam. I did not take the matter lightly but studied it carefully, and there was a time when not many people had more information about Vietnam at hand than I did.

I have written and spoken and marched against the war. One of the national organizers of the Vietnam Moratorium is a close friend of mine. After I left Arkansas last summer, I went to Washington to work in the national headquarters of the moratorium, then to England to organize the Americans here for demonstrations Oct. 15 and Nov. 16. Interlocked with the war is the draft issue which I did not begin to consider separately until 1968. For a law seminar in Georgetown I wrote a paper on the legal arguments for and against allowing, within the selective service system, the classification of selective conscientious objection for those opposed to participation in a particular war. Not simply to participation in war in any form. From my work I came to believe that the draft system itself is illegitimate. No government really rooted in limited, parliamentary democracy should have the power to make its citizens fight and kill and die in a war they may oppose, a war which even possibly may be wrong, a war which, in any case, does not involve immediately the peace and freedom of the nation. The draft was justified in World War II because the life of the people collectively was at stake. Individuals had to fight, if the nation was to survive, for the lives of their countrymen and their way of life. Vietnam is no such case. Nor was Korea an example where, in my opinion, certain military action was justified but the draft was not, for the reasons stated above.

Because of my opposition to the draft and the war, **I am in great sympathy with those who are not willing to fight, kill, and maybe die for their country** (i.e. the particular policy of a particular government) right or wrong. Two of my friends at Oxford are conscientious objectors. I wrote a letter of recommendation for one of them to his Mississippi draft board. A letter which I am more proud of than anything else I wrote at Oxford last year. One of my roommates is a draft resister who is possibly under indictment and may never be able to go home again. He is one of the bravest, best men I know. His country needs men like him more than they know. That he is considered a criminal is an obscenity.

The decision not to be a resister and the related subsequent decisions were the most difficult of my life. I decided to accept the draft in spite of my beliefs for one reason: to maintain my political viability within the system. For years I have worked to prepare myself for a political life characterized by both practical political ability and concern for rapid social progress. It is a life I still feel compelled to lead. I do not think our system of government is by definition corrupt, however dangerous and inadequate it has been in recent years. The society may be corrupt but that is not the same thing. And if that is true we are all finished anyway. When the draft came, despite political convictions, I was having a hard time facing the prospects of fighting a war I had been fighting against and that is why I contacted you. ROTC was the one way left in which I could possibly though not positively avoid both Vietnam and resistance. Going on with my education even coming back to England played no part in my decision to join ROTC. I am back here and would have been at Arkansas Law School because there is nothing else I can do.

In fact I would like to have been able to take a year out perhaps to teach in a small college or work on some community action project. And in the process to decide whether to attend law school or graduate school and how to begin putting what I have learned to use. But the particulars of my personal life are not nearly as important to me as the principles involved.

After I signed the ROTC letter of intent I began to wonder whether the compromise I had made with myself was not more objectionable than the draft would have been, because I had no interest in the ROTC program in itself and all I seemed to have done was to protect myself from physical harm. Also, I began to think I had deceived you, not by lies--there were none--but by failing to tell you all the things I'm writing now. I doubt I had the mental coherence to articulate them then.

At that time, after we had made our agreement and you had sent my 1-D deferment to my draft board, the anguish and loss of my self-regard and self-confidence really set in. I hardly slept for weeks and kept going by eating compulsively and reading until exhaustion brought sleep. Finally, on Sept. 12, I stayed up all night writing a letter to the chairman of my draft board, saying basically what is in the preceding paragraph, thanking him for trying to help in a case where he really couldn't, and stating that I couldn't do the ROTC after all and would he please draft me as soon as possible.

I never mailed the letter, but I did carry it on me every day until I got on the plane to return to England. I didn't mail the letter because I didn't see, in the end, how my going in the army and maybe going to Vietnam would achieve anything except a feeling that I had punished myself and gotten what I deserved.

So I came back to England to try to make something of this second year of my Rhodes scholarship. And that is where I am now, writing to you because you have been good to me and have a right to know what I think and feel. I am writing too in the hope that my telling this one story will help you to understand more clearly how so many fine people have come to find themselves still loving their country but **loathing the military** to which you and other good men have devoted years, lifetimes of the best service you could give. To many of us it is no longer clear what is service and what is disservice, or if it is clear the conclusion is likely to be illegal. Forgive the length of this letter but there was much to say. There is a lot to be said but it can wait. Please say hello to Colonel Jones for me. Merry Christmas.

Sincerely, Bill Clinton

THE WHITE HOUSE

WASHINGTON

October 7, 1993

Mr. and Mrs. James H. Smith
10 Mallard Lane
Long Valley, New Jersey 07853

Dear Mr. and Mrs. Smith:

Hillary and I were very sorry to learn of the loss
of your son. Specialist James E. Smith's death
is a great loss for our nation, as well as for us
personally, and our hearts go out to you in your
sorrow.

Our efforts in Somalia have helped bring security
and stability where anarchy, famine, and suffering
once prevailed. You should know that your son and
his fellow service men and women have preserved the
lives of hundreds of thousands of Somalis. Your
son's courage, and his commitment to the ideals on
which America was founded, will long be remembered
with pride by his fellow citizens.

Our thoughts and prayers are with you.

Sincerely,

Bill Clinton

                    10 MALLARD LANE
               LONG VALLEY, N.J., 07853

                         President William Clinton
                         The White House
                         1600 Pennsylvania Avenue
                         Washington, D.C., 20500

                         October 25, 1993

President Clinton:

As a warrior who was disabled in the Vietnam War and as a
father of a warrior killed in action in Somalia, I cannot
accept your letter of condolence for the death of my son
Ranger Corporal James E. Smith. To accept your letter would
be contrary to all the beliefs I, my son and the Rangers hold
so dear, including: loyalty, courage and tenacity.

During the battle for Anzio, in World War II, an inept
indecisive field commander sent the Rangers into battle where
they were slaughtered. Fifty years later the Rangers again
were ordered into battle, where they were surrounded and
outgunned. But this time it was not the fault of the field
commanders. No - this time it was the fault of the Commander
in Chief, the President of the United States. Your failure
to provide the requested combat support reveals a lack of
loyalty to the troops under your command and an extreme
shortage of moral courage.

I had the honor to meet the Rangers who fought along side my
son and were with Jamie when he died. I heard of magnificent
acts of courage and sacrifice. I had Rangers, with tears in
their eyes, apologize for letting my son die or their failure
to break through and rescue the trapped Rangers. The failure
is not theirs, it is yours. Trucks and Humvees cannot
replace the requested tanks, armored personnel carriers and
Spectre gunships.

As a combat veteran I know that there are no certainties on
the battlefield; however, as an Infantry Officer I will
always speculate that significantly less casualties would
have resulted if you, as Commander in Chief, provided the
Rangers with the requested combat support - equipment with
which Rangers routinely train and for which approval should
have been automatic. The Rangers were pinned down for twelve
hours - long hours when the Rangers were fighting for their
lives and a Delta Force medic fought to save my son. Jamie
bled to death because the requested armor support was not
there to break through to the Rangers.

Rangers pride themselves on the Ranger Creed. "Driving on to the Ranger objective", or "Surrender is not a Ranger word" are not hollow phrases to the men of the black beret. These soldiers understand the word tenacious and wanted to complete their mission. As Ranger after Ranger told me, they were hitting Aidid's forces and command structure hard. But, the United Nations was actually impeding Ranger missions by offering sanctuary to Aidid's supporters. Your willingness to allow this dangerous situation demonstrates a lack of resolve in supporting the men you sent into battle.

My son is no longer here to "Lead The Way"; however, I am. Until you as President and Commander in Chief are either willing or able to formulate a clear foreign policy, establish specific objectives and, most important, support the men and women in uniform, I will "Lead The Way" in insuring that you no longer send America's finest to a needless death. When you are capable of meeting these criteria, then I will accept your letter of condolence.

Sincerely,

James H. Smith
Captain/Infantry (Retired)

RANGER CORPORAL JAMIE SMITH

February 16, 1972 - October 3, 1993

Jamie, from Long Valley, NJ, died courageously in the attempt to rescue a surrounded helicopter crew in Mogadishu, Somalia. This fine young man's death was unnecessary.

APPENDIX B

The lights come up.

The audience silently remains seated, stunned by what they've just seen. They feel anger, frustration, sadness, denial. They can only shake their heads.

It's June 1994; one of the first public screenings of *The Clinton Chronicles* video.

Today, this scene is being repeated daily all over the country, in towns across America. From groups of two or three huddled around TV's and VCR's, to thousands jammed into auditoriums. People are slowly beginning to learn the truth about our government, about the mainstream media, about Bill Clinton.

Indeed, the video's shocking impact is the result of seeing all of the criminal allegations pertaining to Bill Clinton in one sitting. For many, it is the first time the pieces in this hideous puzzle have fallen together.

1994 To date, every attempt to get this evidence presented in court has been systematically blocked through political and legal manuevering by Clinton appointees. In fact, it was the inability to get the information heard which prompted the individuals who appear in *The Clinton Chronicles* to step forward. All have expressed a willingness to repeat their testimony, under oath in a court of law or at Congressional hearings. Their hope is that justice can be served. Their prayer is that this nation can still be saved.

Reports from the FBI, DEA, and the Arkansas State Police, along with published sources are cited in this chapter to corroborate and further document the allegations presented by the eyewitnesses in the video. The corroborating sources are not limited to those listed here.

The following individuals' testimonies appear in the video, *The Clinton Chronicles*. Their interviews are on file with Citizens For Honest Government, P.O. Box 220, Winchester, CA 92596. The date of their interviews are in parentheses.

Judge Jim Johnson: Former Arkansas State Senator and State Supreme Court Justice (Feb. 3, 1994).
Nora Waye: Former Business Partner of Bill Clinton's Stepfather (Feb. 13, 1994).
Larry Nichols: Former Director of Marketing for the Arkansas Development Finance Authority (Feb. 4, Feb. 10, Mar. 13, Apr.1, & Apr.17, 1994).
Doc DeLaughter: Former Arkansas State Police Investigator in Charge of Dan Lasater Investigation (Apr. 21, 1994).
Bill Duncan: Former Internal Revenue Service Treasury Agent in Charge of Mena Investigation (Apr. 30, 1994).
Russell Welch: Former Arkansas State Police Investigator in Charge of Mena Investigation (Apr. 12, 1994).
Winston Bryant: Arkansas State Attorney General (Apr. 16, 1994).
Linda Ives: Mother of Kevin Ives (Feb. 4, 1994).
Charles Black: Polk County Deputy Prosecutor (Apr. 12, 1994).
Gary Johnson: Former Attorney for Larry Nichols (Feb. 13, 1994)
Paula Jones: Former Employee with the Arkansas Industrial Development Commission (Apr. 9, 1994).
Steve Jones: Husband of Paula Jones (Apr. 9, 1994).
Gary Parks: Son of Murder Victim Jerry Parks (Mar. 12 & Apr. 19, 1994).
Tom McKenney: Lt. Col., USMC, Retired (Apr. 18, 1994).
William Dannemeyer: Former U.S. Congressman (Mar. 4, 1994).

ARKANSAS DEVELOPMENT FINANCE AUTHORITY (ADFA)

- Bill Clinton creates ADFA; lies to the public about it's true purpose.
- ADFA is structured with no oversight protection, Clinton retains total control.
- Clinton signs/approves all ADFA loans personally.
- ADFA hands out taxpayer guarenteed loans to Clinton's friends.
- Clinton receives campaign contributions from ADFA loan recipients.
- Hillary's Law Firm receives payments for structuring ADFA bonds.
- ADFA finances Clinton's sexual liaisons.
- ADFA launders drug money through the Bank of Credit & Commerce International (BCCI was long known by financial experts and law enforcement agencies as a haven for drug money launderers and was affectionately dubbed The Bank of Crooks and Criminals International. BCCI collapsed in the early 1990's, which cost depositors and taxpayers tens of billions of dollars, making it the worst banking scandal in world history).

- Arkansas Development Finance Authority Act 1062, Chapter 5, May 1, 1985, pp. 110-133
- Arkansas Development Finance Authority, 1987-1988 Fiscal Year Annual Report, pp. 1-52
- James Ward, "The Villain and the Victim: More Trading Scandals Occur in Arkansas Bond Market", *Arkansas Business*, Sept. 26, 1988, pp. 10-11, 16-19
- Constance Mitchell, "Fast Talking Brokers In Little Rock Target Small-City Treasuries", *The Wall Street Journal*, Apr. 12, 1989, pp. 1, 3C
- Wythe Walker Jr., "Little Rock Firms Concerned over Bond Daddies Image", *Arkansas Democrat-Gazette*, Apr. 13, 1989, p. 5A
- Joe Nabbefeld, "Alleged Bribe Spurs Clinton to Delay Beverly Bond Deal", *Arkansas Democrat-Gazette*, Oct. 12, 1989, pp. 1D, 8D
- Hal Brown, "Clinton, Basset Named in Brother's Suit", *Arkansas Democrat-Gazette*, Oct. 19, 1989, p. 3D
- John Starr, "ADFA Board Ready to Reject Proposed Bond Boondoggle", *Arkansas Democrat-Gazette*, Oct. 19, 1989
- Dave Wannemaker, "Stephens Defends Role in Bond Deal", *Arkansas Democrat-Gazette*, Oct. 19, 1989, pp. 1B, 2B
- Joe Nabbefeld, "Forbes Cites Abuse of Tax-Exempt Funds",

Arkansas Democrat-Gazette, Dec. 1, 1989, pp. 1D, 3D
- John Starr, "Hoofman in Fantasyland Where ADFA Done Good", *Arkansas Democrat-Gazette*, Dec. 28, 1989, p. 11B
- Circuit Court of Pulaski County, Arkansas, 7th Division, Larry Nichols v. Wooten Epes, Bill Clinton, Arkansas Development Finance Authority, Sept. 12, 1990, case #90-4258
- U.S. District Court, Eastern District of Arkansas, Larry Nichols v. Bill Clinton, Wooten Epes, Arkansas Development Finance Authority, Oct. 25, 1990, Case #LR-C-90-746.
- Paul Barton, "Little Rock on BCCI Route to Power", *Arkansas Democrat-Gazette*, Aug. 14, 1991
- Hal Brown, "Report Links Stephens, BCCI", *Arkansas Democrat-Gazette*, Dec. 7, 1991
- Ambrose Evans-Pritchard, "Little Rock's Mean Machine", *Sunday Telegraph*, Mar. 13, 1994, p. 26
- L.J. Davis, "The Name of Rose", *New Republic*, Apr. 4, 1994, pp. 14-23
- Joe Stumpe, "ADFA's Return to Lending Fraught with Controversy", *Arkansas Democrat-Gazette*, Apr. 18, 1994, pp. 1B, 3B
- Micah Morrison, "Another Arkansas Tale", *The Wall Street Journal*, May 2, 1994
- Rob Wells, "Top BCCI Executive Accepts Plea Deal", *The Washington Times*, July 9, 1994

THE MENA AIRPORT DRUG SMUGGLING OPERATION

- $100 million in cocaine is being smuggled into Mena each month.
- Park-O-Meter, Webb Hubbell and Seth Ward's company is linked to Mena.
- Money from Mena is laundered through ADFA along with other local, state and national banks.
- Cocaine is dropped from Mena's planes.
- Massive investigations are suddenly shut down.
- Numerous prosecutions are scheduled to occur, but don't.

- Editors, "When Uncle Sam Deals Dope", *Vanguard Press*, Apr. 7, 1988, pp. 1-4
- Letter from Arkansas Congressman Bill Alexander to Governor Bill Clinton, Re: Mena Drug Smuggling Operation, Jan. 26, 1989, on file, CFHG
- Editors, "The Drugging of America", *Freedom*, May/Jun. 1989 (Part 1) and Jul./Aug. 1989 (Part 2)
- Maria Hensen, "Attorney General to Check into Mena Drug Case

Progress, Alexander Says", *Arkansas Democrat-Gazette*, Sept. 14, 1989
- Rodney Bowers, "Tale Brings Iran Contra to Arkansas", *Arkansas Democrat-Gazette*, Oct. 21, 1990
- Joint Investigation by the Arkansas State Attorney General's Office and the U.S. Congress, "Oral Depositions of Richard J. Brenneke, William C. Duncan, and Russell F. Welch", June 21, 1991 (There are also tens of thousands of documents from the Mena investigations of Welch, Duncan, and Charles Black, proving political corruption at the highest levels of government)
- Rusty Turner, "Brenneke Tells of CIA Connections to Mena", *Springdale Morning News*, June 25, 1991
- Rusty Turner, "Bryant to Ask Walsh to Investigate Mena Airport", *Springdale Morning News*, July 11, 1991
- Scott Morris, "Clinton: State Did All It Could in Mena Case", *Arkansas Democrat-Gazette*, Sept. 11, 1991, pp. 1B, 7B
- Associated Press, "Feds Interested in Mena Link", *Northwest Arkansas Times*, Sept. 26, 1991
- Alexander Cockburn, "More Shoes Are Dropping on Clinton, Scandal May Overturn Bandwagon", *Los Angeles Times*, Mar. 23, 1992, p. B5
- Frank Snapp, "Clinton and the Smugglers' Airport", *Village Voice*, Apr. 14, 1992, pp. 15-18
- Editors, "Bill Clinton's Narcotics-Contra Links Raise Question", *Executive Intelligence Review*, Apr. 13, 1992
- Terry Lemons and Jane Fullerton, "Perot Called Clinton About Mena Inquiry", *Arkansas Democrat-Gazette*, Apr. 19, 1992, pp. 1A, 16A
- Alexander Cockburn, "Beat the Devil", *The Nation*, May 4, 1992, p. 582
- Ambrose Evans-Pritchard, "Shadow of Iran-Contra Affair Falls on Clinton", *Sunday Telegraph*, Mar. 27, 1994, p. 22
- L.J. Davis, "The Name of the Rose", *New Republic*, Apr. 4, 1994, pp. 14-23
- Edward Epstein, "On the Mena Trail", *The Wall Street Journal*, Apr. 20, 1994
- Ambrose Evans-Pritchard, "Lawsuit Timebomb Ticks Under Clinton", *Sunday Telegraph*, May 29, 1994, p. 31
- Micah Morrison, "Mysterious Mena", *The Wall Street Journal*, Jun. 29, 1994
- Ambrose Evans-Pritchard, "Smugglers Linked to Contra Arms Deals," The *Sunday Telegraph* of London, Oct. 9, 1994, p. 3.

BILL CLINTON AND DAN LASATER

- Dan Lasater is hired by Clinton to handle ADFA's bonds.
- Lasater uses cocaine to seduce underage girls.
- Lasater uses cocaine to influence business transactions.
- Lasater is best friends with the Clintons.
- Lasater pays off Roger Clinton's drug debts.
- Lasater is arrested and convicted of cocaine distribution along with Roger Clinton.
- Lasater is pardoned by Governor Clinton.
- Lasater becomes financially linked to the Governor's office, to the Arkansas State Police, and to the Rose Law Firm.
- Lasater is linked to child pornography investigation.

- Drug Enforcement Administration, Narcotics Investigation Report, Mar. 12, 1984, File GJ-83-Z001
- Arkansas State Police Records, Criminal Investigation Division, Mar. 20, 1985, File #I16819
- Organized Crime Information Center, Letter from Nelda Wilson to Lt. Stephens, May 15, 1986, File #I-16283
- Arkansas State Police Records, Criminal Investigation Division, Jun. 26, 1986, File #56-686-86
- Arkansas State Police Records, Criminal Investigation Division, Aug. 21, 1986, File #58-686-86
- Arkansas State Police Records, Criminal Investigation Division, Aug. 28, 1986, File #58-689-86
- Arkansas State Police Records, Criminal Investigation Division, Sep. 11, 1986, File #58-689-86
- Arkansas State Police Records, Criminal Investigation Division, Sep. 15, 1986, File# 58-689-86
- Arkansas State Police Records, Criminal Investigation Division, Sep. 22, 1986, File #58-686-86
- Arkansas State Police Records, Criminal Investigation Division, Sep. 25, 1986, File #58-686-86
- Arkansas State Police Records, Criminal Investigation Division, Oct. 2, 1986, File #58-689-86
- Federal Bureau of Investigation Report, Oct. 10, 1986, File #LR245F-2
- Federal Bureau of Investigation Report, Oct. 14, 1986, File #LR245F-2
- Arkansas State Police Records, Criminal Investigation Division, Oct. 22, 1986, File# 58-689-86
- Arkansas State Police Records, Criminal Investigation Division, Oct. 27, 1986, File #58-689-86
- Steve Barns, "Bond Daddies: Greed, Lust, and Bust on the

Financial Frontier", *Southern Magazine*, Jan. '89, pp. 31-34, 65-67
- C.S. Heinbockel, "From Prison to Business Partners", *Arkansas Democrat-Gazette*, Jan. 16, 1990
- Dan Bailey, "Bank, (Lasater) Named in Suit for $120 Million", *Arkansas Democrat-Gazette*, Sep. 1, 1990
- Andrew Moreau, "Ex-dealers Turn Sights on Work in Mortgages", *Arkansas Democrat-Gazette*, May 14, 1991
- Jo Beth Briton, "Agency Denies Lasater License", *Arkansas Democrat-Gazette*, July 27, 1991
- Larry Ault, "Who's Lasater's Worst Enemy, the Media or Himself," *Arkansas Democrat-Gazette*, Aug. 23, 1991
- Jerry Seper, "Second Whitewater Cash Link Probe", *The Washington Times*, Feb. 16, 1994
- Editors, "Hillary's Legal Ethics", *Human Events*, Feb. 18, 1994
- Ellen Joan Pollock, "Special Counsel's Probe of Whitewater Includes Bond Dealer Linked to Clinton", *The Wall Street Journal*, Mar. 24, 1994, p. A20
- Don Johnson & Noel Oman, "Clinton Helped Lasater Get Bond Contract", *Arkansas Democrat-Gazette*, Mar. 24, 1992, pp. 1A, 7A
- Joe Stumpe and Noel Oman, "Clinton Campaign Denies Times Story", *Arkansas Democrat-Gazette*, Mar. 25, 1992, pp. 12A-14A
- Joe Stumpe, "Legislators Easily Approved Radio System Purchase on 2nd Vote", *Arkansas Democrat-Gazette*, Mar. 26, 1992
- Andrew Moreau, "Lasater, Partners Made Best Bond Offer, Officials Say", *Arkansas Democrat-Gazette*, Mar. 27, 1992
- Don Johnson, "Ex-lawyer Pardoned by Governor", *Arkansas Democrat-Gazette*, Apr. 11, 1992, p. 16A
- Jonathan Groves and Doug Thompson, "Deals Entwine Lasater, and Rose Partner", *Arkansas Democrat-Gazette*, Mar. 25, 1994, pp. D1, D2
- Editors, "The Lasater Affair, Ghosts of Carelessness Past", *The Economist*, May 7, 1994, pp. 30-31
- Dick Lyneis, "Fiske Eyes Angel Fire Ex-Owner, Lasater Tied to Clintons", *The Sunday Journal*, May 8, 1994, pp. A1, A12
- Ambrose Evans-Pritchard, "The Enforcer and the Broken Man, the Clinton Controversy", *Sunday Telegraph*, May 8, 1994, p. 21
- Jerry Seper, "Longtime Friend Probed as Source of Clinton Funds", *The Washington Times*, May 12, 1994, pp. A1, A11
- Tony Snow, "Hillary's Turn in the Spotlight", *The Washington Times*, May 29, 1994
- Jerry Seper, "Whitewater Probe Eyes Drug-Profit Laundering", *The Washington Times*, June 9, 1994, p. A11
- Lisa Hoffman, "Whitewater Probe Leads to Coke Dealer", *San Francisco Examiner*, July 3, 1994, p. B10
- Ambrose Evans-Pritchard, "Smugglers Linked to Contra Arms Deals," The *Sunday Telegraph* of London, Oct. 9, 1994, p. 3.

BILL CLINTON AND COCAINE

- Governor Clinton uses cocaine while in office.
- Clinton discontinues mandatory drug testing for White House staff members.
- Clinton eliminates 121 positions with the National Drug Control Policy Office.
- Clinton appoints Jocelyn Elders U.S. Surgeon General despite her well known desire to legalize drugs.

  - Larry Nichols Press Release, Oct. 19, 1990, p. 4
  - U.S. District Court, Eastern District of Arkansas, Larry Nichols v. Bill Clinton, Wooten Epes, and Arkansas Development Finance Authority, Oct. 25, 1990, Case #LR-C-90-746
  - White House Press Release, Feb. 9, 1993
  - Isabel Wilkerson, "They Kick My Baby Around So Much, Elders' Mother Laments", *Arkansas Democrat-Gazette*, Dec. 31, 1993, p. 3B
  - Susan Roth, "Elders Still Firm that Legalizing Drugs an Option", *Arkansas Democrat-Gazette*, Apr. 15, 1994, pp. 1B, 9B
  - Joyce Price, "Elders Urges Girl Scouts to Admit Lesbians, Suggests Controlled Drug Giveaways", *The Washington Times*, June 2, 1994
  - John McCaslin, "Ship Adrift", *The Washington Times*, July 6, 1994
  - Ambrose Evans-Pritchard, "Clinton Took Cocaine While in Office", *Sunday Telegraph*, July 16, 1994, pp. 1,5
  - Jane Parks, Video Interview, Jul. 19, 1994, on file, CFHG. (Jane Parks was manager of the Vantage Point Apartments where Roger Clinton resided. On several occasions during 1984, while performing managerial duties, she witnessed Governor Bill Clinton using cocaine inside Roger's apartment. Her story is corroborated by other residents).
  - Dr. Samuel Houston, Video Interview, Aug. 2, 1994, on file, CFHG. (Dr. Samuel Houston, personal physician to Hillary's Father, Hugh Rodham, states that his colleague, Dr. Suen, has treated Bill Clinton for cocaine related sinus problems at the Medical Center in Little Rock. Other medical personnel, names temporarily withheld, attest to treating Clinton for cocaine addiction on several occasions during the 1980's. Records have since been destroyed).
  - Sharline Wilson, Video Interview, Sept. 23, 1994, on file, CFHG. (Sharline's grand jury testimony of December, 1990 during a federal investigation into public official corruption in Arkansas, identifies Bill Clinton as a regular user of cocaine).

BILL CLINTON AND DON TYSON

- Tyson Foods counselor James Blair helps Hillary get a $100,000 return on a $1,000 investment.
- Hillary's investment gains appear illegal to experts.
- Clinton enacts state regulations benefiting Tyson Foods.
- Tyson receives a $10 million loan from Clinton's ADFA.
- Don Tyson, president of Tyson Foods, is known to be heavily involved in cocaine trafficking.

  - Arkansas State Police Records, Criminal Investigation Division, Aug. 22, 1973, File# I-3378
  - Arkansas State Police Records, Criminal Investigation Division, Dec. 27, 1974, File# I-4835
  - Arkansas State Police Records, Criminal Investigation Division, Jan. 28, 1975, File# I-3378
  - Arkansas State Police Records, Criminal Investigation Division, Feb. 10, 1975, File# I-4835
  - Arkansas State Police Records, Criminal Investigation Division, July 2, 1975, File# I-2953
  - Arkansas State Police Records, Criminal Investigation Division, Aug. 27, 1975, File# I-3378
  - Arkansas State Police Records, Criminal Investigation Division, Sep. 12, 1975, File# I-4835
  - Arkansas State Police Records, Criminal Investigation Division, Mar. 22, 1976, File# I-7465
  - Arkansas State Police Records, Criminal Investigation Division, Oct. 22, 1976, File# I-7465
  - Arkansas State Police Records, Criminal Investigation Division, Apr. 2, 1979, File# I-7465
  - Arkansas State Police Records, Criminal Investigation Division, Feb. 5, 1980, File# I-7465
  - Arkansas State Police Records, Criminal Investigation Division, Oct. 24, 1980, File# I-4835
  - Arkansas State Police Records, Criminal Investigation Division, Jan. 21, 1981, File# I-4835
  - Arkansas State Police Records, Criminal Investigation Division, Oct. 26, 1981, File# I-14838
  - Drug Enforcement Administration-Narcotics Investigation Report, Dec. 14, 1982, File# GFGJ-83-9052
  - Drug Enforcement Administration-Narcotics Investigation Report, July 9, 1984, File# GFMQ-84-4046
  - Mick Normington, "Tyson, Lumber Firm, Government in Dispute Over Transaction", *Arkansas Democrat-Gazette*, Apr. 13, 1992
  - Bruce Ingersoll, "Tyson Foods, With a Friend in the White House,

Gets Gentle Treatment from Agriculture Agency", *The Wall Street Journal,* Mar. 17, 1994, p. A16

- D.R. Stewart, "Critics Say Tyson Rules USDA Roost", *Arkansas Democrat-Gazette,* Mar. 18, 1994, pp. 1A, 13A
- Daniel Puzo, "USDA More Lax on Poultry Laws, Secret Study Says", *Arkansas Democrat-Gazette,* Mar. 26, 1994, pp. 1D, 2D
- Jeffery Taylor and Bruce Ingersoll, "Hillary Clinton's Commodities Broker Was Disciplined for Variety of Violations", *The Wall Street Journal,* Mar. 29, 1994, p. A16
- Jeffrey Taylor and Bruce Ingersoll, "Clinton's Broker Ran Afoul of Regulators", *Arkansas Democrat-Gazette,* Mar. 30, 1994, pp. 1D, 6D
- Andrew Moreau, "Tyson Once Fined for Tricks in Egg Trade", *Arkansas Democrat-Gazette,* Mar. 30, 1994, 1D, 2D
- John M. Broker, "Mrs. Clinton Turned $1,000 Stake Into $99,000 Profit", *Los Angeles Times,* Mar. 30, 1994, pp. A1, A20
- Jeff Gerth, "Blair Led First Lady to $100,000 Windfall", *The New York Times,* Mar. 30, 1994, p. 1A
- Maurice Weaver, "Wall St. Amazed at Mrs. Clinton's Midas Touch", *The Daily Telegraph,* Mar. 31, 1994
- Sara Fritz and John Broder, "First Lady's Broker Used Improper Block Trading", *Los Angeles Times,* Apr. 5, 1994, pp. A1, A14
- David Brandon, "The Mystery of Hillary's Trades", *The Wall Street Journal,* Apr. 7, 1994
- Mark Hosenball, et. al., "Hillary Clinton: Saint or Sinner?", *Newsweek,* Apr. 11, 1994, pp. 25-27
- Hillary Clinton, White House News Conference, Apr. 22, 1994
- Frank Muray, "Hillary Denies Ethical Lapses, Regrets Stalling", *The Washington Times,* Apr. 23, 1994, pp. A1, A14
- Greg Gordon, "Exchange Finds Mrs. Clinton's Trading Records", *The Washington Times,* Apr. 28, 1994, p. A3
- Scripps Howard News Service, "Brokerage Broke Rules for Hillary", *The Washington Times,* May 27, 1994
- Jerry Seper, "Espy Investigated for Reported Favors from Tyson Foods", *The Washington Times,* June 10, 1994
- Sara Fritz, "Clinton Ties to Tyson Scion Still Drawing Critics Fire", *Los Angeles Times,* June 12, 1994
- Jeffery Birnbaum, "President Clinton Becomes Embroiled in Another Controversy Over Finances", *The Wall Street Journal,* July 14, 1994
- Jerry Seper, "Clinton Loans Raise New Questions", *The Washington Times,* July 15, 1994, pp. A1, A12
- Michael Isikoff and Mark Hosenball, "The Chicken King Plays Hard-Boiled Politics", *Newsweek,* July 18, 1994, pp. 33-36
- Dan McGraw, "The Birdman of Arkansas", *U.S. News & World Report,* July 18, 1994, pp. 42-46

Tyson Chicken Millionaire

- Michael Kramer, "How the Chicken Got Loose", *Time*, July 25, 1994, pp. 29-30
- James Adams, "The Ties That Blind", *The American Spectator*, Aug. 1994, pp. 40-46
- Thomas Rosenstiel, "Reno May Request Independent Counsel for Espy Investigation", *Los Angeles Times*, Aug. 8, 1994
- Combined Sources, "Independent Inquiry Ordered in Espy Case", *The Press Enterprise*, Aug. 10, 1994
- Tony Munroe, "Some Crow at Tyson's Pull in White House", *The Washington Times*, Aug. 15, 1994, pp. A1, A20
- Doug Frantz, "One Truck, Out of Gas, Was Humble Start of Tyson Empire", *Arkansas Democrat-Gazette*, Aug. 29, 1994, pp. 1D, 5D
- Ambrose Evans-Pritchard, "Bill Clinton and the Chicken Man," *The Sunday Telegraph*, Oct. 9, 1994, page 1.

THE MURDERS OF KEVIN IVES AND DON HENRY   1988

- Kevin and Don are murdered after witnessing a drug drop; their bodies are then placed on railroad tracks and run over by a train.
- State Medical Examiner Fahmy Malak rules their deaths accidental.
- Malak's ruling is overturned, boys had indeed been murdered.
- Malak is kept in office at the insistence of Governor Clinton despite public outcry.
- Malak covers up for Clinton's mother, Virginia Kelley, in wrongful death suit.
- Malak rules death by natural causes for a decapitation victim.
- Clinton says Malak is just overworked.
- Clinton says Malak is underpaid and gives him a $14,000 raise.
- Malak resists court orders and commits perjury.
- Six police informants in Kevin and Don's murder investigation are murdered themselves.
- Clinton appointees cover up the boy's murders.
- Conspirators in the boy's murders receive cushy jobs from Clinton.

- Lynda Hollenbeck, "Jury Convenes to Study 2 Deaths", *The Benton Courier*, Apr. 28, 1988, pp. 1A-2A
- Affidavit of Betsey Wright, Saline County Circuit Court, May 26, 1988
- Report of the Grand Jury, Saline County Circuit Court, Dec. 28,

1988
- Editors, "Malak an Untouchable?", *Arkansas Democrat Gazette*, Aug. 13, 1989
- James Merriweather, "Clinton Says Malak Stressed Out", *Arkansas Democrat-Gazette*, Aug. 11, 1989, pp. 1B-2B
- Max Parker, "Committee Slices 41% Raise for Malak", *Arkansas Democrat Gazette*, Oct. 26, 1989
- Memorandum to Chuck Banks & Mac Dodson from Bob Govar, Re: Saline County Narcotics Investigation, Feb. 13, 1990, pp. 1-20
- Rod Lorensen, "The Malak Files", *Arkansas Times*, June 1990, pp. 32-37, 91-96
- Suzanne Brown, "Memorandums Link Drug Dealers to 2 Local Deaths", *Benton Courier*, Dec. 13, 1990, pp. 1, 14
- Linda Hollenbeck, "Trial Testimony Ties Dead Man to Ives-Henry Deaths", *Benton Courier*, Mar. 7, 1991, p. 1
- Joe Nabbefeld, "Disputes Trail Medical Examiner", *Arkansas Democrat-Gazette*, Mar. 24, 1991, p. 1A, 17A
- John Brummett, "Out of Control", *Arkansas Times*, Jul. 1991, pp. 44-51
- Meredith Oakley, "Sheltering Malak Raw Deal for State's Taxpayers", *Arkansas Democrat-Gazette* Sep. 13, 1991
- Nancy McFarland,"Malak's New Job Looks Like a Bribe", *Arkansas Democrat-Gazette*, Sep. 18, 1991
- Doug Thompson, "Son's Death Thrusts Ives Into Politics", *Arkansas Democrat-Gazette*, Dec. 8, 1991
- Mara Leveritt, "The Boys on the Tracks", *Arkansas Times*, Jan. 1992, pp. 40-45, 65-71
- James Risen and Edwin Chen, "Clinton's Ties to Controversial Medical Examiner Questioned," *Los Angeles Times*, May 19, 1992, pp. A1, A12
- Jean Duffey, Video Interview, Mar. 18, 1994, on file, Citizens for Honest Government
- John Brown, Video Interview, Jul. 18, 1994, on file, Citizens for Honest Government

THE MURDER OF JERRY PARKS

- Private investigator Jerry Parks compiles a detailed file documenting Governor Clinton's extra-marital sexual encounters and drug usage from 1984 through 1990
- Parks is appointed Chief of Security for Clinton's Presidential Campaign Headquarters
- The Parks home is burglarized and the Clinton files are stolen
- Parks is executed while driving home in September 1993

- Jerry's son Gary Parks accuses Clinton of having his father killed to save the President's political career
- Detective Tom James is pulled off the case after linking Clinton to the murder of Jerry Parks

   - Editors, "Clinton Campaign Headquarters Security Chief Gunned Down", *Human Events*, Mar. 11, 1994, p.3
   - Tim Brooks, "Roland Man's Death, Ties to Clinton, Spark Interest", *Arkansas Democrat-Gazette*, Mar. 19, 1994
   - Ambrose Evans-Pritchard, "My Father Spied on Clinton", *Sunday Telegraph*, Mar. 20, 1994, p. 26
   - Deroy Murdock, "Are Attacks Linked to Whitewater?", *New York Post*, Mar. 23, 1994, pp. 14, 21
   - Deroy Murdock, "A Pattern of Violence", *Orange County Register*, Mar. 24, 1994
   - Editors, "Whitewater Curiouser", *The Economist*, July 9, 1994, pp. 29, 30
   - Ambrose Evans-Pritchard, "Clinton Took Cocaine While In Office", *Sunday Telegraph*, July 17, 1994, pp. 1, 5
   - Jack Wheeler, "The Arkansas Body Count", *Strategic Investment*, July 20, 1994, pp. 5, 6
   - Jane Parks, Video Interview, Jul. 29, 1994, on file, Citizens for Honest Government

BILL CLINTON AND ADULTERY

- Gennifer Flowers receives a government job to keep quiet about her affair with Governor Clinton.
- Flowers' neighbor, attorney Gary Johnson accidentally captures Clinton at Flowers' apartment on his home video security system.
- Johnson is nearly beaten to death. His attackers demand the video.
- Flowers publicly admits her affair with Clinton.
- 60 Minutes producer, Don Hewett admits to saving Clinton's presidential campaign with a doctored news story denying Flowers affair.
- Media smear campaigns are prepared against 26 additional women who can ruin Clinton's chance at the presidency.
- State vehicles and troopers are used at taxpayers' expense to shuttle Clinton back and forth to rendezvous points with women, including Sally Perdue.
- Perdue is offered a federal job to keep quiet about her affair

with Clinton or threatened with physical harm if she talks.
- Perdue receives threats, loses her job, and has the rear window of her car shot out after she talks.
- Perdue tapes interviews with television networks which are never aired.
- Clinton's former bodyguards (Arkansas State Troopers Perry, Patterson, Ferguson, Anderson, and Brown) provide detailed information about Governor Clinton's sexual activities.
- Governor Clinton's sexual partners number over 100.
- Phone logs and other corroborating evidence back these reports.
- *American Spectator* Magazine's offices suffer three separate breakins while preparing a story on Clinton's adulterous activities.
- The Clinton administration urges Trooper Ferguson to lie.
- The Clinton administration levies false charges of fraud against Perry and Patterson. They are later cleared.
- Clinton attempts to seduce state employee Paula Jones in a Little Rock Hotel.
- Reporter Mike Isikoff is suspended by *The Washington Post* for writing an article favorable to Paula Jones.
- Jones files a lawsuit against Clinton (and Trooper Ferguson) claiming sexual harassment.
- A Massive media smear campaign against Jones is launched.
- Other Clinton sex partners are given prominent positions in the government and national media in exchange their for silence.

- Circuit Court of Pulaski County, Arkansas, 7th Division, Larry Nichols v. Wooten Epes, Bill Clinton, Arkansas Development Finance Authority, Sept. 12, 1990, Case #90-4258. (also, Objection and Request for Disqualitication filed Oct. 22, 1990)
- Larry Nichols, Press Release, Oct. 19, 1990, p. 3
- U. S. District Court, Eastern District of Arkansas, Larry Nichols v. Bill Clinton, Wooten Epes, and Arkansas Development Finance Authority, Oct. 25, 1990, Case #LR-C-90-746 (also, witness list, filed Oct. 8, 1991)
- Gennifer Flowers, Press Conference, Jan. 1992
- Noel Oman, "Troopers Tell of Amazing Clinton Trysts", *Arkansas Democrat-Gazette*, Dec. 20, 1993, pp. 1A-3A
- William Rempel and Douglas Frantz, "Troopers Say Clinton Sought Silence on Personal Affairs", *Los Angeles Times*, Dec. 21, 1993, pp. A1, A24, A25

- Jane Fullerton, "From Sexgate to Silence, Coverage Reflects Debate", *Arkansas Democrat-Gazette*, Dec. 21, 1993, p. 8A
- Rex Nelson, "Clinton's Calls Leave Paper Trail", *Arkansas Democrat-Gazette*, Dec. 22, 1993, pp. 1A, 18A
- Rex Nelson, "Troopers Scared, Alone in Whirlwind", *Arkansas Democrat-Gazette*, Dec. 23, 1993, pp. 1A, 9A
- Elizabeth Caldwell, "2 Troopers Entangled in Traffic Crash Suits", *Arkansas Democrat-Gazette*, Dec. 23, 1993, p. 8A
- Randy Lilleston and June Fullerton, "Clinton Confirms Trooper's Charges", *Arkansas Democrat-Gazette*, Dec. 23, 1993, pp. 1A-8A
- Joe Stumpe and Rex Nelson, "Wright Urged 3rd Trooper (Ferguson) to Alter Story", *Arkansas Democrat-Gazette*, Dec. 24, 1993, pp. 1A, 8A
- Meredith Oakley, "At Issue: Abuse of Office, Not Sex", *Arkansas Democrat-Gazette*, Dec. 26, 1993, p. 5J
- Susan Roth, "Lawyers Eye Significance of Affidavit in Trooper Case", *Arkansas Democrat-Gazette*, Dec. 30, 1993, 1A, 8A
- David Brock, "Living With the Clintons", *American Spectator*, Jan. 1994, pp. 18-30
- Amand Mitchison, "The First Mistress", *Independent Magazine*, Jan. 15, 1994, pp. 24-30
- Ambrose Evans-Pritchard, "I Was Threatened After Clinton Affair", *Sunday Telegraph*, Jan. 23, 1994, pp. 1-5
- Reuters, "Clinton Sought Sex, Woman Says", *Arizona Republic*, Feb. 12, 1994, p. B10
- Randy Lilleston, "Clinton Made Advances, Woman Says", *Arkansas Democrat-Gazette*, Feb. 12, 1994, pp. 1A, 10A
- Robert Shogan, "Ex-Arkansas State Worker Says Clinton Harassed Her", *Los Angeles Times*, Feb. 12, 1994
- Noel Oman, "Judge Drops Suit Involving 2 Who Accused Clinton", *Arkansas Democrat-Gazette*, Mar. 18, 1994, p. 1A
- Deroy Murdock, "Are Attacks Linked to Whitewater", *New York Post*, Mar. 23, 1994, p. 14
- Editors, "Censored in Arkansas", *The Wall Street Journal*, Mar. 23, 1994, p. A12
- Ambrose Evans-Pritchard, "Clinton Accused of Grotesque Sex Harassment", *Sunday Telegraph*, Mar. 27, 1994, p. 1
- Daniel Wattenberg, "Love and Hate in Arkansas: The L.D. Brown Story", *American Spectator*, April/May, 1994, pp. 32-42
- Julie Malone, "Critics Say Media Buried Sex Harassment Charge Against Clinton", *Arkansas Democrat-Gazette*, Apr. 7, 1994, p. 9A
- Noel Oman, "Why 3rd Trooper (Brown) Came Forward", *Arkansas Democrat-Gazette*, Apr. 17, 1994, 1A, 16A
- Ambrose Evans-Pritchard, "Trooper Solicited 100 Girls for Clinton", *Sunday Telegraph*, Apr. 10, 1994, p. 1
- Don Hewitt, video interview, May 1994

60 Minutes
Producer ~ best friend of Mike Wallace

case pending

- U.S. District Court, Eastern District Arkansas, Paula Corbin Jones v. William Jefferson Clinton and Danny Ferguson, Civil Action Suit, May 6, 1994, Case #LR-C-94-290 (Jones' co-worker, AIDC employee Pamela Blackard, has signed a legal affidavit corroborating Jones' allegations)
- Combined Sources, "Sex Harassment Suit Accuses Clinton", *Press Enterprise*, May 7, 1994, pp. A-1, A-8
- Rod Ducher, "Jones Gets Her Day in Print by Taking Clinton to Court", *The Washington Times*, May 7, 1994, p. A7
- Nancy Roman, "Sex Suit Against Clinton is Filed Under Arkansas Tort Law", *The Washington Times*, May 7, 1994, p. A6
- Sam Fritz and John Broden, "$700,000 Lawsuit Accuses Clinton of Sex Harassment", *Los Angeles Times*, May 7, 1994, p. A4
- Bill Clinton, White House News Conference, May 8, 1994
- Joyce Price, "Portrait of Sex Harasser: Habitual, Power Hungry Man", *The Washington Times*, May 8, 1994, A15
- Reuters, "Most Doubt Clinton on Lawsuit", *The Washington Times*, May 8, 1994, A15
- Joe Klein, "The Politics of Promiscuity", *Newsweek*, May 9, 1994, pp. 16-20
- COX News Service, "Talk of Clinton Defense Fund Stirs Ethics Debate", *Press Enterprise*, May 10, 1994
- Mark Hosenball and Ginny Carroll, "No Laughing Matter", *Newsweek*, May 16, 1994, pp. 22-24
- Matthew Cooper and Greg Ferguson, "The New FOB's: Foes of Bill", *U.S. News & World Report*, May 16, 1994, pp. 20-31
- Paul Richter, "White House Seeks Study of Presidential Immunity", *Los Angeles Times*, May 19, 1994
- Melinda Bech, et. al., "Paula Jones' Credibility Gap", *Newsweek*, May 23, 1994, pp. 42-43
- Sara Fritz and William Rempel, "Trooper Faces Dilemma as Clinton Suit Co-Defendent", *The Los Angeles Times*, May 23, 1994, pp. A1, A20
- David Ellis, et. al., "The Perils of Paula", *People*, May 23, 1994, pp. 88-94
- Editors, "Distinguishing Characteristics", *New Republic*, May 30, 1994, pp. 7-8
- Deroy Murdock, "Arkansas Trail of Tears", *Orange County Register*, June 8, 1994
- Douglas Jehl, "Clinton Aid Fund Planned", *Press Enterprise*, Jun. 28, 1994, p. A1, A20
- Editors, "Whitewater Curiouser", *The Economist*, July 9, 1994, pp. 29-30.
- Jerry Seper, "Clinton Seeks Immunity in Sexual Misconduct Suit", *The Washington Times*, Aug. 11, 1994, p. A3
- From Washington Post, "Justice Dept. Backs Clinton on Immunity",

Los Angeles Times, Aug. 19, 1994, A19

THE DEATH OF VINCE FOSTER

- Vince Foster, appointed White House Deputy Counsel by Clinton, allegedly shoots himself in the mouth at Fort Marcy Park on July 20, 1993. However intial reports indicate...
- There is very little blood at the scene.
- There is no gun powder residue in his mouth or on his face.
- There are no broken teeth or damaged lips.
- No bullet is ever found.
- The gun is still in Foster's hand, which would be highly unlikely due to natural reflexes and the recoil of the gun.
- The gun is found in Foster's right hand, Foster is left-handed.
- Death is ruled a suicide before an autopsy or balistics test is performed.
- Film of crime scene is "accidentally ruined during developing".
- Surviving Polaroid photos don't match location where body is supposedly found.
- Members of Clinton's staff ransack Foster's office the night he dies removing Whitewater and other files.

  - U.S. Department of the Interior, National Park Service Supplemental Criminal Incident Record and Mobile Crime Lab Report, July 20, 1993, Case #3050
  - Report of Autopsy, Vincent Foster, Office of Chief Medical Examiner, Commonwealth of Virginia, July 28, 1993, Case #353/93
  - Gwen Ifill, "Files of Dead Clinton Aide Are Dispensed to Legal Staff", *The New York Times*, Aug. 12, 1993
  - David Johnston, "New Gap Arises in Inquiry into Death of Clinton Aide", *The New York Times*, Aug. 14, 1993
  - Michael Isikoff, "Diary Emerges in Foster Suicide", *The Washington Post*, Dec. 18, 1993
  - AP, "Whitewater, Other Papers Taken from Foster's Office", *Arkansas Democrat-Gazette*, Dec. 21, 1993, p. 3A
  - William Saffire, "Foster's Ghost is Haunting White House", *New York Times*, Jan. 17, 1994
  - Christopher Ruddy, "Doubts Raised On Foster's `Suicide'", *New York Post*, Jan. 27, 1994, pp. 5, 18
  - Christopher Ruddy, "Foster Gun Was Never Tested", *New York Post*, Jan. 28, 1994
  - Christopher Ruddy, "Politics Kept FBI Off Foster Case", *New York*

misspelled SAFIRE (Nat'l Press Award as best of 1995)

Post, Feb. 3, 1994
- Pierre Thomas, "Park Police Ruled Suicide, Then Sought Tests on Foster Weapon", *Arkansas Democrat-Gazette*, Feb. 4, 1994, p. 5A
- Ambrose Evans-Pritchard," White House Death Riddle Deepens", *Sunday Telegraph*, Feb. 6, 1994, p. 1
- Christopher Ruddy, "Fumbling Feds Change Story on Foster Suicide", *New York Post*, Feb. 10, 1994
- Memorandum from M.S. Wheatley to David P. Boszien, Fairfax County, Virginia, Feb. 17, 1994. Includes interview transcripts of George Gonzales and Cory Ashford of Fairfax County Fire and Rescue, Mar. 4 and Mar. 11, 1994
- Christopher Ruddy, "Cops Made Photo Blunder at Foster Death Site", *New York Post*, Mar. 7, 1994
- Christopher Ruddy, "Foster Coroner Has Been Dead Wrong", *New York Post*, March 8, 1994
- Christopher Ruddy, "Foster File Shocker: 2nd Set of Papers Taken From Safe", *New York Post*, March 9, 1994
- Michael Hodges, "Foster Case's Coroner Erred in '89 Killing", *Washington Post*, Mar. 9, 1994, pp. A1, A5
- Editors, "Who Is Patsy Thomasson", *The Wall Street Journal*, Mar. 10, 1994, p. A18
- Thomas Hargrove, "Ask Thomasson About Foster Files, Republican Urges", *Arkansas Democrat-Gazette*, Mar. 17, 1994, p. 13A
- Erich Eichman, "Tabs Tangle Over Foster Death", *The Wall Street Journal*, Mar. 21, 1994, p. A14
- James Risen, "White House To Give Fiske All Files on Foster", *Los Angeles Times*, May 6, 1994
- Jerry Seper, "Gonzales Rejects Panel Probe into Death of Foster", *The Washington Times*, June 21, 1994, p. A3
- Michael Frasby, "White House's Thomasson Keeps Ties to Clintons Strong Despite Controversy and GOP Criticism", *The Wall Street Journal*, Jun. 21, 1994, p. A16
- Jerry Seper, "Leach Criticizes Narrowed Hearings: Foster's Death Not on Agenda", *The Washington Times*, June 30, 1994
- Robert Fiske Jr., "Report of the Independent Counsel in Re Vincent L. Foster, Jr.", Washington, D.C., June 30, 1994
- Editors, "Fiske on Foster: There Was No Foul Play", *U. S. News & World Report*, July 11, 1994, p. 12
- Ambrose Evans-Pritchard, "Doubt Lingers Over Death of Clinton Aide", *Sunday Telegraph*, Jul. 31, 1994, p. 24
- Michael Isikoff, "Why Vince Foster Died", Newsweek, July 11, 1994, p. 17
- Jerry Seper, "Foster's Death Still a Puzzle", *The Washington Times*, July 19, 1994, pp. A1, A18
- Jerry Seper, "Congress Eyes Motives in Foster Office Search", *The Washington Times*, July 20, 1994, p. A1, A12

- Christopher Bond, "Why is Foster's Death Still a Mystery", *The Washington Times*, Aug. 1, 1994, p. A19
- AP, "White House Misled Media on Foster Papers", *The Washington Times*, Aug. 3, 1994, p. A12
- Paul Roberts, "Fiske's Exit Reopens Hope on a Mystery", *Los Angeles Times*, Aug. 7, 1994, p. M5
- Paul Roberts, "Muzzled on Foster", *The Washington Times*, Aug. 8, 1994
- Sidney Blumenthal, "The Suicide", *The New Yorker*, Aug. 9, 1994, pp. 41-45
- Paul Rodriguez, "Man Who Found Foster's Body Says He Saw No Gun", *The Washington Times*, Aug. 11, 1994, p. A15

BILL CLINTON AND WHITEWATER

- The Clintons claim Whitewater is a simple money losing investment.
- The Clintons use Whitewater to skim federally insured deposits for themselves and their associates causing a savings & loan to fail, obligating U.S. taxpayers to pick up the $60 million tab.
- The Clintons continually change their story as more information is uncovered and revealed to the public.
- The Clintons receive value from Whitewater in excess of resources invested.
- Taxpayer guaranteed Whitewater funds find their way into Clinton's campaigns.
- The U.S. Government's regulatory system is intentionally violated to protect Clinton.

- United States District Court, Eastern District Arkansas, United States of America v. James McDougal, Order, Dec. 21, 1989, Case #LR-CR-89-161
- Gloria Borgen, "Why the Secrecy About Whitewater", *U.S. News & World Report*, Jan. 24, 1994, p. 30
- George Church, "The Tangled Web", *Time*, Jan. 24, 1994, pp. 31-34
- Howard Fineman, et al., "How Bad Is It?", *Newsweek*, Jan. 17, 1994, pp. 14-21
- William Rempel and Douglas Frantz, "Fallout From Collapse of S&L Shadows Clinton", *Los Angeles Times*, Feb. 11, 1994, p. A17
- U.S. District Court, Eastern District of Arkansas, United States of America v. David L. Hale, Charles Matthews, and Eugene Fitzhugh, Supersedes Indictment, Feb. 17, 1994, Case #LR-CR-93-147
- Terry Lemons, "White House Briefed on Madison Inquiry", *Arkansas Democrat-Gazette*, Feb. 25, 1994, pp. 1A, 15A

- Sam Fritz, "Clinton Name Tied to Deal, Witness Says", *Los Angeles Times*, Mar. 1, 1994
- Douglas Jehl, "Clinton Attacks Cover-Up Claims", *Daily News*, Mar. 8, 1994, pp. 1, 13
- Don Balz, "First Lady Says She and President Truthful About Whitewater Loss", *Fort Worth Star-Telegram*, Mar. 15, 1994, p. A7
- Bill Turque, et. al., "Whitewater Torture", *Newsweek*, Mar. 14, 1994
- Randy Lilleston, "Strategy on Whitewater Shifts to Damage Control", *Arkansas Democrat-Gazette*, Mar. 20, 1994, pp. 1A, 10A
- Bill Turque, et al., "The Unsinkable Scandal", *Newsweek*, Mar. 21, 1994
- Terry Lemons, "Gonzales Kills Hearings, Fears Lies", *Arkansas Democrat-Gazette*, Mar. 22, 1994, pp. 1A, 9A
- William Rempel, "Ex-Judge Hale Pleads Guilty Over Arkansas Loan Fraud", *Los Angeles Times*, Mar. 23, 1994, pp. A1, A21
- Richard Kell, "Ex-Judge Cuts Deal With Whitewater Counsel", *Press Enterprise*, Mar. 23, 1994, p. A9
- Angie Cannon, et al., "Clinton Defends Arkansas Venture", *Press Enterprise*, Mar. 25, 1994, p. A1
- Ronald Ostrow and William Rempel, "Letter Shows Official Doubts on Whitewater Prosecution", *Los Angeles Times*, Mar. 26, 1994, p. A22
- Editors, "Arkansas Secrets", *The New York Times*, Mar. 31, 1994, A18
- Susan Schmidt, "RTC Staff Ties S&L's $60,500 to '84 Campaign", *Arkansas Democrat-Gazette*, Apr. 3, 1994, pp. 1A, 19A
- Editors, "The Congressional Cover Up", *The Wall Street Journal*, May 19, 1994
- John Solomon, "Probe Reveals Check Kiting at Whitewater", *The Washington Times*, June 9, 1994, p. A11
- Eugene Methuin, "Understanding Whitewater", *Readers Digest*, June, 1994, pp. 95-100
- Carl Bernstein, "A Matter of Honesty: Bill Clinton and Whitewater", *Los Angeles Times*, July 17, 1994, pp. M1, M6
- John Malone, "Documents Withheld by White House", *Press Enterprise*, July 28, 1994, p. A9
- Mike Feinsilber, "Clinton Aids Swear They Did Nothing Wrong", *Press Enterprise*, July 29, 1994, p. A3
- Excerpts from Whitewater Hearings, "White House Concealed, Disguised, Distorted the Truth", *The Washington Times*, July 30, 1994, p. A7
- Michael Ross and Sara Fritz, "Altman Lied About Probe Contacts, GOP Senators Say", *Los Angeles Times*, July 30, 1994
- Editors, "Ethics, Lies and Whitewater", *The Washington Times*, Aug. 1, 1994, p. A18

- Donald Lambro, "Hearings Bolster Public Disaffection with White House", *The Washington Times*, Aug. 7, 1994, pp. A1, A12
- Michael Duffy, "Culture of Deception", *Time*, Aug. 15, 1994, pp. 15-19
- James Risen, "Altman Resigns Over Whitewater", *Los Angeles Times*, Aug. 18, 1994, p. A1, A10
- Jeff Gerth, "Investigation Explores Clinton Campaign Funds", *Press Enterprise*, Aug. 20, 1994

DOCUMENTS DESTROYED

- The Rose Law Firm begins shredding documents the same week the special counsel is hired to investigate Whitewater.
- Also that same week, a fire at the Worthen Bank building destroys a CPA firm housing Whitewater documents.
- Most of Bill Clinton's campaign contribution records in Arkansas have been destroyed.

  - Secretary of State, Office of Records, Campaign Contributions, Little Rock, Arkansas
  - Stephen Engelberg, "Jury Reportedly Told Clinton Aide's Papers Shredded", *Press Enterprise*, Mar. 4, 1994, p. A3
  - Sara Fritz, "Rose Firm Aides Shredded Foster Papers", *Los Angeles Times*, Mar. 5, 1994, p. A18
  - Noel Oman, "Rose Aide Tight-Lipped on Contents of Foster Files He Shredded", *Arkansas Democrat-Gazette,* Mar. 5, 1994, p. 15A
  - Stephen Engleberg, "Man Ties Shredding, Naming of Counsel: Law Firm Courier Says Foster Papers Destroyed After Investigator Picked", *Dallas Morning News*, Mar. 9, 1994, p. 1A, 19A
  - Editors, "Document Shredding: Destruction of Papers Raises Red Flag", *Dallas Morning News*, Mar. 11, 1994, p. 20A
  - Deroy Murdock, "Are Attacks Linked to Whitewater", *New York Post*, Mar. 23, 1994
  - L. J. Davis, "The Name of Rose", *The New Republic*, Apr. 4, 1994, p. 23
  - Ellen Pollock, "Two Who Shredded Documents at Rose Law Firm Resign", *The Wall Street Journal,* Apr. 7, 1994

Did J. Reno realize she was being used — or was she in on the scam?

CLINTON AND THE NOT-SO-INDEPENDENT COUNSEL ROBERT FISKE

- Clinton, through Attorney General Janet Reno, appoints Fiske as the independent prosecutor to investigate Whitewater. (It is never mentioned to the public that attorney Fiske represented Clark Clifford and BCCI, the bank ADFA had been laundering its drug money through. Clinton dismissed the charges against Clifford and BCCI prior to Fiske's appointment as independent counsel! A thorough investigation of Whitewater would have eventually lead to BCCI. Fiske knew in advance he could never complete his investigation since it is illegal to prosecute a former client).
- Fiske begs Congress not to hold public hearings.
- Fiske succeeds in obstructing Whitewater hearings and keeping vital information from the public during his stay as independent prosecuter.
- Fiske is fired as special prosecutor in August 1994.

   - John Broder and David Lauter, "Clinton Calls For Special Counsel to Probe Land Deal", *Los Angeles Times*, Jan. 13, 1994, pp. A1, A18
   - Editors, "Too Much Baggage", *The Wall Street Journal*, Jan. 21, 1994, p. A12
   - Catherine Wilson, "Legal World Lauds Fiske, Expects Him to Give us an Honest Count", *Arkansas Democrat-Gazette*, Jan. 23, 1994, p. 6A
   - Joe Stumpe, "Fiske's Jurisdiction Reaches Far and Wide", *Arkansas Democrat-Gazette*, Feb. 26, 1994, p. 1B, 5B
   - Wall Street Staff, "Fiske Acts to Block Release of Reports on Death of Foster", *The Wall Street Journal*, March 1, 1994, p. A4
   - Terry Lemons, "Congressional Hearings Too Risky, Fiske Contends", *Arkansas Democrat-Gazette*, March 8, 1994
   - John Broder and Michael Ross, "Avoid Hearings, Whitewater Counsel Says", *Los Angeles Times*, Mar. 8, 1994, p. A17
   - Editors, "The Fiske Coverup", *The Wall Street Journal*, March 9, 1994, p. A14
   - Terry Lemons, "Fiske Fends off GOP Clamor for Hearings", *Arkansas Democrat-Gazette*, March 10, 1994, pp. 1A, 13A
   - Sara Fritz, "Fiske Sends a Message: Don't Interfere", *Los Angeles Times*, March 13, 1994
   - Editors, "The Fiske Cover Up II", *The Wall Street Journal*, March 14, 1994
   - Letter from Congressman James Leach to Robert Fiske published Mar. 14, 1994 in *The Wall Street Journal*

- Robert Bartley, "What Mr. Fiske Can't Do With the Facts", *The Wall Street Journal*, March 30, 1994, p. A17
- David Bowermaster and Greg Ferguson, "The Clinton-Fiske Face-Off", *U.S. News & World Report*, Apr. 4, 1994, pp. 20-22
- Paul Rodriguez, "No Indictments Against Any Senior Officials, Fiske Says", *The Washington Times*, Apr. 30, 1994
- AP, "Fiske Hopes to Sidestep Role in Bank-Fraud Trial", *The Washington Times*, June 20, 1994
- John Broder, "Sense of Relief at White House After Initial Phase of Fiske's Probe", *Los Angeles Times*, July 1, 1994, p. A18
- Letter from Senator Lauch Faircloth to Attorney General Janet Reno, Re: Independence of Robert Fiske, July 1, 1994, on file, Citizens For Honest Government
- Jerry Seper, "Reno Seeks a Change in Fiske Status", *The Washington Times*, July 2, 1994, pp. A1, A16
- AP, "Reno Asks Court to Appoint Fiske as Independent Counsel", *Los Angeles Times*, July 2, 1994
- Jerry Seper, "Fiske Says No to House Hearings", *The Washington Times*, July 9, 1994, pp. A1, A14
- Major Garrett, "Fiske Again Refuses to Testify in House Before Bank Panel", *The Washington Times*, July 13, 1994
- Editors, "The Fiske Hangout", *The Wall Street Journal*, July 26, 1994, p. A14
- Sara Fritz, "Fiske Ousted in Whitewater Case, Move is Surprise", *Los Angeles Times*, Aug. 6, 1994, pp. A1, A18
- Lisa Hoffman, "Fiske Out of Clinton Inquiry", *Press Enterprise*, Aug. 6, 1994, p. 1
- Ronald Ostrow and John Broden, "Starr to Build Upon Fiske Probe", *Los Angeles Times*, Aug. 11, 1994, pp. A10, A11

CLINTON'S CIRCLE OF POWER

- Clinton appoints corrupt judges, attorneys, and police officers to oversee drug trafficking operations in Arkansas.
- Clinton gives friends involved in illegal activities in Arkansas high level government positions in Washington.
- White House staff members are allowed access to restricted areas without proper security clearances.

- Drug Enforcement Administration, Narcotics Investigation Report, Mar. 12, 1984, File #GJ-83-Z001
- Federal Bureau of Investigation Report, Oct. 16, 1986, File #LR245F-2
- Durable Power of Attorney, Pulaski County, Jan. 14, 1987, pp. 1-8

- Memorandum from Bob Govar to Chuck Banks and Mac Dodson, re: Saline County Narcotics Investigation, Feb. 13, 1990, pp. 1-20
- Seventh Judicial District Drug Task Force, Letter from Steve A. Cook to John Garner, Nov. 12, 1990
- Seventh Judicial District Drug Task Force, Letter from Steve A. Cook to John Garner, Nov. 12, 1990
- Chris Day, "Three Undercover Agents Quit Drug Task Force", *Arkansas Democrat-Gazette*, Nov. 14, 1990
- Lynda Hollenbeck, "Agent Resigns to Back Duffey", *The Benton Courier*, Nov. 14, 1990
- Chris Day, "Investigation Targets Saline Drugs", *Arkansas Democrat-Gazette*, Nov. 27, 1990
- Doug Thompson, "Corruption Investigation Confirmed", *Arkansas Democrat-Gazette*, Nov. 27, 1990
- Suzanne Brown, "Document Links Harmon to Federal Grand Jury Probe", *Benton Courier*, Dec. 12, 1990
- Chris Day, "Probe Targets Prosecutor", *Arkansas Democrat-Gazette*, Dec. 12, 1990, pp. 1A, 11A
- Doug Thompson, "Prosecutor-Elect Alleged Target of Investigation", *Arkansas Democrat-Gazette*, Dec. 12, 1990, p. 8A
- Scott J. Lewellen, Press Release, Dec. 12, 1990
- Rosy Mathews, "Duffey Gets Client's Support for Fighting Drug Trafficking", *Arkansas Democrat-Gazette*, Dec. 13, 1990
- Doug Thompson, "Memo Linking Harmon, Drugs Leaked from Office", *Arkansas Democrat-Gazette*, Dec. 13, 1990
- Gazette Staff, "More Officials Corrupt, Ex-Investigator Claims", *Arkansas Democrat-Gazette*, Dec. 13, 1990, p. 6B
- Benton Staff, "Govar: Testimony to Implicate Harmon", The Benton Courier, Mar. 15, 1991
- Lynda Hollenbeck and Suzanne Brown, "Federal Witness Arrested Friday", *The Benton Courier*, Mar. 18, 1991
- George Wells, "Ruling to Open Saline-Linked Drug Trial Today", *Arkansas Democrat-Gazette*, Apr. 2, 1991
- John Brummett, "Out of Control", *Arkansas Times*, July, 1991, pp. 44-51
- Jake Sandlin, "Lasater Associate to Lead State Democrats", *Arkansas Democrat-Gazette*, Aug. 31, 1992
- Editors, "Arkansas Forbearance", *The Wall Street Journal*, Feb. 22, 1994, p. A12
- Susan Schmidt, "Law Firm Probing Hubbell" *The Washington Post*, Mar. 2, 1994, pp A1, A7
- Editors, "Patsy Takes the Fiske", *The Wall Street Journal*, Mar. 10, 1994, p. A18
- Editors, "Who Is Patsy Thomasson?", *The Wall Street Journal*, Mar. 10, 1994, p. A18
- Ann DeVroy, "100-plus Work at White House Without Security

Hubbell was Chief Justice of Arkansas Supreme Court; left for ASSIS'T ATT'Y GENED in Wash DC — now in prison

Check", *Arkansas Democrat-Gazette*, Mar. 14, 1994, p. 2B
- David Johnston, "A Senior Official Quits Justice Post as Pressure Rises", *The New York Times*, Mar. 15, 1994, pp. A1, A10
- Steve McGonigle, "Justice Official Quits Post Amid Billing Dispute", *The Dallas Morning News*, Mar. 15, 1994, pp. A1, A11
- John Broder and Ronald J. Ostrow, "Hubbell Quits; Top Justice Aide, Clinton Friend", *Los Angeles Times*, Mar. 15, 1994, pp. A1, A18
- Bruce Ingersoll and Michael Frisby, "SEC Investigating Arkansas Investors In Probe into Possible Insider Trading", *The Wall Street Journal*, Mar. 18, 1994
- Jean Duffey, Video Interview, Mar. 18, 1994 and Aug. 5, 1994, on file, Citizens For Honest Government
- White House Personnel Records, Senate Testimony of Patsy Thomasson, Mar. 25, 1994, pp. 530-565
- Kenneth H. Bacon, "RTC Asserts Hubbell's Father-In-Law Helped Cause Madison Guaranty to Fail", *The Wall Street Journal*, Mar. 31, 1994
- L.J. Davis, "The Name of Rose", *The New Republic*, Apr. 4, 1994, p. 23
- Ambrose Evans-Pritchard, "The Enforcer and the Broken Man, the Clinton Controversy", *Sunday Telegraph*, May 8, 1994, p. 21
- Robert D. Novak and Zelda Novak, "Oh, What a Tangled Webb..." *The American Spectator*, June, 1994, pp. 24-29
- Michael Frisby, "White House's Thomasson Keeps Ties to Clintons Strong Despite Controversy and GOP Criticism", *The Wall Street Journal*, June 21, 1994, p. A16
- Alan Fram, "Senate Wants Information on Drug Tests for White House Aide", *Associated Press*, June 22, 1994
- Combined Dispatches, "Senate Votes to Query Clinton on Drug Tests", *The Washington Times*, June 23, 1994, A1, A12
- Ambrose Evans-Pritchard, "Clinton Took Cocaine While in Office", *Sunday Telegraph*, July 17, 1994, p. 1, 7
- Audio Interview with Eyewitness, Name Temporarily Withheld, July 18, 1994, on file, Citizens For Honest Government
- John Brown, Video Interview, July 18, 1994, on file CFHG
- Ambrose Evans-Pritchard, "Smugglers Linked to Contra Arms deals," The *Sunday Telegraph* of London, Oct. 9, 1994, page 3.

DEATHS, ATTACKS, AND COVER-UPS

- Arkansas State Police Investigator Russell Welch nearly dies after being poisoned with military grade Anthrax.
- Federal Agent Bill Duncan, a 15-year veteran with a permit to carry a gun, is arrested for carrying a weapon, then hand-

cuffed to a pipe in the basement of the Washington, D.C. police station and later released. This incident effectively brings the Mena drug smuggling/money laundering investigation to a halt. Duncan is later instructed by his superiors to lie to a Federal Grand Jury regarding the results of his investigation. When he refuses, he is forced to resign.

Arkansas State Police Investigator Doc DeLaughter is forced to resign after successfully leading the investigation which resulted in the cocaine distribution conviction of Clinton's friend and associate Dan Lasater.

- In 1988, Polk County Prosecuting Attorney, Charles Black personally requests funds from Governor Clinton to continue the Mena airport investigation. Clinton claims to authorize $25,000, but the money never comes. Later, Black's mother is brutally killed in her home. Police insist there is no connection.

- Jean Duffey, former head of the Arkansas Drug Task Force, receives numerous threats to her life after courageously presenting evidence to Congress which links Governor Clinton's administration to drug trafficking in Arkansas.

Ronald Rogers, who possessed important information about Bill Clinton, is killed in a suspicious plane crash just hours before his scheduled interview for The Clinton Chronicles.

- In February 1994, veteran journalist L.J. Davis is beaten in his Little Rock hotel room. His attacker tears pages from his notebook which contains information about the inner workings of the Rose Law Firm.

- In March 1985, Wayne Dumond is castrated and subsequently imprisoned for allegedly raping Bill Clinton's 17 year-old cousin. Even after it is proven that Dumond had been falsely accused and is completely innocent, Clinton blocks his release from prison.

- On August 15, 1993, John Walker, an RTC investigator who had uncovered ties between Whitewater Development, Madison Guaranty and the Clintons, falls to his death from the Lincoln Towers in Arlington, Virginia. Investigators rule his death a suicide.

- On July 28, 1994, police informant Calvin Walraven is found dead after testifying against U.S. Surgeon General Jocelyn Elder's son, Kevin, at Kevin's cocaine distribution trial. Although Walraven's testimony puts his life in jeopardy, Little Rock Police insist he committed suicide.

- In May 1994, Kathy Ferguson, ex-wife of former Clinton body

guard Danny Ferguson, who was named as co-defendant in
the Paula Jones lawsuit against Bill Clinton, is found dead in
her apartment less than a week after Jones files suit. Medical
personnel who examined the body claim her wounds point to
homicide, yet the police, as expected, rule suicide as the
cause of death. Four weeks later, Ferguson's fiancee, police
officer Bill Shelton, is also found dead. His death is labeled a
suicide as well.

- "The Reporters", FOX-TV, Nov. 11, 1988
- "20/20", ABC-TV, Jan. 13, 1989
- Letter from Arkansas Congressman Bill Alexander to Governor
  Clinton, Re: Mena drug smuggling operations, Jan. 26, 1989, on
  file, Citizens for Honest Government.
- Memorandum from Bob Govar to Chuck Banks and Mac Dodson,
  Re: Saline County Narcotics Investigation, Feb. 13, 1990
- Joint Investigation by the Arkansas State Attorney General's Office
  and the U. S. Congress, "Oral Deposition of William C. Duncan
  and Russell F. Welch, June 21, 1991.
- Mara Leveritt, "The Boys on the Tracks", *Arkansas Times*, Jan.
  1992, p. 70.
- "Current Affair", FOX-TV, Jan. 29 and Apr. 16, 1992
- Ambrose Evans-Pritchard, "Little Rock's Mean Machine", *Sunday
  Telegraph*, Mar. 13, 1994, p. 26
- Jean Duffey, video interviews, Mar. 18 and Aug. 5, 1994, on file,
  Citizens For Honest Government
- Deroy Murdock, "Are Attacks Linked to Whitewater?", *New York
  Post*, Mar. 23, 1994, p. 14
- Editors, "Censored in Arkansas", *The Wall Street Journal*, Mar. 23,
  1994, p. A12
- Deroy Murdock, "A Pattern of Violence", *Orange County Register*,
  March 24, 1994, p. M9
- Dan Rather, "Eye on America", *CBS Evening News*, Mar. 25, 1994.
- Martin Yant, "Ohio Native Battles Clinton-Clan 'Justice'", *The Ohio
  Observer*, May, 1994, pp. 7-12
- Arkansas State Crime Laboratory, Medical Examiner Division,
  Coroner's Report on Kathy Ferguson, May 11, 1994, Case #ME-
  371-94
- AP, "Arkansas Trooper's Ex-Wife Apparent Suicide", *Los Angeles
  Times*, May 14, 1994.
- Michael Hedges, "Ex-wife of Sued Trooper Kills Self", *The
  Washington Times*, May 14, 1994.
- Ambrose Evans-Pritchard, "Congress Backs off Clinton Hearings",
  Sunday Telegraph, May 15, 1994, p. 1
- Deroy Murdock, "Arkansas Trail of Tears", *Orange County
  Register*, June 8, 1994, p. M7

- Oliver Uyttebrouck, "Officer Can't Stand It, Follows Fiancee in Suicide at Grave", *Arkansas Democrat-Gazette*, Jun. 14, 1994, p. 1A
- Editors, "Curiouser", The Economist, Jul. 9, 1994, pp. 29, 30
- AP, "Surgeon General's Son Is Convicted of Selling Cocaine", *The Washington Times*, July 19, 1994
- AP, "Death of Figure in Elders' Case Called a Suicide", *Los Angeles Times*, July 30, 1994.
- Video Interviews with Eyewitnesses, Names Temporarily Withheld, July 30 and Aug. 2, 1994, on file, Citizens For Honest Government

APPENDIX C

THE DOCUMENTS WHICH FOLLOW ARE ACTUAL COPIES OF OFFICIAL GOVERNMENTAL INVESTIGATIONS OR REPORTS OBTAINED FROM SOURCES DEEMED RELIABLE. HOWEVER ANY ALLEGATIONS OF CRIMINAL ACTIVITY CONCERNING PERSONS NAMED IN THESE DOCUMENTS, OR PERSONS SUBJECT TO ANY GOVERNMENTAL INVESTIGATIONS, ARE NOT ESTABLISHED FACTS UNLESS OR UNTIL PROVEN IN A COURT OF LAW OR IMPEACHMENT PROCEEDINGS.

BILL ALEXANDER, M.C.
ARKANSAS

COMMITTEE ON
APPROPRIATIONS

233 CANNON HOUSE OFFICE BUILDING
WASHINGTON, DC 20515
(202) 225-4076

Congress of the United States

January 26, 1989

Gov. Bill Clinton
State Capitol
Little Rock, Arkansas

Dear Bill:

The investigation into alleged drugs and gun smuggling at Mena
airport can be cleared up by a local grand jury that will require
state funds. Deputy Prosecutor Charles Black of Mt. Ida, the state
police and congressional investigators are interested in convening
such a grand jury, which is probably the only way that the matter
will be resolved and laid to rest once and for all.

Black estimates that about $25,000 will be required, because
witnesses will have to be brought in from out of state. This figure
cannot be paid for out of local resources. Black knows of witnesses
who will testify that planes loaded with guns went to Central America
and returned loaded with drugs.

Certain DEA agents have stated that the late convicted smuggler Barry
Seal was flying weapons to Central America in violation of U.S.
foreign policy and in return, the federal government secretly allowed
Seal to smuggle drugs back into the United States. Congressman Bill
Hughes' Subcommittee on Crime has learned independently that at the
time Seal was working on the famous Nicaraguan "sting" operation for
the DEA and the CIA in 1984, he was still running drugs. Sources in
Mena indicate that smuggling activities at Mena continued after
Seal's murder in 1986 and are still continuing.

My involvement in the case stems from two sources: I initiated a
General Accounting Office investigation into drug trafficking from
Latin America to the United States, and secondly, because of my
position as the senior ranking Democrat on the Appropriations
Subcommittee that handles Justice Department funding.

Prosecutor Black, State Police Investigator Russell Welch, and others
who have been involved in the investigation have done an exemplary
job, but they have been frustrated by the failure of some federal
officials to proceed with the case. The only way to get the matter
cleared up is to convene the local grand jury. Otherwise it will
continue to fester and be a thorn in the side of local, state and
congressional resources. I hope you will grant Mr. Black's request
for funding in this matter.

With kindest regards, I am

Sincerely,

BILL ALEXANDER
Member of Congress

1

CRIMINAL INVESTIGATION DIVISION

ASP-3-A

DATE: September 11, 1986
DICTATED BY: INV. J. N. "DOC" DELAUGHTER
DATE TYPED: September 12, 1986
COPIES TO: INV. J. N. "DOC" DELAUGHTER
TERRY DERDEN

INTERVIEW OF WITNESS

White Female
27 Years Old
██████ Lane, Little Rock, Arkansas
Phone ██████
Employed at ██████, Little Rock, Arkansas
Office ██████

██████ was interviewed on August 28, 1986 at the United States Attorney's Office in Little Rock, Arkansas by J. N. "DOC" DELAUGHTER. She reports as follows.

I ██████ state that I reside at Number ██████ Lane, Little Rock, Arkansas.

In April 1983, I saw DAN LASATER at a COLLINS LOCK and LASATER party at the Arlington Hotel in Hot Springs, Arkansas. There was a glass table in the Suite where the party was held with five or six lines of cocaine arranged on it.

"ROGER CLINTON a friend of mine and I used some of the cocaine. I did not see LASATER use any cocaine during the twenty minutes or so I was at the party. The cocaine was free".

"ROGER and I went to DAN LASATER'S Quapaw Towers Apartment and ROGER asked DAN if he was interested in any of MAURICE RODRIGUEZ'S cocaine". LASATER said no he didn't want anything to do with MAURICE. DAN LASATER, ROGER and I used some cocaine that was already at LASATER'S apartment.

FILE NUMBER: 58-689-86   CRIME: Criminal conspiracy to possess
                                           controlled substance

2

ASP-3-A

DATE: 9-22-86
DICTATED BY: INV. J. M. (DOC) DELAUGHTER
DATE TYPED: 9-23-86
COPIES TO: INV. J. M. (DOC) DELAUGHTER
TERRY DERDEN

<u>INTERVIEW OF WITNESS</u>

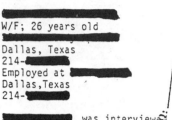

W/F; 26 years old

Dallas, Texas
214-
Employed at
Dallas, Texas
214-

was interviewed at the United States Attorny's Office in
Little Rock, Arkansas on September 17, 1986, by this investigator. She
reports as follows.

I _____ am willing to give a statement about my use of
cocaine.

I first used cocaine approximately two times in college. After my college
days I went to work for CL&L of 1982. A month later <u>DAN LASTER</u> invited me
to his apartment 12D in the <u>Quapaw Towers in Little Rock</u>, Arkansas. The
people I remember at the apartment were DAN LASTER, GEORGE LOTT, DAVID COLLINS,
a few other white females, and myself. DAN LASTER produced a one gram bottle
of cocaine with a <u>spoon on it</u>. DAN took a bump of the cocaine and I handed
the bottle to the person next to him. When the bottle reached me I also took
a bump of the cocaine. The best that I can remember was that everyone in the
room snorted some of the cocaine. After this particular evening I started
doing cocaine on a regular basis. I later reached the point with my use of
cocaine that if I was out late the night before I would sometimes get up and
snort cocaine in order to start my day.

The next time I remember DAN LASTER giving me cocaine was approximately four
or five weeks later. DAN LASTER, GEORGE LOTT, CARRIE TRACEY, PAT PATTERSON,
his girl friend FNU LNU, and myself flew on DAN LASTER's six seater jet from
Little Rock, Arkansas to Las Vegas, Nevada. Following the trip out to Las
Vegas DAN produced a one two gram bottle of cocaine. DAN LASTER, GEORGE LOTT,
CARRIE TRACEY, and myself all snorted cocaine from DAN LASTER's bottle of
cocaine. I remember snorting cocaine several times on the way to Las Vegas.

FILE NUMBER: 58-686-86
58-689-86

CRIME: CRIMINAL CONSPIRACY OF POSSESSI
OF A CONTROLLED SUBSTANCE

AS1-3-A

DATE: September 11, 1986
DICTATED BY: INV. J. N. "DOC" DELAUGHTER
DATE TYPED: September 11, 1986
COPIES TO: INV. J. N. "DOC" DELAUGHTER
TERRY DERDEN

INTERVIEW OF WITNESS

███████████
A K A ████████
White Female
22 years old
████████ Avenue, North Little Rock, Arkansas
Phone █████████
Employed at ████████████ .in Little Rock, Arkansas

████████ was interviewed on September 8, 1986 at the United States
Attorney's Office in Little Rock, Arkansas by investigator J. N. "DOC"
DELAUGHTER. She reports the following.

I ████████████ am willing to give a statement about my possession
of cocaine.

I recieved cocaine from GEORGE LOCK and DAN LASATER approximately ten
times each from the middle of 1984 to the first of 1985. The first time
I met DAN LASATER and GEORGE LOCK was at GEORGE LOCK'S apartment located
off Cantrell Road in Little Rock, Arkansas. On this particular evening
GEORGE LOCK gave me approximately ten snorts of cocaine. I received approx-
imately eight to ten snorts from DAN LASATER. The next time I remember
receiving cocaine was on April of 1984 when DAN LANSTRUM, GEORGE LOCK,
MITCHELLE COCHRAN, CLARENCE LNU, myself flew on DAN LASATER ' jet to Las
Vegas, Nevada. While flying from Little Rock to Las Vegas I recieved Ten
bumps of cocaine from GEORGE LOCK and approximately ten bumps from DAN
LASATER. We stayed at the Riviera Hotel in Las Vegas. I stayed with
GEORGE LOCK and MITCHELLE COCHRAN stayed with DAN LASATER. We ran out of
cocaine while we were in Las Vegas, so we didn't have any to snort on the
return trip. The main times I received cocaine from DAN LASATER and GEORGE
LOCK were at GEORGE LOCK'S apartment off of Cantrell Road in Little Rock,
Arkansas.

I contacted GEORGE LOCK on August 25, 1986 and asked him to help me get
a job at the Black Eyed Pea. The Black Eyed Pea is owned by DAN LASATER.
I started to work approximately on August 27, 1986 at the Black Eyed Pea.
Approximately three days later I called GEORGE LOCK and told him that I got
the job. During the conversation GEORGE LOCK said "do you know a
guy by the name of "DOC" DELAUGHTER that works at the State Police?"

FILE NUMBER: 58-689-36   CRIME: Criminal conspiracy to posse
                                      controlled substance

4

ASI-3-A

DATE: September 11, 1986
DICTATED BY: INV. J. N. "DOC" DELAUGHTER
DATE TYPED: September 11, 1986
COPIES TO: INV. J. N. "DOC" DELAUGHTER
                 TERRY DERDEN

INTERVIEW OF WITNESS

White Male
42 years old
███████████████████, Boca Raton, Florida
Phone 305-████████
Employed at ████████████████████████████
Office 305-████████████

███████████ was interviewed on August 26, 1986 at his office in Boca Raton,
Florida by investigator J. N. "DOC" DELAUGHTER. He reports as follows.

I ██████████████ am willing to give a statement about seeing DAN LASATER,
DAVID COLLINS in possession of cocaine.

In December of 1983 DAN LASATER had a Christmas party for his firm at
the Marriott Hotel in the Casablanca room in Fort Lauderdale, Florida.
DON BUSZANASKI and myself drove home from work. In the process in going
home DON told me I got to drop something off to DAN LASATER. From this
statement I don't have any doubt that he was talking about cocaine. We
drove to the Mariott and I stayed in the car. GEORGE LOCK came outside
and asked me, upstairs but I told him I had to get home. The time of day
was approximately 5:30 p.m. That day or the next day we had the Christmas party
at approximately 8:30 p.m. The people attending the party were DAN LASATER,
GEORGE LOCKE, BUSZANASKI, GUY GARDOKI, MARK KERKEL, BILL FORTNER, myself and
several other people from the office. DAN LASATER, GEORGE LOCK, and DON
BUSZANASKI, and myself went into the bathroom together, while in the bathroom
DAN said, "I am happy to have you back in the firm." DAN produced approximately
one eighth ounce container of cocaine. I saw DAN LASATER snort four or five
bumps of cocaine in the bathroom, DON BUSZANASKI and myself were given cocaine
in the bathroom which we snorted in front of DAN LASATER. I would venture to
say that there were approximately a hundred people at the party. In May 1984
DAN LASATER and myself went into the ROWLAND'S Restaurant in Fort Lauderdale,
Florida. We both went to the bathroom and DAN LASATER produced a container
of cocaine. DAN offered me some of it but I can't remember if I snorted it
or not. DAN LASATER then snorted some of the cocaine in my presence.

I have observed through my relationship with DAN LASATER that the LASATER
forces security people through employment pressure to engage in the use of
cocaine usually provided by him LASATER.   I have seen LASATER employees
family relationships and professions practically destroyed.

FILE NUMBER: 58-686-36   CRIME: Criminal conspiracy to posses
                 58-639-36   controlled substance

1. PROGRAM CODE	2. CROSS FILE	RELATED FILES	3. FILE NO. GJ-83-2001	4. G-DEP IDENTIFIER DP1-C1

5. BY: AT: DEATF Sgt. Don Sanders
Little Rock, AR

6. FILE TITLE

WELLS, Al

7. ☐ Closed ☐ Requested Action Completed ☐ Action Requested By:

8. DATE PREPARED
March 12, 1984

9. OTHER OFFICERS:

10. REPORT RE:
Application for Exemption for Special Landing Requirements

DETAILS:

1. Reference is made to all previous Reports of Investigation (ROI's) under instant fil concerning the alleged activities of Dan R. LASATER of LASATER AND COMPANY INVESTMENT BANKERS, Little Rock, Arkansas.

2. The following information was determined from U.S. Customs Agent Ed Walker of Nashvi Tennessee, in regards to a request by LASATER AND COMPANY, of Little Rock, Arkansas, to issued an exemption (overflight) for special landing requirements. The exemption would allow LASATER AND COMPANY to fly from points outside the United States, south of the 30t parallel and clear customs at Little Rock, Arkansas.

3. Information from Agent Walker indicated that LASATER AND COMPANY utilize business addresses of 312 Louisiana Street, Little Rock, Arkansas, telephone 501-376-0069, and #1 Corporate Plaza, Penthouse D, 110 E. Broadway Boulevard, Fort Lauderdale, Florida, telephone 305-467-3088.

4. LASATER AND COMPANY requests exemptions for the following aircraft and designated personnel.

REGISTRATION	REGISTERED OWNER	A/C TYPE	COLOR
N-600DL	Dan R. LASATER ▓▓▓▓▓▓ Little Rock, AR	Canadian CL600/Jet	White w/Bl Trim
N-200DL	LFI CORPORATION (leased) COLLINS, LOCK, LASATER DEVELOPMENT 312 Louisiana Little Rock, AR	IAI 1124 Westwind, Jet	White w/re maroon tri

11. DISTRIBUTION:	12. SIGNATURE (Agent)	13. DAT
REGION		3/1
DISTRICT LRPD Narcotics ASP Narcotics	14. APPROVED (Name and Title)	15. DAT
OTHER HQS, ARI & OC	Gary G. Worden, RAC	3/1

T-16082

N-100DL   Dan R. LASATER   Gates Learjet   White w/blu
                                                               24B   Trim

NAME	ADDRESS	DATE OF BIRTH
Dan R. LASATER Passenger	Little Rock, AR 72205	1/2/43
George E. LOCKE Passenger	Little Rock, AR 72205	5/20/35
Larry D. MALONE Passenger	Little Rock, AR 72212	8/13/46
Patsy L. THOMASSON Passenger	Little Rock, AR 72205	12/27/47
Joe MARFOGLIO Passenger	Little Rock, AR 72207	12/30/41
Rolland ZILLER Chief Pilot	Little Rock, AR.	12/7/40
Tony GOCZALK Crew Member	Little Rock, AR	3/13/58
Marty QUICK Crew Member	Little Rock, AR	11/26/51
Clarence STRAHAM Crew Member	Little Rock, AR	9/27/56

5. The exemption request listed flights of LASATER AND COMPANY to originate outside th
United States from the Caribbean, Latin America and South America.

INDEXING SECTION:

1. Dan R. LASATER - NADDIS #141475.

DEA Form — 6a
(May 1980)

DEA SENSITIVE
DRUG ENFORCEMENT ADMINISTRATION
This report is the property of the Drug Enforcement Administration.
Neither it nor its contents may be disseminated outside the Agency to which loaned.

Previous edition may be used.

7

stated that he has seen CLARENCE STRAHAN use cocaine approximately
five times and that STRAHAN has had the responsibility
of holding his (LASATER's) cocaine on numerous occasions.
He stated that CLARENCE STRAHAN has bought cocaine for
him approximately three or four times but that the money
used for the purchase always came from himself.

Mr. LASATER admitted doing cocaine with GEORGOE
HALL and HERBIE DOUGLAS in the past, with one of the occasions
occurring at the KING ARTHUR'S CLUB on Markham in 1982
or early 1983. He did not recall to whom the cocaine belonged
at the time.

He is familiar with LARRY KELLY, but he has never
done cocaine with KELLY, and he has never given KELLY any
cocaine.

He is unfamiliar with an individual by the name
of BUD GUY. Mr. LASATER advised that he has snorted cocaine
with DON BUZANOWSKI, who worked in the Fort Lauderdale,
Florida, office. He snorted cocaine with him on one or
two occasions and has given him cocaine in bump amounts.

He is only slightly familiar with OMAR BUTTARI
as BUTTARI worked in the Fort Lauderdale, Florida, office.
He had no drug dealings with BUTTARI.

He is familiar with TOM CARTER, with whom he
has snorted cocaine on several occasions in which the cocaine
would be both his and TOM CARTER's at the time.

Mr. LASATER related that he has given PAULA COLLINS
cocaine ranging from fifteen (15) to twenty-five (25) times
in small amounts. He denied ever ordering CHUCK BERRY
to give PAULA COLLINS cocaine but was aware that BERRY
had given her cocaine in the past. He knows PAULA COLLINS
as being the former wife of DAVID COLLINS.

Regarding ROGER CLINTON, Mr. LASATER advised
he met CLINTON through MITCHELL WOOD sometime around 1981
or 1982 during the time CLINTON played in a band in the
Hot Springs area. CLINTON was employed by him at one time
in which Governor BILL CLINTON requested LASATER to hire
him. ROGER CLINTON was employed as a stable hand at his
Ocala, Florida, horse farm. Mr. LASATER stated he has
done cocaine with ROGER CLINTON, and they have shared their
personal supplies of cocaine as each of them always had
it with them.

8

MICHAEL DRAKE was very instrumental in working out the legislative problem surrounding the bill and additional amendments. DRAKE worked very closely with JOHNNY SIMPSON, Arkansas State Police Commissioner, and they eventually formed a consultant partnership after DRAKE left LASATER AND COMPANY.

There was considerable lobbying done for the contract, but Mr. LOCKE said he felt because LASATER AND COMPANY backed the right individual in Governor CLINTON, LASATER AND COMPANY received the contract.

There was no under-the-table payment of money to legislators involved, and to his recollection, the only opposition LASATER AND COMPANY had that was on the Arkansas State Police Commission was GENE RAFF of Helena.

Mr. LOCKE stated he was aware DAN LASATER had given TOMMY MITCHUM $500 in the past for past campaign debts but this had no influence at the time of the communications bond issue.

However, TOMMY MITCHUM is the brother to JOHNNY MITCHUM, a member of the Arkansas State Police Commission.

Mr. LOCKE speculates DAN LASATER developed a relationship with MIKE MAHONE, Arkansas State Police, through his friendship with ROGER CLINTON or ROGER's mother, VIRGINIA CLINTON.

As he recalls, subsequent to the SAM ANDERSON trial, a black male individual was a frequent visitor of VIRGINIA CLINTON's box seats at OAKLAWN race track, Hot Springs, Arkansas. This individual was subsequently identified as MIKE MAHONE.

While in Chicago, Illinois, he was contacted three to six months ago by DAN LASATER, who advised MIKE MAHONE was coming to Chicago, and DAN LASATER requested he get his friend a room.

LOCKE stated he made a room reservation in his (LOCKE's) name and paid for the reservation on his (LOCKE's) credit card. The room was for MIKE MAHONE, and he and DAN LASATER met MAHONE and paid for his meal. During the first meeting, MAHONE stated he needed an attorney as his mother's home in Chicago was being foreclosed on. MAHONE asked for assistance in obtaining a lawyer, and DAN LASATER asked him (LOCKE) to try and retain an attorney to help MAHONE. LOCKE said his efforts were

9

Approximately two months ago, LASATER asked
him to get MAHONE a room for one night. He obtained a
room at the AMBASSADOR WEST HOTEL, Chicago, and MAHONE
stayed there. He met MAHONE the next morning, and over
breakfast, MAHONE, DAN LASATER, and he discussed the ongoing
drug investigation surrounding DAN LASATER and himself.
MAHONE stated LARRY GLEGHORN and DOC DE LAUGHTER, both
investigators for the Arkansas State Police, had a "hard
on" for LASATER. LOCKE said he was familiar with GLEGHORN
and DE LAUGHTER and knew them to frequent "SPANKY'S" in
Little Rock, and to be close friends with DANIEL BARNETT.

During this breakfast meeting with MAHONE, MAHONE
advised him that he (LOCKE) would be subpoenaed before
a Federal Grand Jury (FGJ) but did not think there was
any evidence that would convict him of drug charges.

MAHONE stated, "If there is no evidence, there
is no way they could convict us."

In addition, MAHONE told them to be circumspect
in the use of the telephone as the telephones may be tapped.

At this meeting in Chicago, MAHONE gave DAN
LASATER a beeper with which he (MAHONE) could contact
LASATER in case an emergency arose.

Mr. LOCKE advised he was aware the attorneys
for DAN LASATER opposed LASATER having anything to do
with MIKE MAHONE.

Mr. LOCKE stated MIKE MAHONE never did any personal
favors for him.

Mr. LOCKE stated he recalls cocaine present
during a reception given in honor of ROSALYN CARTER, wife
of President JIMMY CARTER. The reception was at the UNION
LIFE BUILDING, Little Rock, and he attended the affair
with BENNY RYBURN, PATTY THOMASON, and BILL CALHOUN, all
personal friends. The year was 1980.

During the reception, he (LOCKE) was offered
to do a line of cocaine by CRAIG CAMPBELL, who he knows
to be employed by STEPHENS AND COMPANY, INC., Little Rock.
CRAIG CAMPBELL and an unknown individual who owned and
operated a television station in Fort Smith, Arkansas,
had approximately three lines of cocaine layed out on
a table inside the men's lounge area. Mr. LOCKE said
he saw the two men snort the cocaine, then refused to
snort the cocaine himself, then left the room.

LR 245F-2

Continuation of FD-302 of _____ GEORGE EDWARD LOCKE _____ On __10/10/86 &__ Page __9__
                                                                    10/17/86

Mr. LOCKE advised it was his understanding that CRAIG CAMPBELL was the source of cocaine for ▮▮▮▮▮▮▮▮▮▮▮ during a time ▮▮▮▮▮▮▮▮▮▮ was having problems regarding alcohol consumption.

GEORGE LOCKE is described as a white male, date of birth May 20, 1935, residence ▮▮ North ▮▮▮▮▮▮▮▮ Drive, Chicago, Illinois, telephone (312) ▮▮▮▮▮▮▮, height 5'10", weight 178 pounds, hair gray, eyes blue, Social Security Account Number ▮▮▮▮▮▮▮▮▮.

CRIMINAL INVESTIGATION DIVISION

ASP-3-A
DATE: 10/27/86
DICTATED BY: INV. J. N. "DOC" DELAUGHTER
DATE TYPED: 11/4/86
COPIES TO: INV. J. M. "DOC" DELAUGHTER

INVESTIGATOR'S NOTES

This particular case is a continuation of an investigation that I
have conducted on Collins and Associates Government Securities Incorporated. It was revealed through signed statements and memorandums
to the case file that DAN LASATER was using Cocaine as a tool to
manipulate individuals around him for business and sexual gratifications.
The heaviest Cocaine used ran from the first of 1980 until the middle
of 1985. In 1985 DAN LASATER realized that he and his associates
were projecting a bad image to the public, therefore, DAN lunged a
campaign to project a better image. This was done through his
becoming involved in the FLORENCE CRITTENDEN Home Services for
Unwed Mothers, the Arthritis Foundation, and the Gyst House for
Drug Abuse. Then also attempted to project this good image through
his socializing with different Law-Enforcement Agency personnel.

In 1981 through 1985 DONALD GLEN BRADLEY was responsible for supplying
approximately one kilo of Cocaine per month to the Little Rock area.
From 1981 through 1982 one of BRADLEY'S purchasers of Cocaine was
DAVE GINGRASS. GINGRASS would distribute his Cocaine in the following
order.

1. MICHAEL STANDRIDGE
2. DAN LASATER
3. DAVID COLLINS
4. GEORGE LOCKE

In 1982 after GINGRASS became unreliable DONALD GLEN BRADLEY started
selling to LARRY GUCCIARDO. GUCCIARDO would distribute his Cocaine
in the following order.

1. DAVIE GINGRASS
2. MICHAEL STANDRIDGE
3. DAN LASATER
4. LASATER & ASSOCIATES

In the early part of 1981 through the early part of 1984 BRADLEY distributed his Cocaine to BUCKY CLAYTON who in return distribued it in
the following order.

FILE NUMBER: 58-689-86

CRIME: CRIMINAL CONSPIRACY TO P
OR DISTRIBUTE A CONTROLLED SUBS

12

ASP-3-A

DATE:
DICTATED BY:
DATE TYPED:
COPIES TO:

August 21, 1986
INV. J. N. DELAUGHTER
August 27, 1986
Inv. Doc DeLaughter

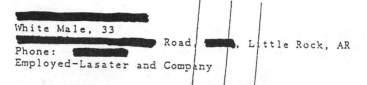

INTERVIEW OF WITNESS

White Male, 33

███████████████ Road, ████, Little Rock, AR

Phone: ███████

Employed-Lasater and Company

███████████ was interviewed on August 20, 1986 at the United-States Attorney's Office in Little Rock, Arkansas by INV. J. N. "DOC" DELAUGHTER. ████████ reports the following information.

I, ███████████, am willing to give a statement abotu receiving cocaine from DAN LASATER and DAVID COLLINS.

On November 6, 1981, DAN LASATER had a bachelor's party for me at his apartment, 12B, at the Quapaw Towers in Little Rock, Arkansas. The people at the party were DAN LASATER, DAVID COLLINS, ERIC WESTERMAN, GEORGE LOCKE, CURTIS McCLENDON, ROGER CLINTON, LASATER's girl friend by the name of FNU LNU, and approximately twenty (20) other people that I can't remember their names. I saw one or two grams of cocaine poured into a plate at the dining room table. I saw DAN LASATER make two to three lines of cocaine from the plate at a time. DAN did this approximately six (6) times while I was present. I also saw DAN LASATER, GEORGE LOCKE, ERIC WESTERMAN, and CURTIS McCLENDON snort the cocaine from the table. While at this party, I snorted cocaine twelve to fifteen times at no expense to me. I saw DAN LASATER, GEORGE LOCKE, and DAVID COLLINS in the same bed, having sex, with two (2) white females and one black female.

On December 20, 1983, I remember DAN LASATER offered me some cocaine while we were at the Christmas party

FILE NUMBER: 58-686-86   CRIME: CRIMINAL CONSPIRAC
                58-689-86   POSS. A CONT. SUBS

13

<u>INTELLIGENCE</u>

```
CID- 3C
DATE:                      3-20-85
DICTATED BY:               MORROW
COUNTY:                    JONESBORO, AR/CRAIGHEAD
SOURCE OF INFORMATION:     R.O.C.I.C.
TOPIC OF INFORMATION:·     TELEPHONE SUBSCRIBERS
DATE TYPED:                3-21-85
COPIES TO:                 MORROW
                           JENKINS
```

At the request of Sergeant JIM JENKINS on 3-14-35, this investigator researched subscriber information on ten (10) telephone numbers provided by Sergeant JENKINS. The request was involving an investigation in regards to child pornography and the suspect was listed as JOHN ████████, white male, DOB: 7-13-54.

The following is a list of telephone numbers and the subscriber information.

1. 501-661-0402, Southwestern Bell Telephone Number, indicates that this is not a good working number.

2. 501-376-0069, Southwestern Bell Telephone Number, indicates that it is listed to <u>LASITER AND COMPANY</u>. <u>INCORPORATED</u> at 312 Louisiana Street, Little Rock, Arkansas.

3. 501-████████, United Telephone of Rola, Missouri, final account for ████████, Attorney, which is also a joint account with ████████.

4. 501-████████, United Telephone of Rola, Missouri, listed to ████████ and ████████. ████████ Street, P. O. Box ██, Truman, Arkansas. Billing information has a Social Security Number listed of ████████, believed to be that of ████████, lists his father as ████████, ████████ in Jonesboro, Arkansas, telephone number ████████.

5. 501-████████, United Telephone of Rola, Missouri, registered to ████████ and ████████ at Route ██, Box ██, Truman, Arkansas. Billing information has the father as ████████, also listed with the telephone number ████████.

The following subscriber information was received through R.O.C.I.C., on 3-20-85, at approximately 3:15 p.m.

FILE NUMBER: I-16819   I-16283

14

Kenneth D. Reasonover
DIRECTOR

Telephone
(615) 366-1197

May 15, 1986

Lt. Doug Stephens
Arkansas State Police
P. O. Box 5901
Little Rock, AR   72215

Dear Lt. Stephens:

I would appreciate your assistance in obtaining any criminal/
intelligence-information on the following individual. The request
is being made by the Attorney General's Office in Sante Fe, New
Mexico in reference to narcotics trafficking via aircraft with possible
Organized Crime ties.

Dan R. Lasater
w/m, dob 1-2-43
address: 312 Louisiana N.E., Little Rock, AR
aka: Dan R. Lassiter

If you have any questions, please call. Thank you for your
assistance.

Sincerely,

Nelda Wilson
Intelligence Technician

6/4/86 Contacted Joe Stinson, ROCIC + advised
him ASP had on going investigation on This Subject.
Stinson was Requested To have New Mexico Attny
Generals office To Contact Capt Doug Stephens
So Capt Stephens could get his investigator in
Touch with ASP Inv Doc Delaughter, who is ASP
Case Agent. R. Hughes

TO:_____ DATE_____
TO:_____ DATE_____
TO:_____ DATE_____
TO:_____ DATE_____
TO:_____ DATE_____
TO:_____ DATE_____
TO:_____ DATE_____

I-16283

15

UNITED STATES DISTRICT COURT
EASTERN DISTRICT OF ARKANSAS

UNITED STATES OF AMERICA)
)   NO. LR-CR-86-
         v.   )   21 U.S.C. § 846
)
DAN R. LASATER   )

INDICTMENT

THE GRAND JURY CHARGES THAT:

COUNT I

From on or about December 15, 1981 and continuing to
on or about September 15, 1985, in the Eastern District of
Arkansas and elsewhere,

DAN R. LASATER

did knowingly, willfully, and intentionally conspire, combine
and confederate with Donald Glenn Bradley, Roger Clinton, David
Collins, George Locke, and Lee Curtis Berry, named herein as
unindicted co-conspirators, and with other persons known and
unknown to the Grand Jury to violate a law of the United
States, that is, to knowingly and willfully possess with the
intent to distribute and to distribute cocaine; a Schedule II
Narcotic Controlled Substance, a violation of Title 21, United
States Code, Section 841(a), thereby violating Title 21, United
States Code, Section 846.

                                A TRUE BILL

                        _____
                        FOREMAN

16

T. Karam
BRANCH
DATE Sept. 26, 1984
T. Karam
$ ***9,900

CASHIER'S CHECK

№ 3 7

⑂0074940⑂ ⑂122401367⑂ 003-0006999⑂

LITTLE ROCK, ARK. _____ AUGUST 6 _____ 19 84 No. 0814

WORTHEN Bank & Trust Company, N.A.
Member FDIC

PAY TO THE
ORDER OF _____ T. KARAM
$ 9,000.

WORTHEN E 39,000 AND 00 CTS

CASHIER'S CHECK

Marsha Do

⑂0814⑂ ⑂0820000731⑂ 6601-150-3⑂

EXHIBIT 116

CD-00000437

17

~5976264~ ⑆122240⑉ 14:8803210010⑈ 751

First Interstate Bank

FIRST INTERSTATE BANK
OF NEVADA, N.A.
LAS VEGAS, NEVADA

38-584576

94-36
1224

PURCHASER T. Karam

DATE September 26, 1984

Pay to the order of ************T. Karam*************************** $**9,900.00*********

$ ──OFFICE─9,900 dll's 00 cts
33

CASHIER'S CHECK

AUTHORIZED SIGNATURE

⑆584576⑈ ⑆1224003644:8803210010⑈ 751

First Interstate Bank

FIRST INTERSTATE BANK
OF NEVADA, N.A.
LAS VEGAS, NEVADA

38-617812

94-36
1224

PURCHASER Only Karam

DATE September 25, 1984* * *

Pay to the order of * W.J. Karam* * * * * * * * * * * * * * * * * $*9,997.00* * * * * * *

$ ──OFF.CE─9,997
126

CASHIER'S CHECK

AUTHORIZED SIGNATURE

⑆617812⑈ ⑆1224003644:8803210010⑈ 751

CD-00000435

EXHIBIT 114

18

REPORT OF INVESTIGATION

1. PROGRAM CODE	2. CROSS FILE	RELATED FILES	3. FILE NO. GTGJ-83-9052	4. G-DEA IDENTIFIER DA1-CO
5. BY: H. Dean Gates, S/A AT. Oklahoma City, Oklahoma	☐ ☐ ☐ ☐		6. FILE TITLE REFERRALS FROM STATE LAW ENFORCEMENT AGENCIES	
7. ☐ Closed ☒ Requested Action Completed ☐ Action Requested By 9. OTHER OFFICERS:			8. DATE PREPARED December 14, 1982	

10. REPORT RE:

Identification of associate of Jerry PRIDEAUX.

DETAILS:

1. Reference is made to DEA-6 by S/A Robert Morris, Little Rock, Arkansas, dated 11/30/82 concerning the arrest of Jerry BLACKWELL and Tina JONES.

2. On December 14, 1982, S/A Gates had a telephone conversation with Detective Sgt. Frank Myres of the Tulsa Police Department concerning Jerry PRIDEAUX. Sgt. Myres advised that he had received information from confidential sources indicating that PRIDEAUX' source for cocaine is a Don TYSON, who owns TYSON INDUSTRIES in Springdale, Arkansas. Sgt. Myres also advised that his source said that TYSON smuggles cocaine from Colombia, South America inside race horses to Hot Springs, Arkansas. No further amplification or clarification as to exactly how the drugs were concealed in the horse was made. It was unknown by Sgt. Myres and S/A Gates that horses were brought to the race tracks at Hot Springs from Colombia.

3. Sgt. Myres' source also stated that a Dale LNU is a runner for TYSON and drops cocaine to PRIDEAUX. Sgt. Myres' source was under the impression that Dale LNU lives in Stilwell, Oklahoma rather than the Sallisaw area where, according to the referenced report, Dale WARD resides.

4. Sgt. Myres advised that PRIDEAUX has been a target by the Tulsa PD for several years and in fact PRIDEAUX has been arrested numerous times for illegal gambling. PRIDEAUX owns the STING BAR, 9411 East 31st, Tulsa, Oklahoma, telephone 918/627-9983 and is part owner of the PARADOX CLUB, 6214 South Lewis, Tulsa, Oklahoma, telephone 918/742-9386.

INDEXING SECTION:

1. PRIDEAUX, Jerry - NADDIS 1427803, DOB 12/04/34, Tulsa PD# 39086, OSBI# 85101
2. TYSON, Don J. - NADDIS 470067, aka "CHICKEN MAN", owns Tyson Industries, Springdale, Arkansas.
3. WARD, Dale - NADDIS 1427854.

11. DISTRIBUTION:	12. SIGNATURE (Agent)	13. D
REGION	H. Dean Gates, S/A	1.
DISTRICT Dallas, Little Rock	14. APPROVED (Name and Title)	15. C
OTHER HQT OC	Mel D. Ashton, RAC	4.

DEA Form - 6
(Mar. 1980)

T-17927 (DALE WARD)

Page 1 of 3

1. PROGRAM CODE	DESTROY	2. CROSS FILE	JOINT TO FILES	3. FILE NO. GFHQ-84-4046	4. G-DEP IDENTIFIER DA1-CO

5. BY: S/A Anthony J. Coulson
AT: Tucson, Arizona

6. FILE TITLE

TYSON, Donald J. et al

7. ☐ Closed ☐ Requested Action Completed ☐ Action Requested By:

8. DATE PREPARED

July 9, 1984

9. OTHER OFFICERS:
Tucson Police Detective Roy LeBlanc

DA1CO

10. REPORT RE:
Debriefing of SMQ-84-0019 Re: Donald TYSON Drug Trafficking Organization

DETAILS:

DRUG-RELATED INFORMATION:

1. On July 5, 1984, SMQ-84-0019 telephoned S/A Anthony Coulson at the Tucson District Office concerning narcotic trafficking by Donald J. TYSON in and around the area of Fayetteville, Arkansas. The Cooperating Individual (CI) had information concerning heroin, cocaine and marijuana trafficking in the States of Arkansas, Texas, and Missouri by the TYSON Organization. On that same day, S/A Coulson and Tucson Police Detective Roy LeBlanc met with SMQ-84-0019 to debrief that CI. The CI advised S/A Coulson that in January, February and March of 1978 the CI had contact with Alex MONTEZ and Donald KEMP, who are believed to be Lieutenants for Donald TYSON. The CI stated that MONTEZ owns a restaurant named CASA MONTEZ and distributes cocaine from that restaurant.

2. The CI got involved with the TYSON Organization through James and Harmon CURRY. The CURRY brothers are believed to be smugglers for Donald TYSON. The CI stated that Harmon CURRY, AKA BUTTER, used the CI's vehicle to smuggle marijuana and cocaine throughout Arkansas. Harmon CURRY is believed to be living in Cement, Oklahoma, working for a construction/excavation company approximately forty miles from Oklahoma City.

3. The CI stated that a Jacqueline SMITH, who used to live in Fayetteville, Arkansas, married to George SMITH, had an affair back in 1978 with Donald KEMP. It was from SMITH that the CI learned of a location called "THE BARN" in which TYSON used as a "stash" location for large quantities of marijuana and cocaine. "THE BARN" area is located between Springdale and Fayetteville, Arkansas and, from the outside, the appearance of "THE BARN" looks run down. On the inside of "THE BARN" it is quite plush. The CI also learned that Donald TYSON has all of the narcotics related meetings at the Ramada Inn in Fayetteville, Arkansas, and those meetings are usually concerning the business in and around "THE BARN."

11. DISTRIBUTION:	12. SIGNATURE (Agent)	13. DATE
REGION Little Rock R.O.	ANTHONY J. COULSON, Special Agent	8-10-84
DISTRICT ARI, PCFZ, OIE	14. APPROVED (Name and Title)	15. DATE
OTHER HQS-OC-Direct	H. T. FERNANDEZ, Group Supervisor	8/11

DEA Form - 6
(May 1980)

RMB/8/10/84

CIS - 3C
DATE:
DICTATED BY:
COUNTY:
SOURCE OF INFORMATION: CI
TOPIC OF INFORMATION: Drug Trafficking
DATE TYPED: October 27, 1981
COPIES TO: Sgt. Sanders, Inv. Best

10-26-81
Sgt. Sanders
Pulaski

The following information received from SGT. JOEY COX, Training Division, Little Rock, Arkansas.

The reliability of the information is unknown and has not yet been verified.

SGT. COX advised that he received information from an informant who told that DON TYSON of Tyson Food Industries in Springdale, Arkansas, owns a company aircraft, which is being utilized to smuggle drugs from Florida to Springdale. The informant told that the aforementioned information had been received from a ████████████ of Beaver Shores, Telephone number believed to be ████████, address ████████ Street.

████████ indicated to the CI that he would be willing to talk to an investigator reference to the above information he alleged to the CI. A check with directory information was made to obtain the above telephone number and address of ████████ at Beavershores.

Sanders
Best
CFO 10
Jm Beach

FILE NUMBER: I-14838

CIS - 3C
DATE: 3/22/76
DICTATED BY: INV. DOUG FOGLEY
COUNTY: Washington
SOURCE OF INFORMATION: Sheriff HERB MARSHALL
TOPIC OF INFORMATION: Criminal Activity
DATE TYPED: 3/25/76
COPIES TO: CAPT. GEORGE MOYE
                           LT. CARROLL EVANS
                           INV. FOGLEY

VERY CONFIDENTIAL

This information was related to this agent on the morning of March 22, 1976 by Sheriff HERB MARSHALL.

No dissemination is to be made of this information other than to this agent, Captain MOYE and Lieutenant EVANS.

Several hotels in the southern United States including Arkansas are owned by the Teamsters Union as legitimate businesses which the various factions of the somewhat questionable Teamsters Union use to "clean" their money. Two such hotels are the Downtowner Inn in Fayetteville and the Aristocrat Hotel in Hot Springs. The Teamsters Union goes out of its way to keep these hotels highly legitimate and of unquestionable reputation. The manager or overseerer employed by the Teamsters Union for the two hotels in Arkansas (plus others) is BOB FORSHEE, a white male. Recently a private club called the Brass Monkey was established in the basement of the Downtowner Inn in Fayetteville, Arkansas. This club of somewhat questionable reputation has lately caused the Teamsters certain anxiety about it being in one of their hotels. The club is leased and the license holder for the private club are DON TYSON, a white male and BILLIE SNYDER, a white female.

DON TYSON needs no introduction to the State Police CID or for that matter. any law enforcement agency in Northwest, Arkansas. He is an extremely wealthy man with much political influence and seems to be involved in most every kind of shady operation especially narcotics, however, has to date gone without implication in any specific crime. TYSON likes

FILE NUMBER:\ I-2465

22

to think of himself as the "King of the Hill"
in Northwest, Arkansas and quite possibly this
might not be erroneous.

BILLIE SNYDER is a very close friend of
DON TYSON, is financially comfortable by anyone's
means and also has a great deal of influence both
financial and political in the Northwest, Arkansas
area. BILLIE SNYDER is on a first name basis with
many of Arkansas' top politicians.

Since TYSON and SNYDER have been working·
the Brass Monkey, prostitution and gambling have .
run rampant in the club. Two employees, RED SMITH
and FNU TAYLOR allegedly push drugs from behind the
bar. Needless to say, this situation causes the
Teamsters a certain amount of worry since the hotels
are used as a legitimate front and their reputation
must be kept above reproach.

According to Sheriff HERB MARSHALL, the
representative of the Teamsters Union have advised
TYSON and SNYDER to vacate the premises of the club
in the Downtowner Inn in Fayetteville. Allegedly
TYSON and BILLIE SNYDER slightly refused in very
blunt terms.

The Teamsters Union dispatched "an investigator"
from the St. Louis Office named Mr. WAYRICK who
is an attorney employed by the Union to "correct
the situation".

It is the opinion of Sheriff MARSHALL and Mr.
BOB FORSCHEE, District Manager for the hotels,
that if simple reasoning does not cause the TYSON-
SNYDER partnership to vacate the premises "other
methods" will be employed by the Teamsters Union to
accomplish these ends.

Since law enforcement will not become involved
until a crime has occurred, it was decided by
Sheriff MARSHALL that he would wait to see what
happened in the above described situation.

It is the personal opinion of this investigator
that knowing TYSON and his pride, he will slightly
refuse to vacate the premises and in knowing the
Teamsters Union, it will more or less be insisted
upon above TYSON's objections. The reason this

FILE NUMBER: CRIME: Criminal Activity

intelligence report is dictated is to document
the information already obtained on the situation
for a possible future use. It is felt that it will
be interesting to see what transpires from the
situation as whether or not TYSON thinks that he
is a big leaguer.. He is most assuredly dealing
with the "big boys" now in the form of the
Teamsters Union.

TO: _Fcalcu_____ DATE __
TO: _cuaso___ DATE __
TO: _4 __ DATE __
TO: _CE009___ DATE __
TO: _____ ____ __
TO: _____ ____ __
TO: _____ ____ __
TO: _____ ____ __
TO: _____ ____ __
TO: _____ ____ __

FILE NUMBER: CRIME: Criminal Activity

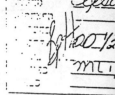

CID- 3C
DATE:
DICTATED BY:
COUNTY:
SOURCE OF INFORMATION:
TOPIC OF INFORMATION:
DATE TYPED:
COPIES TO:

January 21, 1981
SERGEANT HALE
WASHINGTON
CONFIDENTIAL INFORMANT
DRUG AND STOLEN PROPERTY DEALERS
January 17, 1981

The following information was received from Inmate ▮▮▮▮▮ at the Tucker Unit of the Arkansas Department of Corrections. The informant has been confined since 1978 and the reliability of his information is not known at this time, but he states he had been updated on happenings with in the county by other inmates.

The dissemination of this information should remain within confidential sources.

The inmate states that DON TYSON, white male, in his 50's, that lives in Springdale and operates the Tyson Chicking Processing Plant in that city is involved in drug traffic and stolen property. The informant states that TYSON has been operating a Crystal Methamphetamine lab that was located at the Swepco Generator Plant in a small shed located on Highway 68 west of Springdale between Siloam Springs and Gentry. The security on this drug lab was over seen by BILL ELVINS and his son, BILL, JR.. The above two are affilliated with a security company there in Springdale. The plant was moved approximately 4 months ago to Baldwin, Arkansas and set up in a mobile home behind the Speedy-Mart Store. Most of the produ of this drug lab are being passed on the campus of the University of Arkansas at Fayetteville. TYSON brings in his supplies for his lab in his trucks that haul frozen chickens.

An assosicate of TYSON was now ex-sheriff HERB MARSHALL. Ex-sheriff MARSHALL was to have been furnishing confiscated weapons to TYSON for sale. The information is that in July, 1980, ex-sheriff MARSHAIL confiscated a large amount of guns in a mobile home and that these guns were turned over to TYSON.

Also involved with the stolen guns is JOE FRED STARR, white mal approximately 57 years of age, operator of Springdale Farms. STARR also is involved in purchasing Cocaine and Marijuana and hires the runners to distribute it. STARR and TYSON work together in the

FILE NUMBER:

narcotics and stolen gun dealings.

Inmate ████ stated he has information that the gun that was confiscated from him, that he used in the shooting which he was convicted of, was used also in an armed robbery of the Monteray (phonetic) Seafood Cafe. The robbery was committed by a black male, who is now said to be serving time in Cummins for the crime.

The stolen guns are often said to end up in the "71" Gun Shop in Fayeteville.

CLINT SPENCER, white male, approximately 60, 185 pounds, operator of the Spencer Bonding Agency in Fayettevi le is said to work for TYSON as a hit man. Drug dealers that owe TYSON money were tracked down by SPENCER and said to have been found missing and to be heard of again.

Runners for TYSON are said to be ; 1. RICK DOLAN, white male, 23, 6'4", 170 lbs. 2. BOBBY CARSLIE, white male, 45, 6', 180 pounds (said to be Mayor of Farmington). 3. CHARLES AGEE, white male, 60, 6', 190 pounds, manager of the IGA Grocery, Fayetteville. 4. LARRY HACKINS, white male, 26, 5'10", 175 lbs., was the jailer at the Washington County Jail. 5. MORTON MARSHALL, white male, 24, 5'8", 220 lbs., also jailer at the Washington County Jail.

Also information that the Am-Vet's Club in Fayeteville, Highway 62 west, has the same ownership as TOMMY'S Lounge in Sprindgale, being CHUCK last name unknown, white male, 6'5", 280 lbs., was paying the Washington County Sheriff's Office for protection in the past and some of TYSON'S drugs goes through these clubs.

TO:	DATE 1/30
TO:	DATE 1/30
TO:	DATE
TO:	DATE
TO:	DATE
TO:	DATE
TO:	DATE
TO:	DATE
TO:	DATE
TO:	DATE

ILE NUMBER: CRIME:

ASP-3-C   CRIMINAL INVESTIGATION DIVISION

INTELLIGENCE

DATE: 7-31-81
DICTATED BY: Inv. Don Taylor
COUNTY: Crawford
SOURCE OF INFORMATION: Confidential Informant
TOPIC OF INFORMATION: Murder for Hire
DATE TYPED: 8-3-81
COPIES TO: Inv. Don Taylor
           Lt. Evans

The confidential informant has furnished reliable information
in the past. His accessibility to this type of information
has not been established.

This information has been furnished to Lt. EVANS by public
service. Due to the sensitivity of this information no
further dissemination of this information should be made
without authorization of Lt. EVANS or this investigator.

The confidential informant advised that a short time ago
he was talking with RONNIE TEAGUE'S wife who lives in
Mountainburg and is in the process of getting a divorce.
She told the confidential informant that she thought RONNIE
TEAGUE was a hit man for DON TYSON of Springdale. In the
same sentence she asked if anyone had been arrested for the
recent murder of the man at the Country Club in Tulsa, Oklahoma.

The confidential informant advised that he got the impression
from talking with her that she thought RONNIE had been involved
in the killing.

TO: Taylor   DATE
TO: Evans   DATE
TO: Swesley   DATE
TO: EFOOL   DATE
TO: DATE
TO: DATE
TO: DATE
TO: DATE
TO: DAT
TO: DA

Tyson Foods, Inc. P.O. Box 2020 • Springdale, AR 72765-2020 • Phone (501) 290-4000

July 21, 1994

Mr. Larry Nichols
862 Farris Road
Conway, AR 72032

Dear Mr. Nichols:

A disturbing report has come to my attention. You are being quoted in a publication called "For The People News Reporter" dated June 27, 1994 as having talked to a talk show host named Chuck Harder on June 9, 1994 on something called "For The People Broadcast".

The "News Reporter" quotes you as having said on the radio, "Don Tyson was in the middle. He has been. He used his chicken trucks to haul cocaine."

If you said this, it is obviously slander, libel and defamation of the most vicious sort.

I am compelled to ask you, "What do you have to say for yourself?"

Did you say these things?

Do you claim you were misquoted?

Do you have any justification for spreading these vicious lies, if you weren't misquoted?

Do you have anything you want to show me to justify your conduct?

Will you publicly take it back and admit it is not true?

Will you apologize to me and my company?

Are you aware that "For The People" is broadcast into many states, some of which have criminal libel and defamation statutes.

Do you realize you cannot with impunity destroy people's reputation without cause anymore than you can destroy their lives and property?

Will you give me the courtesy of a definitive reply?

Yours truly,

Don Tyson
Chairman

Feeding you like family.™

28

Dear Mr. Tyson:

If you're wondering whether I have said what you asked in your letter, I have, and will continue to do so. You asked why, but you should know the answer. It's because it's all true.

So that you understand why I'm doing this, it's because of your friend, Bill Clinton. You've used him to build your company at the expense of Arkansas, and you plan to do the same for America.

I've enclosed a couple of documents from the Arkansas State Police files and other agencies. These are already all over the nation. I will tell the truth about you and Bill Clinton.

So that you know, people from the FBI, the Arkansas State Police and the Drug Enforcement Agency have told me not to mess with you because you have money and power and would have me killed. You're now on notice. Fire the shot whenever you want; I can't stop you. I can only tell you to call ahead of time and get my schedule. It may be tough to fit you and yours in between talk shows. But I'm sure something can be worked out.

Let's do lunch.

Larry

Love, Larry

United States Senate

WASHINGTON, DC 20510-3305

July 1, 1994

The Honorable Janet Reno
Attorney General of the United States
United States Department of Justice
Tenth and Constitution Avenue, N.W.
Washington, DC 20530

Dear Attorney General Reno:

As you know, the President yesterday signed into law the reauthorization of the Independent Counsel Act. In signing it, he referred to the act as a "foundation stone for the trust between the government and our citizens."

In your attached letter to me of January 11, 1994, in which you outlined your opposition to appointing a special counsel, you wrote that "Any such counsel appointed by me would not be regarded as truly independent.."

Now that the Independent Counsel Act has been reauthorized, given the appearance of not being truly independent which you referenced, it would be highly improper for you to recommend to the Independent Counsel Panel of the U.S. Court of Appeals that the current special counsel, Robert Fiske, be appointed Independent Counsel.

The "Washington Post" put it well when it said that "Its purpose is to ensure investigations free from political interference or the appearance of such interference." However, you put it __best__ when you told me in your November 4, 1993 testimony to the Senate Banking Committee, "..I support that in every way possible to avoid any appearance of conflict..."

Further, in addition to appearances, very real questions about Mr. Fiske's independence have been raised. Prior to your appointment of him as special counsel, Mr. Fiske collaborated on at least one high-level Clinton appointment - The Director of the FBI, who is now overseeing criminal investigations involving a number of Clinton Administration officials.

Mr. Fiske also enjoyed a professional relationship with Bernard Nussbaum - former White House Legal Counsel and current subject of the Fiske probe - which included Mr. Nussbaum referring clients to Mr. Fiske, Mr. Nussbaum recommending Mr. Fiske for a job with former Iran/Contra prosecutor Lawrence Walsh, and Mr. Nussbaum and Mr. Fiske being involved on the same side in at least two legal cases.

Continued

Mr. Fiske also collaborated with the President's Lawyer, Robert Bennett, in the defense of Clark Clifford and Robert Altman in the BCCI case. As you know, your Deputy Attorney General, Jamie Gorelick also attempted to get the money to pay Mr. Fiske's and Mr. Bennett's bills from the trustee of First American/BCCI. Further, BCCI has been implicated in various allegations surrounding the Whitewater affair, including allegations concerning possible illegal activities in Mena, Arkansas, and questionable activities surrounding the Arkansas Development Finance Authority.

I am also told that Mr. Fiske served as legal counsel to the firm which initially sold the land to the Clinton's Whitewater partnership, a possible conflict of interest which many obviously find quite troubling.

Given both the appearance of lack of independence which you referenced, and the relationship between Mr. Fiske and the Clinton Administration, Mr. Fiske should not be appointed Independent Counsel. While a new, truly independent counsel, might choose to retain Mr. Fiske in some capacity in order to insure continuity, his appointment as Independent Counsel would guarantee that the current cloud of doubt and suspicion hanging over his appointment would remain.

Therefore, I urge you not to recommend the appointment of Robert Fiske as Independent Counsel, and I urge you to actively encourage the Independent Counsel Panel of the U.S. Court of Appeals to appoint a new, truly independent, counsel that will enjoy the confidence of those who seek truth and justice, regardless of party.

Sincerely,

Lauch Faircloth
United States Senate
North Carolina

Reno &
Clinton
Chase
Fiske

31

HOUSE OF REPRESENTATIVES
WASHINGTON, D.C.

June 30, 1994

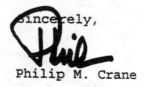

Dear Republican Colleague:

Those of our colleagues who wish a succinct but wide-ranging perspective on all the allegations aired thus far in regard to the involvement of the Clintons and their circle of friends in Whitewater, Tyson Foods, the Madison S&L, the Worthen Bank, Mena drug activities, the Rose Law Firm, etc., are encouraged to view the enclosed video, <u>The Clinton Chronicles</u>.

This tape is one of the most comprehensive summations that I have viewed of the various accusations that have been covered only piecemeal thus far in the media. If full documentary evidence of these allegations is ever allowed to be officially investigated and is ever confirmed, the Clinton Administration will be short-lived indeed.

Observing, of course, the precaution that accusations cannot be equated with legal evidence, I encourage my colleagues to review the tape in order to fully grasp the dimensions of the accusations that have been recited.

Sincerely,

Philip M. Crane

Absolutely no taxpayer's funds were used for the preparation or mailing of this letter.

New Video!
Available: February of '95!

ONLY $19.95

How did the U.S. Attorneys office prevent IRS and State Police evidence from being brought before a grand jury? Who shut down Arkansas Congressman Bill Alexander's investigation? And why was the deputy Prosecuting Attorney ordered not to investigate any public official?

An Arkansas director of the drug task force who uncovered too much, and ultimately had to establish a new identity out of state, is now ready to tell all. Get it straight from CIA, DEA and other law enforcement officials in this hard hitting video that takes you behind the COVER-UP!

ORDER TODAY
1-800-558-4436

A PETITION

We, the American people, exercising our Constitutional right to petition, demand that both Congress and other federal authorities conduct a full investigation into allegations of criminal wrongdoing by Bill Clinton and his political machine in Arkansas.We demand full, unrestricted, public Congressional hearings into allegations of drug trafficking, money laundering, murder, political payoffs and other abuses of power.
Specifically, we are demanding:

1. That the independent counsel reopen the investigation into the death of Vincent W. Foster, Jr., and convene a full grand jury investigation into the death and the subsequent police and federal probes into his death;
2. That the independent counsel release all Whitewater documents that have been hidden by subpoena, including the papers of Judge David Hale for public scrutiny;
3. A full investigation into the execution of Jerry Parks, former Chief of Security for Clinton's presidential campaign headquarters;
4. A full federal investigation be initiated into the murders of Kevin Ives and Don Henry, two Arkansas boys brutally killed, a series of murders that took place after their deaths and the connection between these murders and organized crime activity in Arkansas;
5. A federal investigation into alleged drug trafficking by Don Tyson, his ties to Clinton, and efforts by Arkansas officials to prevent the state police from presenting evidence from their intelligence files before a grand jury;
6. That Congress exercise its oversight duties and conduct full public hearings in a timely manner.

Signed   _____

Address   _____

_____

Please copy and distribute. Add additional sheets for signatures if necessary. Please mail copies to:

Kenneth Starr	Your Congressman	Your Senator
Kirkland & Ellis	The Honorable _____	The Honorable ____
655 15th NW	House of Representatives	U.S. Senate
Suite #1200	Washington, DC 20515	Washington, DC 20510
Wash., DC 20005		

CITIZENS FOR HONEST GOVERNMENT—

producers of the film,
THE CLINTON CHRONICLES—invites you to:

BECOME A MEMBER...JOIN TODAY!

Citizens for Honest Government (CHG) is a nonprofit grassroots organization which promotes honesty and integrity in government. We have intelligence information and a variety of products which can be great resources for you.

We at Citizens for Honest Government want to ensure that these valuable resources are available to more than just a select few who are able to donate large sums to the cause. We provide an opportunity for every concerned citizen to have access to the hottest, most sensitive intelligence information available. Now, for a minimum suggested donation of only $20, you can become a member of CHG (larger donations are gratefully accepted as well). It's easy to sign up! Simply call (**800**) **558-4436** or mail in one of the membership applications on the next page with your check or money order.

NEW MEMBERS IMMEDIATELY RECEIVE...

A copy of the latest video production from CHG—
no charge, no shipping, no handling!

AS A SPECIAL BONUS...

Membership includes a one-year subscription to the CITIZENS INTELLIGENCE DIGEST newsletter, a quarterly publication. It gives you the news that's too hot for the networks to handle—government cover-ups, intrusions and abuse of power—it's all in the CITIZENS INTELLIGENCE DIGEST! You'll be right on the cutting edge of the most sensitive intelligence information available. Also read success reports of how teamwork is helping put America back together. We want to give you the tools you need to effect a positive change in government.

EXTRA EXTRA BONUS!

All members also receive a whopping **20% purchase discount**
on all CHG videos and publications.

WE URGE YOU—DON'T DELAY! SIGN UP TODAY!

MEMBERSHIP APPLICATION
CITIZENS FOR HONEST GOVERNMENT

PLEASE SPECIFY DONATION AMOUNT ON REVERSE SIDE
($20 MINIMUM DONATION)

_____
APPLICANT NAME

_____
ADDRESS

_____
CITY   STATE   ZIP CODE
( )
_____
TELEPHONE

MEMBERSHIP APPLICATION
CITIZENS FOR HONEST GOVERNMENT

PLEASE SPECIFY DONATION AMOUNT ON REVERSE SIDE
($20 MINIMUM DONATION)

_____
APPLICANT NAME

_____
ADDRESS

_____
CITY   STATE   ZIP CODE
( )
_____
TELEPHONE

MEMBERSHIP APPLICATION
CITIZENS FOR HONEST GOVERNMENT

PLEASE SPECIFY DONATION AMOUNT ON REVERSE SIDE
($20 MINIMUM DONATION)

_____
APPLICANT NAME

_____
ADDRESS

_____
CITY   STATE   ZIP CODE
( )
_____
TELEPHONE

MEMBERSHIP APPLICATION
CITIZENS FOR HONEST GOVERNMENT

PLEASE SPECIFY DONATION AMOUNT ON REVERSE SIDE
($20 MINIMUM DONATION)

_____
APPLICANT NAME

_____
ADDRESS

_____
CITY   STATE   ZIP CODE
( )
_____
TELEPHONE

MEMBERSHIP APPLICATION
CITIZENS FOR HONEST GOVERNMENT

PLEASE SPECIFY DONATION AMOUNT ON REVERSE SIDE
($20 MINIMUM DONATION)

_____
APPLICANT NAME

_____
ADDRESS

_____
CITY   STATE   ZIP CODE
( )
_____
TELEPHONE

MEMBERSHIP APPLICATION
CITIZENS FOR HONEST GOVERNMENT

PLEASE SPECIFY DONATION AMOUNT ON REVERSE SIDE
($20 MINIMUM DONATION)

_____
APPLICANT NAME

_____
ADDRESS

_____
CITY   STATE   ZIP CODE
( )
_____
TELEPHONE

MEMBERSHIP APPLICATION
CITIZENS FOR HONEST GOVERNMENT

PLEASE SPECIFY DONATION AMOUNT ON REVERSE SIDE
($20 MINIMUM DONATION)

_____
APPLICANT NAME

_____
ADDRESS

_____
CITY   STATE   ZIP CODE
( )
_____
TELEPHONE

MEMBERSHIP APPLICATION
CITIZENS FOR HONEST GOVERNMENT

PLEASE SPECIFY DONATION AMOUNT ON REVERSE SIDE
($20 MINIMUM DONATION)

_____
APPLICANT NAME

_____
ADDRESS

_____
CITY   STATE   ZIP CODE
( )
_____
TELEPHONE

SEND CHECK OR MONEY ORDER TO:

CITIZENS FOR HONEST GOVERNMENT
P.O. BOX 220 , WINCHESTER, CA 92596
OR CALL: **(800) 558-4436**

CHECK ONE: ☐$20 ☐$50 ☐$100 ☐OTHER $____

TO CHARGE YOUR MEMBERSHIP, PLEASE FILL OUT THE FOLLOWING
CREDIT CARD INFORMATION:

CIRCLE ONE: VISA   M/C   AMEXP   DISCOVER

NUMBER: _____ / _____ / _____

EXPIRATION DATE: _____
CARDHOLDER
SIGNATURE: _____

SEND CHECK OR MONEY ORDER TO:

CITIZENS FOR HONEST GOVERNMENT
P.O. BOX 220 , WINCHESTER, CA 92596
OR CALL: **(800) 558-4436**

CHECK ONE: ☐$20 ☐$50 ☐$100 ☐OTHER $____

TO CHARGE YOUR MEMBERSHIP, PLEASE FILL OUT THE FOLLOWING
CREDIT CARD INFORMATION:

CIRCLE ONE: VISA   M/C   AMEXP   DISCOVER

NUMBER: _____ / _____ / _____

EXPIRATION DATE: _____
CARDHOLDER
SIGNATURE: _____

SEND CHECK OR MONEY ORDER TO:

CITIZENS FOR HONEST GOVERNMENT
P.O. BOX 220 , WINCHESTER, CA 92596
OR CALL: **(800) 558-4436**

CHECK ONE: ☐$20 ☐$50 ☐$100 ☐OTHER $____

TO CHARGE YOUR MEMBERSHIP, PLEASE FILL OUT THE FOLLOWING
CREDIT CARD INFORMATION:

CIRCLE ONE: VISA   M/C   AMEXP   DISCOVER

NUMBER: _____ / _____ / _____

EXPIRATION DATE: _____
CARDHOLDER
SIGNATURE: _____

SEND CHECK OR MONEY ORDER TO:

CITIZENS FOR HONEST GOVERNMENT
P.O. BOX 220 , WINCHESTER, CA 92596
OR CALL: **(800) 558-4436**

CHECK ONE: ☐$20 ☐$50 ☐$100 ☐OTHER $____

TO CHARGE YOUR MEMBERSHIP, PLEASE FILL OUT THE FOLLOWING
CREDIT CARD INFORMATION:

CIRCLE ONE: VISA   M/C   AMEXP   DISCOVER

NUMBER: _____ / _____ / _____

EXPIRATION DATE: _____
CARDHOLDER
SIGNATURE: _____

SEND CHECK OR MONEY ORDER TO:

CITIZENS FOR HONEST GOVERNMENT
P.O. BOX 220 , WINCHESTER, CA 92596
OR CALL: **(800) 558-4436**

CHECK ONE: ☐$20 ☐$50 ☐$100 ☐OTHER $____

TO CHARGE YOUR MEMBERSHIP, PLEASE FILL OUT THE FOLLOWING
CREDIT CARD INFORMATION:

CIRCLE ONE: VISA   M/C   AMEXP   DISCOVER

NUMBER: _____ / _____ / _____

EXPIRATION DATE: _____
CARDHOLDER
SIGNATURE: _____

SEND CHECK OR MONEY ORDER TO:

CITIZENS FOR HONEST GOVERNMENT
P.O. BOX 220 , WINCHESTER, CA 92596
OR CALL: **(800) 558-4436**

CHECK ONE: ☐$20 ☐$50 ☐$100 ☐OTHER $____

TO CHARGE YOUR MEMBERSHIP, PLEASE FILL OUT THE FOLLOWING
CREDIT CARD INFORMATION:

CIRCLE ONE: VISA   M/C   AMEXP   DISCOVER

NUMBER: _____ / _____ / _____

EXPIRATION DATE: _____
CARDHOLDER
SIGNATURE: _____

SEND CHECK OR MONEY ORDER TO:

CITIZENS FOR HONEST GOVERNMENT
P.O. BOX 220 , WINCHESTER, CA 92596
OR CALL: **(800) 558-4436**

CHECK ONE: ☐$20 ☐$50 ☐$100 ☐OTHER $____

TO CHARGE YOUR MEMBERSHIP, PLEASE FILL OUT THE FOLLOWING
CREDIT CARD INFORMATION:

CIRCLE ONE: VISA   M/C   AMEXP   DISCOVER

NUMBER: _____ / _____ / _____

EXPIRATION DATE: _____
CARDHOLDER
SIGNATURE: _____

SEND CHECK OR MONEY ORDER TO:

CITIZENS FOR HONEST GOVERNMENT
P.O. BOX 220 , WINCHESTER, CA 92596
OR CALL: **(800) 558-4436**

CHECK ONE: ☐$20 ☐$50 ☐$100 ☐OTHER $____

TO CHARGE YOUR MEMBERSHIP, PLEASE FILL OUT THE FOLLOWING
CREDIT CARD INFORMATION:

CIRCLE ONE: VISA   M/C   AMEXP   DISCOVER

NUMBER: _____ / _____ / _____

EXPIRATION DATE: _____
CARDHOLDER
SIGNATURE: _____